Advance Praise for *First Fuel*

'This is a thoughtful account of episodes in India's arduous journey towards energy conservation and self-sufficiency. *First Fuel* provides insights into the roles of important players and institutions and of US technical assistance in this effort. Over three decades, Padu Padmanabhan played a key part in shaping this assistance. This book is an insider's account, providing a view of some important hurdles and successes along the way. It offers a thought-provoking perspective of broad interest in the context of continuing challenges'

Romir Chatterjee, energy economist

'No one has seen and perhaps influenced India's energy transition more closely than Padu Padmanabhan. His journey – of traversing through oil shocks and the cleansing of coal, unravelling the nexus of energy and water, creating and scaling up world-class energy efficiency programmes in a complex country and polity and applying renewable energy at scale – is truly amazing. It is also an amazing personal journey. Through the years, despite the inevitable ups and downs, Padu has remained positive and pragmatic, focusing as much on people as on technology. This engaging and enlightening book tells a story never told before'

Anish De, Global Sector Head,
Power & Utilities, KPMG India

'Padu Padmanabhan has spent nearly half a century working on energy and energy efficiency. He has had not just a ringside view, but on many occasions, he has been inside the ring, putting in yeoman's efforts into India's journey – from responding to an international oil crisis with fuel conservation to energy conservation, energy efficiency and finally, to energy productivity. This book is the authoritative story of technology, business, domestic regulation, international cooperation, institution-building, and of individuals who have contributed to one of the world's largest energy systems that continues to push for more with less'

Arunabha Ghosh, CEO, Council on Energy, Environment and Water, India

'This book could not have come at a more opportune time with India and the world grappling with an energy transition of tectonic proportions. Central to this transformation is the ability of the nation to harness the potential that energy efficiency offers. To this end, the lessons from India's historic journey towards embracing energy efficiency as an important strategic resource have been related in an artful and engaging manner. Padu Padmanabhan makes an immensely engaging case for decisively moving from the supply side of the energy equation to the demand side. *First Fuel* is a vital read for everyone wishing to participate in the continual development and growth of the energy efficiency paradigm'

Saurabh Kumar, Executive Vice Chairman, Energy Efficiency Services Ltd Group

'Padu Padmanabhan traces India's energy efficiency odyssey from the fuel efficiency focus of the 1970s to the energy productivity, sustainability and decarbonization focus of today. He was a central participant in many stages of this journey and provides an insider's perspective of what has worked, what hasn't and where we need to go to help shape the future of energy use and emissions in what may soon be the world's most populous country'

Steven Nadel, Executive Director, American Council for an Energy-Efficient Economy

'Reading this book is a joy. Padu Padmanabhan not only articulates and unravels the complex ecosystem around the energy efficiency movement in India in an easy-to-read manner, but also uses his proficiency in blending theory with practice and anchors it with compelling stories of the numerous individuals who contributed to this journey, behind the scenes and at centre stage.

First Fuel offers a comprehensive overview of technology, policy and the institutional and financing landscapes, laid out in a style that entertains, informs and teaches as well. Finding solutions to deliver the "first fuel" (energy efficiency) at scale requires multidimensional thinking, which this book elucidates effectively by building upon a cogent and integrated framework and drawing upon both successful experiences and failures. Rich in substance, it is a must-read for anyone who desires to develop a clear understanding of the past and a guide to the future of energy efficiency in India'

Ashok Sarkar, Senior Energy Specialist, World Bank

first fuel

India's Energy
Efficiency Journey
and a Radical Vision
for Sustainability

first fuel

Padu Padmanabhan

MACMILLAN

First published 2021 by Macmillan
an imprint of Pan Macmillan Publishing India Private Limited
707 Kailash Building
26 K. G. Marg, New Delhi 110001
www.panmacmillan.co.in

Pan Macmillan, The Smithson, 6 Briset St, Farringdon London EC1M 5NR
Associated companies throughout the world
www.panmacmillan.com

ISBN 978-93-90742-23-3

1 3 5 7 9 8 6 4 2

Typeset in Sabon Roman by SÜRYA, New Delhi
Printed and bound in India by
Replika Press Pvt. Ltd.

For Aarthi and Anjana
and
the generations that will follow:
May yours be a more energy-efficient future

CONTENTS

Abbreviations

ACEEE: American Council for an Energy-Efficient Economy
AEE: Association of Energy Engineers, US
AEEE: Alliance for an Energy-Efficient Economy, India
AID/Washington: United States Agency for International Development, Washington
AIP: Dr Ambedkar Institute of Productivity
AP: Andhra Pradesh
ASTAE: Asia Alternate Energy Unit, World Bank
ATF: Aviation turbine fuel
BEE: Bureau of Energy Efficiency
BELP: Bangalore Efficient Lighting Program
BHEL: Bharat Heavy Electricals Ltd
CEA: Central Electricity Authority
CBERD: Centre for Building Energy Research & Development
CEO: Chief Executive Officer
CenPEEP: Centre for Power Efficiency and Environmental Protection
CETEE: Centre of Excellence for Training in Energy Efficiency
CFL: Compact fluorescent lamp
CII: Confederation of Indian Industry
DESL: Development Environergy Services Ltd
DFID: Department for International Development, UK
DNES: Department of Non-conventional Energy Sources
DoE/NETL: Department of Energy's National Energy Technology Laboratory
DSM: Demand-side management
DRUM: Distribution Reform, Upgrades and Management
DPC: Dabhol Power Company
ECBC: Energy Conservation Building Code
ECO: Energy Conservation and Commercialization
EESL: Energy Efficiency Services Ltd
EMC: Energy Management Centre, New Delhi
EPIC: Energy Policy, Innovations and Commercialization
ESCO: Energy service company

e-RA: Electronic reverse auctions
FERA: Foreign Exchange Regulation Act
FPC: Fuel Policy Committee
GBC: Green business centre
GCC: Gulf Cooperation Council
GDP: Gross domestic product
GEP: Greenhouse Gas Emissions Prevention Program
GW: Gigawatt
HVAC&R: Heating, ventilation, air conditioning and refrigeration
IAS: Indian Administrative Service
ICICI: Industrial Credit and Investment Corporation of India Ltd
IDBI: Industrial Development Bank of India
IEA: International Energy Agency
IEN: Integrated energy network
IGBC: Indian Green Building Council
IOC: Indian Oil Corporation Ltd
IRP: Integrated resource planning
ITC: India Tobacco Company Limited
KAPSARC: King Abdullah Petroleum Studies and Research Center
K-EMC: Kerala Energy Management Centre
LED: Light-emitting diode
LEED: Leadership in Energy and Environmental Design
LIMEC: Light Museum and Energy Centre
LNG: Liquefied natural gas
LPG: Liquefied petroleum gas
LRC: Lighting Research Center
M&V: Measurement and verification
MCM: Million cubic metre
MGD: Million gallons per day
MMT: Million metric ton
MoNRE: Ministry of New and Renewable Energy
MSEB: Maharashtra State Electricity Board
MSPGCL: Maharashtra State Power Generation Company Ltd
NAS: National Academy of Sciences, US
NDC: Nationally determined contributions
NETL: National Energy Technology Laboratory, US

NIFES: National Institute of Fuel Efficiency Services, UK
NPC: National Productivity Council
NPM: Non-pesticide managed
NTPC: National Thermal Power Corporation
O&M: Operations and maintenance
OECD: Organization for Economic Cooperation and Development
OPEC: Organization of Petroleum Exporting Countries
PACER: Program for Acceleration of Commercial Energy Research
PAT: Perform, Achieve and Trade
PCRA: Petroleum Conservation Research Association
PMO: Prime Minister's Office
POTUS: President of the United States
PURPA: Public Utility Regulatory and Policy Act
QF: Qualifying facility
RCL: Regional Center for Lighting, Colombo, Sri Lanka
REC: Rural Electrification Corporation
RPI: Rensselaer Polytechnic Institute, New York
RUS: Rural Utilities Service, US
SLSEA: Sri Lanka Sustainable Energy Authority
TERI: The Energy Resources Institute
TNEB: Tamil Nadu Electricity Board
UN-CSD: United Nations Commission on Sustainable Development
UNDP: United Nations Development Programme
UN-SD: United Nations Sustainable Development
UPNEDA: Uttar Pradesh Non-conventional Energy Development Agency
USAID: United States Agency for International Development, India
USDoE: United States Department of Energy
USEPA: United States Environmental Protection Agency
USGBC: United States Green Building Council
VLCC: Very large crude carriers
WEN: Water-energy nexus
WENEXA: Water-Energy Nexus in Agriculture
WESCO: Water Energy Services Company
WI: Winrock International
WISER: Women's Institute for Sustainable Energy Research, Kerala

Foreword

This book is a very worthwhile contribution to the understanding of India's energy odyssey over the past half a century. It is written by someone who was not just an observer but an active player in policies, programmes and projects in the country's energy sector. It recalls both processes and personalities and highlights initiatives and institutions. It is more than a personal memoir having as it does scholarly value as well. A serious and highly technical story is described in a very engaging and reader-friendly manner.

Padu Padmanabhan, whom I have known and interacted with personally for almost four decades, brings to this book long years of professional experience in diverse official and non-official settings. He has seen the government from the inside as well as dealt with it from the outside. He has participated in national endeavours and also helped foster international partnerships. He has spent time in the 'real world' and also in academic institutions. All this gives him a unique perspective on the evolution of India's energy mix, options and choices. His narrative is rich in detail and takes us through many milestones that have marked the making of the country's energy policy from the days it used to be referred to simply as 'fuel policy' and from the time when the overriding emphasis was on simply increasing fuel supplies.

When the author started his career, environmental and climate change concerns did not occupy centre stage as they do now. All through the 1970s and 1980s particularly, greater use of fossil fuels was seen as part of the solution; today, they are indisputably part of the problem. Hence, it is only appropriate that in the latter part of this memoir, he also deals with the ecological context to India's energy future. At the Paris Climate Change Summit of December 2015, India made a significant international commitment to reduce the emissions intensity of its economic growth. Increased energy efficiency is at the heart of reducing this emissions intensity. Padu Padmanabhan was among the earliest group of intrepid thinkers and practitioners to make India aware that improved energy efficiency is both desirable and feasible. This is what gives the present volume credibility and authenticity.

The conventional wisdom of 'grow now, worry later about equity and ecology' is both unwise and simply unacceptable. Economic growth in India must necessarily be rapid, inclusive and sustainable. A growth strategy has to fulfil all of these three objectives simultaneously. Clean energy at affordable prices is an essential pillar of such a strategy. India has lessons to learn from its own energy history. Padu Padmanabhan educates us on what these lessons are and how they should guide us in the years ahead.

JAIRAM RAMESH
Member of Parliament and former Union Minister
November 2020

Preface

Telling It Like It Is

In the spring of 2011, when I was asked to teach a semester at Johns Hopkins University, I was at once trepidant and excited. I checked with the team I worked with in New Delhi and Washington, DC, and they heartily endorsed the idea.

I was to share my experiences in India in the fields of energy and development in a global context. For students of the Western world, this was an alien subject. The first classroom session was held mid-afternoon with about twenty students of the School for Advanced International Studies at the university's campus on Massachusetts Avenue. To someone used to larger student groups in Indian classrooms, I interpreted this as perhaps a lack of interest in matters related to India. The next two classes had about the same number of students. I kept on wondering whether something was wrong.

A week later, as I was chatting with one of the faculty members over coffee, I brought this up. She looked at my perplexed face and grinned, 'You don't seem to have heard what the students are saying.' She looked out of the window at a bunch of them lazing on the lawns. 'Usually, the first day sees a larger number out of curiosity. But the number to have stayed consistent? That shows they are *very* interested. The word in the corridors is that you are a rockstar!' A mid-term evaluation showed very positive feedback. One of the students is said to have told another faculty member, 'Padu is no Socrates. He does not delve too much into theory. He tells it like it is. He has brought India's energy scenarios, its pains and hopes, into the classroom. It is like we are there when he speaks in class.'

In my lectures, I stuck to logical explanations and anchored my thoughts around case studies. I took them through the institutional challenges of an electoral democracy and an opaque bureaucracy.

In a similar way, in the stories these pages recount, I have tried as much as possible to steer clear of hypotheses and academic precepts. The attempt has been to present what worked, what didn't and how things unfurled every time we tried to push the membrane of economic possibility on the frontiers of innovation in the energy sector. Why over-bureaucratizing an institutional framework fails; why energy efficiency processes are more about autonomy and encouraging decision-making down the line; how institutions develop their rhythm in a country like India; why certain issues are not classified as important by the core management in such institutions; why the private sector *alone* is not capable of delivering in a developing country; and how social parameters are of equal, if not greater, concern in economies such as India's.

One example that I presented at the time at Johns Hopkins, and is relevant to this day, is of Noida Power Company and their effort to cut power losses. We, a group of United States Agency for International Development (USAID) advisors at the company, realized soon that the highest levels of competence in technical design and approach are defeated by the walls of resistance that arise from people in government agencies, power utilities and from among energy users too. How do we overcome the human tendency towards resistance to change to foster sustainable attitudes? It was in Kolkata in 2003 that I chanced upon a street-play artist and told her of our predicament about getting the message across. She promised she would conceptualize a few street plays that would weave the theme of energy efficiency into little stories and folk songs which would be staged in and around Noida. I found a small grant that helped this group stage a series of such acts for not only the officials and employees of the power company but also the urban and rural consumers of power in this district to the east of New Delhi, the national capital. It worked like a charm. The play revolved around energy in a rural setting and demonstrated how to save energy and water. A year later when we took stock, we found that the net impact of the plays in terms of energy savings was far in excess of what had been anticipated. Though loss reduction of electrical energy thanks to technology upgrades was certainly tangible, it was dwarfed by what came from voluntary behavioural changes in farmers and homemakers. Back in the classroom, this triggered some animated discussion among students about community-based social marketing; how initiatives to promote behavioural change are often most effective when they are carried out at the *community level* and involve a *direct connect* with people, and why social intermediation in fostering sustainable behaviour is necessary and can make an impact. That the cornerstone of energy management is delivering programmes that are effective in changing people's conduct was a lesson that was driven home.

Quest for the Right Premise

Whenever I have had the time to browse at a bookshop with endless rows of books, it has occurred to me that one more would hardly make a difference unless it is written for truly compelling reasons and to tell a story that really matters. A quick scan of the market shows that there is no book for the lay reader on India's post-Independence wrestle with energy by people with growing numbers of homes, offices, industries and farmlands.

India has come a long way from generating less than a meagre 1.7 gigawatts (GW) of energy post Independence to producing 370 GW today. That makes it the fourth-largest electric power producer in the world. Yet, India is unusually vulnerable to energy market risks because it imports nearly 80% of the petroleum that powers its economy. Energy markets from crude oil to natural gas have been buffeted by political and investment risks, as well as technological disruption. Volatility has grown in the world's major oil-producing regions, especially the Middle East, where the spectre of conflict looms over the region, fuelled by long-standing issues and territorial disputes. The old drivers of cost and security are not enough. So, how do we reshape energy security, make it affordable and sustainable with the least cost to the environment?

Well, it's not just about how much energy we need over the next three decades. It is also about how we use it. We have little choice but to use it efficiently and with the most bang for every buck of energy cost. Every unit of energy saved at the point of end use translates to us having avoided generating 4–5 units. And the cost of doing this is a piffle – one-fifth to a tenth of producing it. It is therefore cheaper and cleaner than other fuels and is competing with alternate energy sources in the generation mix. The more energy efficiency we 'generate', the less coal or oil we need. While we search for other sources of energy, we would be well advised that the real breakthrough in energy is using less.[1] World over, more energy is being saved through efficiency than being generated through fossil fuels – hence the term 'first fuel' to denote energy efficiency. The chorus of voices, first articulated by the Paris-based International Energy Agency (IEA), that claims energy efficiency is indeed the first fuel is growing stronger and louder. India is no exception. Governments, policymakers, power-generating utilities, distribution companies that bring power to your building and consumers have to look anew at how we use this precious 'first fuel' resource.

We have to accept that we live in a world that is terribly

inefficient at choosing energy sources and employs primitive methods of energy conversion. This is something that has bothered me forever. How do we bring about small savings in everyday life that can make a big difference? How do we make energy efficiency our first fuel?[2]

Every story in this book is about this first fuel. Sometimes it is central to the narrative, and at other times, it provides the background. There are sections on the greening of electricity-generating utilities on the supply side with renewable energy forms, but there is simply no getting away from the truth that the only solution for energy deficiency is energy efficiency. Pioneers like P. R. Srinivasan of the National Productivity Council (NPC) of India recognized this and ploughed fresh ground as they fought the tough tide of resistance in those early years of ecological innocence in the country and elsewhere. The battle has since gained energy, to mix a metaphor, with the turn of the millennium. There is more about these pioneers and their organizations later in the book.

From those early years of the 1970s when I began my career in India, I have often questioned the very premise of the inordinate tilt of the national energy establishment towards energy supply. I have had the good fortune of actually being hauled into this career by sheer happenstance. As a young graduate in the seventies, I was by chance drawn into a budding and little-known career in fuel efficiency. Later I was jostled into positions that gave me a ringside view of energy in the developing world and work that demanded a truly interdisciplinary approach to solutions. What is even more fortuitous is that I was in the thick of two grave energy crises that rocked the world. The first one was the unbridled rise in oil prices triggered by the 1973 oil crisis that initiated a major worldwide preoccupation with fuel efficiency. Then a dozen years later, the collapse of crude oil prices in 1985 and the near-simultaneous escalation of public concern about energy and climate change. The search for solutions continued in the years I spent in the US as an energy specialist at the World Bank in Washington, DC, and a decade and a half later, back in Delhi, at USAID. By the turn of the millennium, strident warnings of climate change issued by experts and climate activists had led to institutional shifts and the creation of a clutch of new-gen organizations which this book describes with the aim to inspire the young to engage with such ecosystems of energy transformation. A new key driver in this space is decarbonization, a complex process to mitigate climate change. Decarbonization is the reduction of carbon dioxide emissions through the use of low or zero-carbon energy sources, such as natural gas or hydrogen and renewable energy sources – such as wind and solar – and energy efficiency. Taken to its logical conclusion, total decarbonization of a country's economy can lead to carbon neutrality or net zero. Put simply, net zero refers to the balance between the amount of greenhouse gases produced and the amount removed from the atmosphere through carbon sequestration and the like. Net zero is achieved when the amount added is no more than the amount taken away.

India will need to successfully adapt to a world characterized by technological changes driven by the need to decarbonize. It is this journey from fuel efficiency merely driven by economics, to one that engages with the larger concerns of ecology which arose in the mid-1990s, that you will find within these pages.

It would be easy for us to set this book against the backdrop of the fears that a post-Covid-19 world has raised about public health concerns. Can energy efficiency help revive economies through the targeted deployment of Covid-19 economic stimulus packages that governments are increasingly offering?

This is a simpler question to ask instead of failing to reach a truce with the planet's fragile ecosystem and accelerating the impending Armageddon. The bottom-line financial benefits accrued through energy efficiency could contribute to monetary savings to industry and business to soften the economic shock of the pandemic.

The pandemic is a mere flea bite in the face of the larger threat that looms over the world, and indeed India. As Noam Chomsky said deep into the outbreak of the Covid-19 pandemic: 'We should bear in mind that as severe as this crisis is, there is worse coming. There will be recovery from the pandemic, at terrible cost. There will be no recovery from the melting of the polar ice sheets, the glaciers in the Himalayas or the other dire effects of global warming – which will render much of South Asia uninhabitable if the world persists on its present course.'[3]

The Past Half-century

Energy is a wide-spectrum story. The interplay is between generation (supply) and end use (demand); the insatiable hunger for extracted resources like coal, gas and uranium; and the battle to make the most of what we draw as energy. On the demand side of the energy equation, working on energy saved, and not supplied, must be our outlook towards energy usage. A decisive shift from thinking about the supply side to a national effort on the demand side is part of the story to be written by the next generation of producers and users. This book recounts the four stages in the evolution of energy efficiency in India that led us to this point.

Our crippling dependence on petroleum oil imports led us to the first stage in the 1970s. The stress was on 'fuel efficiency' to reduce this dependence through technical interventions. This led to an expansion of efforts in the 1980s when the scope of fuel efficiency was broadened to 'energy conservation' to also accommodate lifestyle changes and socioeconomic approaches.

This, in turn, gave way to the current term, 'energy efficiency', which focused on an optimum amount of energy used in appliances, equipment and processes.

Today, we are at the threshold of a new concept – 'energy productivity' – based on the principle of maximizing economic value in terms of gross domestic product (GDP) or corporate revenue that countries and corporations obtain from energy through modernization and structural diversification.

It would help if the reader took a moment to step back and understand the journey of energy from a kilogram of coal mined at a 200-metre subsurface to the flick of an electrical switch in their homes. This dynamic and continuing link needs to be first understood and then disrupted as we move towards the future.

Can India as a nation moderate its energy demand at a level that helps mitigate environmental consequences while securing necessary energy supplies and delivering a quality standard of living to its people? Can the country build on its past successes and learn from its failures in mainstreaming energy efficiency in its economy? More importantly, can we tip the energy balance towards the demand side of the equation? It is my belief that it could do so, if the journey thus far is any indication.

The Writer's Quandary

This book is a recount of a journey that is quintessentially Indian. In putting together this book, the greatest challenge has been to write in a way that the few vital facts and figures are sifted from the trivial many. Every effort has been taken to avoid jargon to make the chapters accessible for all readers. The intent is to explain the source-think for many of the projects or programmes that we drove in those thirty years of work with multiple industry stakeholders and researchers who made things happen as we strategized and shuttled between Washington and India.

This is an informally told story of the energy journey India undertook from the time of the first oil crisis of 1973 through the subsequent half-century. This book is a broad investigation of this journey, which may raise as many questions as it answers. If it is successful in stimulating active thought and good research on the questions it raises, the book will have served its basic objective. In this spirit, I urge young, aspiring and practising sustainability professionals to take this guided tour of sorts that a few stalwarts and institutions helped illuminate. Please do accept the baton from an earlier generation that did the little it could and enjoyed doing it. As for the rest, may this book prove to be a gentle prod to nudge you further along on the journey into the energy challenges of the future.

As Isaac Newton had once suggested, how do we stand on the shoulders of those who have pushed the envelope over the decades, and look further with lessons learnt from those vignettes of the history of energy efficiency in India? How do we understand our history of energy use to carve our future endeavours? I hope that these pages will provide more than a few answers.

CHAPTER ONE

The Tryst with Energy, 1974–85

The Oil Shock

When the shadow of the 1973 oil crisis was looming large over India, I was barely into my twenties, having just completed an engineering programme at a peaceable little town in the interior of Tamil Nadu, in Tiruchirappalli, or Tiruchy for short. For over twenty years, India had imported big cars. Taxis would be king-sized American cars with cavernous interiors and soft purring engines that guzzled a litre for every kilometre travelled. No car user flinched at getting such low mileage. It barely made a dent in the pocket of the individual or the economy.

But the landscape of energy prices transformed completely in October 1973 when the smaller Fiat and Standard Herald models hit Indian roads in greater numbers and the large American Buicks and Impalas went off the market. Earlier that month, a war had broken out in West Asia between two ancient peoples – the Jews and the Arabs. It was an eruption of a long-festering wound over the Sinai Peninsula and Golan Heights, two regions that Israel had annexed in 1967 during what is known simply as the Six-Day War. The 1973 conflict lasted about three weeks and would have been buried under the debris of history were it not for an unexpected outcome that left a lasting impact on the world.

It started with the Organization of the Petroleum Exporting Countries (OPEC), established in 1949 and comprising largely the Arab nations, slapping an embargo later in December 1973 on the supply of oil in the aftermath of the war. It was targeted at all nations that were seen to be supporting the Yom Kippur War – named curiously after the last of the ten days of penitence that begins with the Jewish new year, Rosh Hashanah. Ironically, it was also the time of Ramadan, a month of fasting and reflection for Muslim Arabs. The nations targeted were Canada, Japan, the Netherlands, the UK and the US, and the ban was later extended to Portugal, Rhodesia and South Africa.

By the end of the oil embargo in March 1974, the price of oil had risen nearly four times, from $3 per barrel to nearly $12 globally. India's oil import bill rose from ₹204 crores in 1972–73 to ₹560 crores in 1973–74 and further to ₹1,113 crores in 1974–75. This five-fold increase during these three years adversely impacted the country's economy such that 42% of foreign exchange earned was used for imports of crude oil and oil products. In 1974, India topped the United Nations' list of thirty seriously affected developing countries whose balance of payment deficit was estimated to be almost 40% of the total deficit faced by all the affected nations. That year permanently changed the way India looked at the key drivers of the economy. The embargo caused an oil crisis, or 'shock', with many short- and long-term effects on global politics and the global economy. Oil took centre stage in political debates and government policies for the first time and remained the bugbear of every national economy ever since. Things were never to be the same again.

Ever since, stranger things have happened too. In late April 2020, US oil prices turned negative for the first time in history after oil producers ran out of space to store the oversupply of crude oil due to the slowdown of the global economy as a result of the coronavirus crisis, triggering an oil market crash that left oil traders reeling. The price of US crude oil crashed from $18 a barrel to –$38 as rising stockpiles of crude threatened to overwhelm storage facilities and forced oil producers to pay buyers to take the barrels they could not store. The market crash underlined the global impact of the coronavirus outbreak on oil demand as the global economy slumped. President Trump described the negative price as a short-term problem and said that the US was filling up its strategic reserves: 'If we buy it for nothing, we're gonna take everything we can get.' Following the President's off-the-cuff comment, the *Guardian* reported that a record 160 million barrels of oil were being stored in 'supergiant' oil tankers berthed off the US Gulf Coast.[1]

India's Energy Crisis

All through the 1950s until the mid-1960s, electricity generation from hydropower contributed to a quarter of India's commercial energy supply and the balance three-fourths came from coal and petroleum. It was the era of the 'temples of modern India' as Jawaharlal Nehru, India's first prime minister had termed the hydropower projects in Damodar Valley and Bhakra Nangal. By 1974, coal share had dropped to 24% and the share of oil had risen from 40% to 50%. Electricity accounted for the rest. Diesel, petrol and kerosene were largely imported. India tried hard to build self-sufficiency with respect to oil but it just didn't have the natural resources to do so. It has always imported around two-thirds of its oil needs for which it has had to pay precious dollars.

Between coal and oil, India has been caught in a vice-like grip. Throughout the second half of the twentieth century, energy in India – coal for electricity or oil for transportation – was generated only with extracted resources. The push for renewable energy has been faltering due to the intermittent and inconsistent nature of natural energy resources like solar and wind as well as low availability of generation capacity. In addition to this, there is the question of how renewable energy will be integrated with the larger national grid. Incentives are low and the infrastructure for making business easy does not fully exist. Therefore, our import dependence on oil has continued unabated.

Another peculiarity that cropped up post 1973 was India's frenzied effort to scale its coal production. At the time, a Union minister close to erstwhile Prime Minister Indira Gandhi was anonymously reported to have said with much bravado and little understanding of the dire ecological consequence of his intent, 'We produce 80 million metric tonnes (MMT) of coal, a fantastically low figure. Any extra effort is bound to be productive and an extra effort will be made.'[2]

Thus began the ravaging of the forests in central India that continued for the next fifty years. In 2020, India gouged about 675 MMT of coal. Madhya Pradesh (which in 2000 was hived off from the Chhattisgarh mining belts) and Bihar (which had most of the buried minerals in the forests of Jharkhand) bore the brunt of indiscriminate extraction. By mining more coal or importing more oil, we were destroying the intricate, valuable biodiversity hosted by these forests and natural ecosystems and galloping towards the eventual exhaustion of natural resources. There were only two solutions then, even now – hard demand-side management and smart, localized non-fossil-based solutions.

The Sino-Indian War of 1962, the Indo-Pakistan War of 1965 and the drought of 1965 had contributed to the failure of the Third Five-year Plan (1961–66) which led to inflation, and price stabilization became the government's priority. While the target growth rate was 5.6%, the actual annual growth rate was a mere 2.4%. There were no five-year plans implemented in the eight years preceding 1974. This period saw three years of plan holiday (1966–69), plus the Fourth Five-year Plan (1969–74) did not bring about any improvement in the performance of the economy. In fact, the rate of GDP growth or national income decreased further. So had industrial investment, particularly in the sectors producing basic and capital goods. Not only was economic growth not picking up, but the basis of future growth was also being eroded. As an economy that had been suffering from low growth, India had virtually nothing with which it could cushion the sudden deterioration in its ability to pay for the increasing costs of oil imports during the time.

The Aftermath

In 1974, the Indian government found itself paying a staggering amount of ₹1,100 crore against the paltry ₹200 crore they were footing in import bills until the previous year. The oil price hike also caused an across-the-board increase in import prices, especially of food and fertilizers. Since the government had no control over these events, inflation was fanned sharply and India was on the brink of bankruptcy. It had to find a way to sustain the imports of oil, fertilizers and other essential items and prevent catastrophic shortage of food supplies.

'[F]ewer cars are seen on the streets of New Delhi and Bombay, and many businessmen and civil servants are using buses for the first time. The cost of a rickshaw ride has climbed 50 per cent,' wrote the *New York Times* in a 1974 dispatch from India. 'Kerosene rationing is set to start on Feb. 1 in New Delhi. There are long lines to buy cooking oil, some cities, such as Bangalore, have sold oil and kerosene at police stations following riots. Farmers, especially in the fertile Punjab, are complaining about shortages of petrochemical fertilizers and fuel for farm machinery.'[3]

The cost to the consumer at the pump was also steadily increasing. Petrol was sold at less than a rupee per litre in the early sixties. The 1970s saw a rise to ₹2, post the OPEC crisis, it jumped to ₹4 per litre, and by the end of the decade, petrol was valued at ₹8. At the turn of the nineties, it had climbed to ₹11, later ₹18 and was ₹30 by 2000. Ten years into the millennium, India was looking at ₹50 per litre, followed by ₹80 towards the end of 2020, and today, as of March 2021, petrol rates are edging close to ₹100. I cite petrol prices here for we relate better to it as buyers and diesel prices tend to lag only a little behind that of petrol. The demand for diesel rose much more dramatically all through these years, while, by comparison, petrol always rose at a modest 4.5% annually.

The push India needed then as it does now was the reduction in the use of diesel which has always soared sharply at 7.4% year-on-year.[4] The reason is obvious. From toothpaste to steel, the price of every commodity is impacted with every percentile rise in diesel, which is not surprising if one considers the costs of transportation in a country as vast and with distribution as dispersed as in India. Its impact has been felt in average households for which liquefied petroleum gas (LPG) has risen from ₹60 in 1990 to ₹700 for a cylinder in 2020 and thereafter, within a year, reached a peak of ₹845.[5] A lesser-known fact is that the energy used to manufacture petroleum products in refineries and their transportation to consumers had claimed a tidy slice of our oil import expenditures. When the OPEC nations doubled oil prices, petroleum products became so expensive that it adversely affected the supply of fertilizers and hurt farm output. Without naphtha derived from refining petroleum, there was no way to make the production of synthetic fertilizers possible. And India's Green Revolution, which began in 1967, needed all the support that farmers could get.

To complete this picture of then and now, it would be useful to remember that in 1973 the country's population was 580 million, less than half its 2020 population of 1.3 billion.

It produced 115 million tonnes of food grains in 1974, double the 58 million tonnes at the start of the Green Revolution, seven years prior to the oil crisis. Essential uses of crude oil included fertilizers, captive power generation, diesel oil for trains, trucks and tractors, and furnace fuel for industries such as steel, cement, textiles and sugar. No industry was spared when furnace oil prices increased from ₹60 per kilolitre in the sixties to over ₹400 in 1974 and ₹30,000 today. Furnace oil used in industry in boilers and furnaces and diesel used to operate public buses and trucks offered a massive potential for conservation through the adoption of efficient technologies and operational practices then and continues even to this day.

In a sense, the hurt and the crippling economic crisis that the Arab embargo brought to India was at the root of the political crisis that precipitated nearly eighteen months later in June 1975 with the Emergency. The economy had become too fragile to withstand these setbacks without a re-orientation of strong basic policies and stagnated around 3.5% between the fifties and the eighties. This was christened as 'Hindu rate of growth' by Professor Raj Krishna, the Indian economist and professor at Delhi School of Economics who famously argued that the trend growth rate in India will be 3.5% despite any changes in the economy.[6]

The crisis had to be managed without the adoption of unpopular measures. Besides going to the International Monetary Fund, the World Bank and donor countries like the US and the UK for more aid, India's rigid controls and licensing had to be loosened to increase production and promote exports. Large business houses had to be permitted to expand production, which they had not been free to do under Prime Minister Indira Gandhi's reign from 1966 onwards, post Lal Bahadur Shastri's death in harness in Tashkent. To check inflation, the government had to take steps not only to increase the supply of goods but also to restrain demand for them. For this purpose, all wage increases and half of the additional dearness allowance of salaried employees were frozen and converted into compulsory deposits. These measures were condemned as 'anti-working class' by Mrs Gandhi's detractors. She made light of such criticism and avoided making a public comment through the breadth of the crisis of 1973.

The government was vulnerable to criticism for ideological retreat for pursuing anti-market, left-of-centre policies and regulations. While nations like South Korea, Taiwan and Singapore were opening up their economies to global trade, India preferred to head in the opposite direction with strict import controls including imposition of the Foreign Exchange Regulatory Act (FERA). Mrs Gandhi found herself in a difficult situation as she was being pulled in different directions by her professional advisors and her party members. What could have been turned into an opportunity for economic reforms at the most fundamental level, never extended beyond the management of the crisis at hand because of party politics.

Instead, it marked the beginning of a new era of shortages. Management of supply shortages, a euphemism for curtailment, became an art in vogue. On the brighter side, it also signalled baby steps taken on the demand side of the energy equation, aka energy efficiency.

Dawn of the Efficiency Journey

Though India's need for efficiency in fuel oil use manifested nationwide for the first time in 1973, there had been some faint stirrings a few decades earlier. A conference of steam users and boiler inspectors can be traced back as early as 1948, to the erstwhile state of Madras. This conference led to the formation of a voluntary, non-profit organization – emerging largely from the textile industry – led by Binny Limited, a household name in the textile world at the time. It was aimed at improving the efficiency of fuel use, notably coal. In 1953 it was known as the South India Steam & Fuel Users Association and later, in 1965, it took on a national mission and consequently dropped the prefix 'South'. It was perhaps the earliest effort in India by a group of concerned private companies to meet and share information on best fuel efficiency and steam utilization practices in boilers and plant processes. It was a modest step – limited in its geographical scope to the metro cities of Bombay, Calcutta and Madras – and had limited industry coverage. Its publications were popular not least because of the wealth of practical tips and information they provided. One of these, the *New Stokers Manual* was reproduced from a UK source and was widely read by boiler-room firemen for its focus on the art of shovelling coal into boiler furnaces and maintaining its fire line by ensuring burnability.

By the end of the 1960s, the government too had realized the need for understanding the energy supply and demand balances to plan for the current and future energy requirements of the country. The Fuel Policy Committee (FPC), chaired by T. L. Sankar – an Indian Administrative Services (IAS) officer of repute in state and central government energy circles – was set up in 1970 to examine and suggest the country's national fuel policy for the next fifteen years. Its report marked the official recording of energy efficiency or fuel efficiency as it was referred to at that time, the first attempt to define the term by a government-appointed body in India. The efficient use of fuel, weaning of consumption away from petroleum products to coal and biomass as well as promotion of specialized training in fuel efficiency were discussed for the first time in a government study. The FPC report moved the government to action.

One of its fallouts was the establishment of an inter-ministerial body called the Standing Committee on Furnace

Oil in 1971. The purpose of the committee was to determine quotas of furnace oil allocations to industrial units based on established criteria of priority and importance to the economy. It had members from the petroleum, coal, power and railway ministries and was chaired by the Directorate General of Technical Development, an office of the Ministry of Industry responsible for industrial licensing and thus, administering the infamous 'Licence Raj'.

Suddenly the ministry's office was turning to experts who could help in bringing efficiency to fuel use.

NPC was on top of the list of such experts. Established in 1958, NPC was a quasi-governmental autonomous organization engaged in promoting a culture of *productivity* through training and consultancy in Indian industries. Headquartered in Delhi, it had regional offices in the metros (Mumbai, Kolkata and Chennai) and several state capitals and towns in India. In 1964, NPC had established a fuel efficiency consultancy and training cell. But more on that later.

A Career Begins

Meanwhile, oblivious to these upheavals on the world stage, in a sedate Madras – as it was then called – I had picked up a forgettable job in a small engineering firm after graduating from the Regional Engineering College in Tiruchy (now known as the National Institute of Technology). Like many young Indians seeking careers at the time, I didn't realize how these large forces could shape individual fortunes. And one of those pinballs that struck right for me was being picked up by NPC, which was looking for engineers who could lead training, research and consultancy for fuel-efficiency services. It couldn't have been a happier accident. What was never a sexy career before was suddenly the centre of attention.

Of course, as a young man full of hope and aspiration, I

was blissfully oblivious of the war that set me off on a road that has shaped my destiny and led India to innovations in energy. But this chance opportunity got me a vantage view for the next forty years as I saw our economy grow with a hunger for oil imports which was relentlessly continued to be over 80% of our demand.

As a tiny element in the larger scheme of things, I walked into the NPC office on Lodhi Road in New Delhi and into the life of a man with an extraordinary mind, P. R. Srinivasan, in the spring of 1974. PRS, as he was known in his circles, was heading the department for Fuel Efficiency and Technological Services at the organization at the time. The department's function was to provide training and consultancy services to industrial energy users as well as conduct seminars and conferences to discuss and disseminate scientific and technological knowledge and information on fuel efficiency. Moreover, NPC was already working with industry professionals for fuel combustion efficiency on factory shop floors. The wheel had been set in motion in India but I wasn't to know that this tryst with energy which began that fine morning at the Council's office would inspire a great deal of learning in the nearly five decades of my long affair with energy.

Initial Years

In the early 1960s, there were textile manufacturing units in Bombay that sought to switch from coal to oil firing. Importing coal from Bengal and Bihar posed the challenges of rail transportation over the hilly tracts of the Western Ghats and Bombay running out of space for the coal inventory. The textile industry, which was more than a century old, was looking at how Esso and Burmah Shell refineries just off the Bombay docks in Chembur could be a source for residual fuel oil – or furnace oil, as it is commonly referred to – for their steam boilers. The two refineries were set up in 1951 and 1954 respectively, when Western countries such as the UK and the US had sought to make investments in Indian industry and infrastructure. These were nationalized in 1976 during Mrs Gandhi's regime and were rechristened Bharat Petroleum Limited and Hindustan Petroleum Corporation Limited. The idea was simple enough: the refinery plants produced furnace oil as a by-product and were eyeing industry segments looking to switch from coal to fuel oil to bolster their revenues. It made sense to sell to Indian industry which was quite willing to make the change. But they needed help since India was not yet familiar with the use of furnace oil.

With this in mind, the Planning Commission of India invited some experts from the National Institute of Fuel Efficiency Services (NIFES) of the UK for assistance in 1963. NIFES had been set up in the late 1940s after the Second World War, to guide the UK industrial sector on efficient use of fuel. NPC was the commission's natural choice as the catalysing agency mandated to receive know-how from NIFES to assist with the substitution of coal with oil in Indian industry.

Following the visit from the UK experts, PRS set up the fuel efficiency services under NPC at its headquarters in Delhi in 1964. He was one of the first Indians to observe and learn from the evolving energy landscape in the UK where fuel efficiency as a discipline had already taken root. Anything that would bring about savings in public expenditure got the attention of a cash-strapped government, so the programme got off to a decent start in India with extensive campaigns to enhance fuel efficiency. Seeds of planned action to bring fuel efficiency in industrial use were being sown in India. Those were still the years of ecological innocence when the thrust on fuel efficiency was purely economic, and the decision-makers were blissfully unaware of the massive and disastrous ecological impact of the increased use of natural resources.

By the time the oil crisis struck in 1973, NPC had already built some muscle in the sixties with several trained professionals who had blossomed under the diligent tutelage of PRS. NPC was asked by the government's industry ministry to work with corporate leaders to determine the opportunities and potential for fuel oil savings in their factories. This required a technical assessment of how efficiently, or otherwise, oil was being used by these factories and an estimate of where and through what measures its consumption could be reduced. A pan-India survey of over 300 industrial plants by a joint team of NPC and oil companies such as Indian Oil, Bharat Petroleum and Hindustan Petroleum revealed an average of 20%–25% savings with some plants displaying more than 40%–45% savings potential.

A dialogue with the captains of Indian industry followed. It was the first such conference on fuel efficiency in operational practices and technologies in end-use equipment and manufacturing processes. It drove home, for the first time in independent India, the need for energy conservation. Since then, this message has resonated in many boardrooms and strategy meetings of managements across institutions. In hindsight, this conference set off a series of such initiatives across India.

Stepping Forward

The advent and growth of fuel efficiency was a story of savings and bottom-line gains.

Higher conversion efficiencies will indisputably deliver more useful energy. The UK had made gains in the early years following World War II by a combination of gradual improvements in traditional energy converters with improved efficiency in boilers, furnaces and heat (steam) distribution and utilization of equipment and processes. The domestic approach in India post the oil crisis of 1973 was built around maximizing savings by introducing efficient practices and techniques in the use of petroleum fuels ranging from furnace oil in the industrial setting and, in later years, petrol and diesel in transportation and natural gas in power generation. It was a gradual development and grew in rapidity and scale through the eighties and nineties, and beyond, to this day.

The message was simple: how could industries derive twice, or even three times, as much useful energy per unit of primary supply? To carry the message forward, an institutional arrangement was created – among the first in the world – in recognition of the importance of fuel efficiency. The Petroleum Conservation Action Group was set up in 1976 in partnership with NPC and the Indian Oil Corporation Ltd (IOC). Two years later, it evolved into a permanent entity, the Petroleum Conservation Research Association (PCRA) under the Ministry of Petroleum and Natural Gas, to make oil conservation a national priority and movement.

The five years from 1974 to 1979 were a steep learning curve for India with institutions like NPC and PCRA spearheading the national movement to conserve petroleum fuels. They aimed to do this by creating awareness about the importance, methods and benefits of conserving petroleum products and by providing training and technical assistance. At the time, they showed extraordinary foresight, but the bureaucracy moved far too slowly and with little understanding of the outcomes their innovations would foster. Industry, too, toed the conservative line and adopted defensive approaches which had facilitated a quick recovery from the first oil shock in the aftermath of the Yom Kippur War and the Arab oil embargo-led price hike.

The shadow of the oil impact persisted through the seventies. Having seen how the world would, after all, bend to the pressures of oil price spirals, OPEC had gradually and steadily pushed prices to as much as $20 per barrel by 1978. A second oil shock following the deposition of the Shah of Iran due to the Islamic Revolution of 1979, further raised the prices. The price of oil, Iran's main export, had quadrupled in 1973, raising Iranian expectations. Flushed with the newfound national wealth, the Shah accelerated his ambitious modernization plans. Iran's gross national product (GNP) had risen by 34% in 1973 and by 42% in 1974 but fell to 15% in 1976–77. This fall in GNP spelt disaster for a highly mortgaged Iran.[7] It signalled the failure of the Shah's overly ambitious 1974 economic programme that according to a scholar of revolutions, Crane Brinton, created disappointment much greater 'than if people had been left in poverty all along' – consider the adage 'one can't miss what one never had'.

Prices doubled per barrel to $40 in a distraught twelve-month period in 1979. The world reeled under the relentless gaze of OPEC members who turned up the pressure as they generated money hand over fist for the oil economies.

India saw the opportunity in this economic adversity. Every lever was pushed to get to learn from proven and tested past initiatives. Industry captains and production heads were trained by fuel efficiency experts from NPC, PCRA and CII to assess, evaluate and introduce conservation measures in their plants. The results began to emerge slowly at first and gradually picked up speed and spread across different industry segments across geographies.

Efficiency Episodes

I was drawn into this national fuel efficiency movement along with several of my NPC teammates from 1976 thereon. Several industrial visits were undertaken, studies conducted, reports prepared and presented. We had our fair share of hilarious moments, some grim ones and a few that surprised us. Once, when a presentation to the owner of a textile mill and his officials seemed to draw a tepid response, I stopped midway to surprise them with our major proposition. The idea was to retrofit an economizer on the mill's boiler – it is a piece of equipment that saves fuel by recovering waste heat from the boiler's flue gases to preheat boiler water. 'The fuel savings will be 25% and the payback will take less than six months,' I explained. The effect was startling. The owner woke up from his slumber, sprang out of the chair and exclaimed with delight, 'In that case I shall install four of them and save 100% fuel oil!' We had to try our best to contain our laughter.

On another occasion, one of our design change suggestions for a glass furnace got us into trouble. We had suggested using a different insulating brick with a lower heat transfer coefficient and increased thickness to reduce the rate of heat losses from the crown or roof of the furnace. The estimated fuel and hence monetary savings were too attractive for the client to ignore. Not barely a month after incorporating our design specifications and the new furnace being put into action, the furnace roof caved in. The insulating bricks had caused the inner refractory layers to heat up beyond their limit, buckle and collapse. The owner was mortified while we were left embarrassed. Basically, we and industry learnt by doing.

Operation Black Smoke spearheaded by PRS to stress the need to save coal to the textile mills in Bombay is a stirring example of the efforts made by NPC. The city skyline was dotted with chimneys discharging plumes of smoke that wafted over parts of the city. As the day drew to a close, the sea breeze brought with it soot from the smoke that settled down on buildings, parks and public places. People were outraged. The solution to the problem was obvious: complete combustion of the coal in the mills' boilers which would ensure that fewer particulates and less unburnt carbon escaped through the chimney. An indicator of good and complete combustion and thereby fuel efficiency was chimney smoke with a light brown haze.

A mirror fixed outdoors and reflecting the chimney enabled the boiler fireman to assess whether the smoke was of the right shade. With one eye cocked on the mirror, shovelling coal into the boiler furnace was a precarious task. The firemen ensured efficient combustion of the coal by deploying correct firing practices which assured that the coal bed was even, with properly sized coal, and that the fuel and air mixed properly. In short, there was a slew of measures that the firemen were trained to perform so that the smoke at the base of the chimney was not black but rather had a light brown haze.

This action was replicated in scores of mills in the city and beyond to monitor and achieve fuel efficiency.

A Career Triggered

G. C. Datta Roy, an acclaimed and leading energy efficiency professional who founded one of India's premier energy efficiency service companies in the nineties was transfixed by a simple experiment conducted by PRS at the cogeneration plant in his chemical factory in Delhi in the early seventies. With nothing more than a handkerchief in hand and accompanied by Datta Roy, PRS walked around the company's travelling grate and water-tube boilers and marked with chalk the areas in the brickwork where he observed the handkerchief being sucked in. The marked points indicated locations where cold, ambient air was infiltrating through the brickwork and carrying the heat out of the chimney. This indicated poor fuel efficiency and consequently, higher fuel consumption. Reminiscing this many years later, over coffee at his home, Datta Roy said, 'It was a powerful visual experience that has always stayed with me.

An energy efficiency trial conducted with a mere piece of cloth brought home to me the power of simple experimentation and diagnosis. As I look back, I can truly say that inspired me and defined my career path over the next four decades.' His journey eventually led to the creation of an energy efficiency services company – Development Environergy Services Ltd (DESL) – and employed scores of professionals.

Vanishing Savings

We also encountered cheating and craftiness. Once, we were surprised by a call from a client, a pharmaceutical company, complaining that the savings in furnace oil that we had calculated and reported had not materialized. And this was after they had religiously followed up on all our technical recommendations. We visited the plant and met their staff. We combed through the plant inspecting the boiler house, steam pipelines and processing departments – specifically areas which we had earlier studied and recommended changes for. And indeed, the designs reflected the changes we had suggested. 'We thought our monthly oil consumption would reduce by 20% as your report suggested, from 10 kilolitre to 8 kilolitre but it has remained steady, although our product mix and production levels have remained the same,' complained the plant manager in a sharp tone. It was understandable since he had stuck his neck out and convinced his management to invest almost ₹50,000 into fuel efficiency measures, which we had assured would earn them a simple return on investment in just three months. The situation was puzzling with no solution in sight. We returned to the plant the following day. That's when we saw an oil tanker enter the factory gates and decided to observe the decanting of oil into the company's underground storage sumps. The oil in the road tanker was first measured using a dipstick which helped establish the volume of oil in the tank.

Thereafter, the oil was poured into the sump until the torrent was reduced to a trickle and finally the last few drops. It seemed like a normal weekly operation carried out by the private tanker operator and plant staff. On closer observation, we noticed that the tanker was slanted since its rear tires were deflated. One did not require a Sherlock Holmes to deduce its effect on the oil level. A sloping tank would show a higher level at the rear end of the tanker where the dipstick had been inserted. This meant that the company was being short-changed. A quick investigation revealed that the savings were not reflected accurately in the company's purchase records since the actual volume of the oil delivered was less than what was recorded. We left vindicated.

Learning by Sharing

The arguments, chatter and banter among colleagues when we discussed, debated and shared experiences about work held important learnings that could not have been gleaned from books and magazines. We learnt from one another how energy systems and processes are operated in industry. A boiler's chimney that released no smoke is an indication of inefficient combustion just like a chimney that billowed black smoke. The former indicated that too much air was being drawn into the boiler and carrying away some of the heat out through the chimney, and the latter showed that there was a paucity of air for the complete combustion of the fuel which had resulted in black particulates exiting from the chimney as black smoke. A brown haze set against the blue sky indicated that the boiler was operating efficiently. Invisible to the eye, the furnace brickwork that allowed air to infiltrate resulted in fuel wastage. All that was needed was to move a candle flame across the brickwork and watch and mark carefully the locations where the flame appeared to be drawn into tiny cracks and crevices and patch them up.

We also learned that malfunctioning steam traps can waste energy, and how to prevent them from allowing steam to escape instead of discharging condensate. We gathered insights, from our observations and discussions with plant personnel, about the 'factor of safety' syndrome which one wag termed as 'factor of ignorance'. It can be better understood with the following example:

The shop engineer at a factory requisitions for a 3 HP motor based on his experience of the process. The design engineer at the company's R&D department computes the dynamics of the process and arrives at a figure of 4.5 HP. The company's purchase manager, after going through vendor literature, learns that this is a non-standard specification and decides to place an order for a 5 HP motor. The company receives and installs a motor that is 40% larger in capacity than originally specified and operates at a lower efficiency going forward.

Over time, we were forced to ask ourselves a simple question: What are the limitations of energy-efficient designs developed for individual technologies? We realized that our design methods were not inclusive because we had been looking at each equipment in isolation and trying to optimize their operations or functioning without fully understanding their interactions with one another. For instance, we determined the optimal diameter of a pipe to permit the required flow of liquid without taking into consideration the increase or even reduction of dynamic head losses on pump size and performance. This led to an unproductive combination of having installed big pumps and small pipes. At another time, we spent a great deal of effort and money on choosing a light lamp with the highest lumen efficacy without accounting for its application efficacy. We had missed an important question: Is the light illuminating the table or object that we want to light up or is it being scattered across areas of the room that need not be lit? While thinking of ways to insulate hot surfaces to reduce heat losses, our design approach was to work with the thickness of insulating wool. But this individually stylized approach focusing only on insulation technology neglects the capital cost of the heating system, namely the boiler and its auxiliaries. If one were to replace the heating system with a smaller boiler or look at cheaper alternatives such as thermic fluid heaters or heat pumps, the energy savings would be far greater than what just insulation yields. We wrestled with these thoughts while trying to develop integrative energy efficiency design solutions which is an ongoing endeavour for us even today.

And there were, in those early days, many such occasions that brought the satisfaction of successful execution and others that resulted in unintended consequences. But each of these incidents was an article of faith for experimentation and innovation for us. To have failed meant one had tried and success would soon be savoured.

Private Endeavours

The late seventies and the early eighties saw several private-sector initiatives as well. Thermax Private Ltd in Pune, founded in 1980, was among the first private-sector engineering companies involved in energy and the environment that committed to energy efficiency. Thermax advertisements, even in those years, revolved around themes of how money could be saved through well-planned industrial practices and processes. One of their hoardings displayed a sheaf of money coming out of a smokestack. 'Go in for efficient boilers and save money' was the message that blazed across popular Indian dailies. The timing could not have been better.

The country was again in a transition phase. This time India was looking at additional options beyond the substitutes of fuel oil by coal in industry – a reversal of the trend of the

60s when coal firing was abandoned in favour of furnace oil. This was not always possible since coal availability, its quality and its transport to consumers across this vast land was difficult to achieve in practice, and hence, the focus changed from fuel substitution to fuel efficiency. Since 60%–70% of the country's fuel oil consumption was accounted for by industrial boilers, they came under laser-like focus. Textile units, among others, had a battery of Lancashire boilers of various sizes, often referred to as 'museum pieces' and a 'legacy of the British times' having been imported from England during the colonial era. Antique versions of these boilers dating from the early twentieth century fuelled by coal, and later by oil, were generally inefficient but impressively robust. They could tolerate, like the proverbial donkey, a high level of operational abuse. Unlike the modern packaged boiler, the quality of water was hardly a hassle for steam generation for them, and they could run with minimal operator supervision – a very handy attribute during night shifts when operators were likely to be lax. But their efficiency was as low as 50%–55% compared to packaged boilers that could achieve up to 80%–90% efficiency. The reason was simple: heat from the combustion of fuel in a boiler is transferred to the water through the medium of radiation and convection. Radiative heat transfer is the primary process of transfer in shell boilers like the Lancashire boiler, which results in inadequate capture of heat by the water with a large portion of the heat escaping through the boiler chimney.

By way of contrast, packaged boilers offered a combination of radiative and convective heat transfer as well as superior burner management and combustion control systems, and thus, offered efficiencies of greater magnitude.

Right from its early days, PCRA saw shell and tube industrial boilers, such as Lancashire boilers, as a major hindrance to achieving fuel efficiency and had been campaigning for the shift to packaged boilers. Thermax was among the few that manufactured these to meet the surging industrial demand. Gradually, most of the shell-tube boilers in the Indian industry were replaced by packaged boilers between the mid-1980s and 90s. Thermax had led that market drive with success.

Past Ideologies, Current Trends

As a country, we have taken some major steps in industrial energy management, utility demand response programmes and design of efficient processes and end-use equipment. Another area, as the following anecdote reveals, is risk shared business approaches to energy savings. The year was 1978. Those were the days of Licence Raj. I was a junior faculty member for a training programme on industrial fuel efficiency for participants mostly from the public sector. During one of the sessions, I shared an interesting concept I had earlier come across in an article in a magazine: energy savings performance contracts. These contracts had been gaining popularity in the US. The idea was to save energy by implementing measures identified, designed and paid for by another party, and in exchange for their services, one split the savings with them according to a shared or guaranteed savings performance contract. It was an appealing idea that merited some discussions in the class. The participants were bewildered. They had never heard or contemplated such an idea. My bosses were not pleased at all. They felt I was introducing a business idea into what was thought to be a patriotic duty of every citizen, namely, to save energy. Today this call for altruism lies discarded and ideological barriers of the past have made way for contemporary business solutions. The trend of energy service companies who provide turn-key energy efficiency services – ranging from audits through project design and execution in return for shared savings – has gained acceptance.

A Matter of Aggregation and Scale

The emergence of the Energy Efficiency Services Ltd (EESL) in 2009 as a catalyst and a force multiplier for the development and service of energy efficiency markets through the supply of energy efficient products in India at scale has been a key event in this energy story. EESL's forays, first of its kind in the country, into efficient illumination through strategies aimed at aggregating the LED (light-emitting diode) market and reducing consumer prices of LED lamps was a game changer. Behind this and other innovative concepts was EESL CEO Saurabh Kumar. An engineer by training and alumnus of the Indian Revenue Service, Saurabh's first stint in matters of energy efficiency was at the Bureau of Energy Efficiency (BEE) as its secretary in 2007. This allowed him a ringside view as to what ails the efficiency movement in the country. He observed how market-size constraints, non-standardized equipment and high costs proved insurmountable. Saurabh's 2011 stint with the UN in Bangkok provided him with a global perspective and opportunity to explore solutions to this vexing problem. On his return to India in 2013, he was soon propelled to the helm of EESL and granted the opportunity to test his ideas. Saurabh launched a strategic programme of partnership with municipalities, state utilities, governments and donors. Under this arrangement, EESL offered a package of advisory and financial services to invest in, design and implement large-scale efficient street lighting and home systems paid for through energy savings performance contracts. EESL's aggressive but non-subsidized approach to promoting energy efficiency as a commercial activity through the marketing and distribution of LED bulbs, LED tube lights and energy efficient fans resulted in avoided peak demand of 9,724 MW and an estimated annual energy savings of 48 billion kWh, 39 million tonnes of carbon dioxide and monetary savings of ₹19,200 crore in customer electricity bills.[8] LED lights, which were earlier priced upwards of ₹600 for a 9W lamp, saw prices tumble down to as low as ₹65. Within four years, other manufacturers were vying to compete for a share of one of the world's largest and growing lighting market. It was only a matter of time before EESL used its market aggregation approach to include other technologies such as efficient air conditioners, irrigation pumps, electric motors and thereafter branch into providing consulting and design services in building energy management systems, smart meters, distributed solar, trigeneration, electric vehicles and solarization of irrigation pump sets, to mention a few. Triggered by the success in India, EESL has also forayed into international ventures in over ten other countries, including the UK, in a sense, returning the favour bestowed on India by NIFES four decades ago. Indeed, the contribution of EESL under Saurabh's astute leadership to the transformation of energy efficiency markets unleashed through innovative and bold procurement practices was a significant milestone in the country's energy journey.

Uniquely Indian

I recall a meeting in Bangalore in early 1992 with an American co-researcher, Steve Nadel, from the American Council of Energy-Efficient Economy (ACEEE). We had decided to visit a factory in the city to understand how they went about saving energy in their business. It happened so that our visit fell on the day of the Hindu festival Ayudha Puja which means 'worship of tools'. Instead of the usual focus on the worship of one or the other innumerable Hindu gods, this is a day to express gratitude for the tools that are an integral part of our everyday life. The tools and instruments that were being worshipped by the workers on the factory floor were seemingly mundane like lathes, boring machines, drilling machines, electric motors, transformers and other similar equipment found in any industrial workplace. These 'tools' had garlands of marigold strung across them and three short, vertical lines of red vermillion smeared artistically – a devotee's mark of respect to all celestial beings, be they animate or inanimate. Steve was astonished by the colourful display. He listened intently to the factory manager explain the significance of the pooja. On our way back to the hotel, Steve leaned over to me and said thoughtfully, 'Divinity in equipment that uses energy gives a new meaning to efficiency.' It was a dimension that the West had scarcely explored!

Looking back, it is hardly a surprise in the aftermath of the 1973 oil crisis, that the first dozen or so companies in India that had made the greatest progress in achieving furnace oil savings were those with strong management commitment and led by staff who were not afraid to experiment in an area where the science was new and the application nascent. A 1978 NPC publication titled 'Case Studies in Furnace Oil Utilization' listed a dozen companies, private and public, that were successful in using furnace oil. A few years later, the list had expanded to over a hundred companies.

The prices of oil peaked by 1980 and did not subside to pre-crisis levels until the mid-1980s. Nevertheless, an important lesson was learnt. India – and the world – would never again review economic plans without using the petroleum lens. The idea of building resilience through strong demand-side management (DSM) was being gradually etched into the minds of government ministries, regardless of party loyalty and regimes. For India, which had grown fifty times in energy generation capacity since 1947 and was touching 65 GW by the end of the 1980s after a harrowing decade of OPEC's pitiless arm-twisting, there was much to be done in research, capacity building, technology and science as well as innovations on the demand side of the energy equation. However, the first few steps of greening India were underway.

As PRS once said, 'Developed countries like the US waste energy out of a sense of affluence; we waste energy out of a sense of ignorance. The point is, we both waste.'

CHAPTER TWO

Vital Few and Trivial Many, 1975–95

Energy Basics

PRS, the classical energy strategist that he was, used to break into little perorations on the bedrocks of energy every now and then. Mechanical energy, or work, and heat were his favourite themes. They were related by an equivalence that he often shared with those around him. It was described by him thus: 'Any student of physics knows that the correct value for the equivalence of heat and mechanical energy was discovered by the English physicist James Prescott Joule (1818–89). Joule used very sensitive thermometers to measure the temperature of water being churned by an assembly of revolving vanes driven by descending weights; this arrangement made it possible to measure the mechanical energy invested in the churning process with great precision. In 1847, Joule's painstaking experiments yielded a result that many years later, when conducted with instruments of an order of high calibration, turned out to be off by a mere 1% from the actual value.' Behind this description was his sober observation, 'Work is precious and heat is less so. One can obtain heat by burning any combustible material but to obtain work or mechanical energy needs a heat engine, a device that converts heat into mechanical energy. And all the heat cannot be converted into work, since there are irreversible losses that are governed by the laws of thermodynamics.'

Much of thermodynamics concerns the transformation of

heat into work and its little nuances of energy fundamentals that have always fascinated me. The law of conservation of energy – that energy can be neither created nor destroyed but can be converted from one form to another – we all know as the first law of thermodynamics or generally termed as the First Law Efficiency. Basically, it means you cannot cheat (or win) since all the energy must be accounted for. The second law states that all the heat cannot be converted to work without creating some waste heat. This means you cannot break even, since there will always be losses when you convert heat to work. And this fascination has only grown with the trivial realities of, say, a bag of grain or a barrel of crude oil being a low-entropy store of energy. It can do a great deal of useful work once burned.

As Vaclav Smil, a contemporary Canadian energy researcher, puts it, if you now chose to use an electric light to illuminate this page, the electromagnetic energy of that light is only a small part of the chemical energy contained in the lump of coal used to generate it. If as a reader, you used an old incandescent light, then more than 95% of 'delivered' electricity ends up as heat generated by the heated metal of the bulb's coiled filament resisting electric current. The light reaching the page is either absorbed by it or reflected and absorbed by its surroundings and reradiated as heat. The initial low-entropy input of coal's chemical energy dissipates as diffused high-entropy heat that warmed the air above the station, along the wires and around the light bulb, causing an imperceptible increase in temperature above the page. No energy has been lost, but a highly useful form was degraded to the point of no practical utility.

In 2018, coal with thermal power was used to produce nearly 70% of the electricity generated in India. At least 60% of coal's energy is lost as heat through a plant chimney and in cooling water. There are conversion losses as electricity is generated in the turbo-alternators as well as transmission and distribution losses as it is conveyed through the electrical network to your home. Almost five units of input electrical energy are consumed to deliver a single unit of electricity to the end user. Simply put, every time you use an air conditioner for ten hours, there is some coal miner excavating more than a kilo of the black stuff from a mine that is at least 150 m below the earth's surface. Every effort towards energy efficiency is about saving the five units of energy (electrical) that have to be generated and delivered to the busbar of the thermal power plant to supply one unit of electricity at the flick of a switch. If one were to trace the fuel input back to the utility boiler, then it would be at least twenty thermal energy units to deliver a single unit of electricity at the consumer end.

Macro Insights, Micro Approach

One of the advantages of working with NPC and PRS was that I got insights at the macro level. The perspectives I developed on India's response to the oil crisis, decisions the government could make, thrusts on conservation of fuel and measures that industry or the end user could potentially implement with process efficiencies were part of the steep learning curve that my work at NPC offered during those heady years in Delhi. Industry interactions and outcomes in terms of action at the shop floor had us all secure invaluable understanding as energy professionals.

Here is one such simple insight I gained at a conference in the summer of 1975.

'One needs a reliable supply of energy to save energy,' declared an agitated industry owner of an automotive forging plant in the industrial town of Faridabad at a conference of small- and medium-scale industry owners with government officials to discuss the opportunities for fuel efficiency. It was a common refrain in parts of the country where unstable and unreliable power supply, accompanied by voltage fluctuations and sudden interruptions, was causing plants to shut down. The penalty of unreliable supply is severe. For instance, in a forging furnace, unplanned and forced shutdowns cause energy losses due to the dissipation of heat which is further compounded by the additional energy needed to bring the furnace back on stream. The solution: ensure reliable, stable and quality power supply. A backup captive diesel engine could do that but it is a misallocation of scarce capital resources that a small or tiny plant owner can ill afford. 'So it's not all about energy efficiency,' concluded the gentleman, and with a silent nod, we accepted the truth of the remark. A much-needed dose of reality was injected into the deliberations.

One remarkable professional who got me to see the micro end of such strategies was P. Raghavendran or Raghu. When I met Raghu for the first time in 1975, he was heading the regional business of IOC Ltd in Coimbatore. His restless mind was constantly looking for ways to draw in customers or offer them ways to save fuel as well as money. It didn't take long for his company to get Raghu to steer jointly with NPC a campaign that brought him to New Delhi. We shared a house and I got many evenings to delight in animated conversations that he would usually lead. His passion for fuel efficiency was of a rare kind. Some of his ideas were breathtaking in their simplicity but potent in their result. One such idea was in motivating bus and truck drivers to save diesel while driving. I'll come back to the story later.

Raghu is an Indian Institute of Technology gold medallist who had landed a career in IOC after his graduation in 1969 and was posted in Coimbatore, which was then a sleepy little town. It was a quirk of destiny that placed him among the first founders of PCRA by the mid-seventies. In the summer of

1974, IOC Chairman C. R. Dasgupta was visiting Ootacamund or Ooty, the picturesque hill station nestled in the Nilgiris located in the tri-junction of the states of Tamil Nadu, Kerala and Karnataka on the Western Ghats. He summoned Raghu over for a meeting. Raghu excitedly told him of some value-add services that he was launching for his industry customers in Coimbatore, and how the idea had been inspired by a training programme where PRS had been a speaker. The conversation led to talk on the need for a fuel efficiency service for Dasgupta's oil company customers. The Chairman had been asked by the central government to come up with a plan for fuel efficiency, thanks to the insistent demands from industry.

Dasgupta lost no time on his return to Delhi to call PRS to discuss getting NPC to steer the programme. PRS had been working on such a plan for some years, so when he met Dasgupta, he swiftly pulled copies of a short monograph that lay tucked in his briefcase. The piece detailed how industry could save 5% energy with simple solutions. The meeting ended with an invitation to NPC to take up the programme. And that is how Raghu was brought in to work on the country's first fuel-efficiency campaign.

Oil Conservation Traverse

The maiden effort of the campaign involved conducting a survey of 300-plus companies across various industry segments from heavy engineering to tea and paper, from fertilizers and textiles to pharmaceuticals. These diagnostic surveys were carried out by a group of IOC and NPC engineers. The findings were shared with the management of the companies and the consolidated report on the results of the survey was presented to the Standing Committee on Furnace Oil (SCFO). At the request of the Chairman of the SCFO, Brigadier Sawhney, NPC was tasked with organizing a seminar-meeting to present the survey results to industry.

In the August of 1975, I attended a seminar at Delhi's Vigyan Bhavan where industry leaders debated all day long on the technical aspects to measure conversion efficiency, heat losses in furnaces, boiler efficiency, storage and filtration of oils and so on. The survey found favour with industry leaders who engaged. They suggested the formation of a permanent mechanism to assist industry.

In deference to their request, PCRA was launched in 1977 and staffed with officials from IOC, like Raghu, and NPC. Two years later, I joined PCRA on deputation from NPC. This gave me the opportunity to work on a nationwide educational campaign for fuel efficiency. Raghu was a strategist with foresight even as early as 1976. The devil lay in the details for him. He would spend endless hours on questions raised in surveys or making little how-to booklets on the efficient use of LPG and kerosene for kitchen use or diesel for trucks and petrol in cars and two-wheelers. He was among the first few in the country to foresee the geometric rise in demand for diesel; however, he never saw the demand for petrol as much of a threat. India was moving from cars to two-wheelers, he would say based on, not research data, but rare intuition. Petrol was no more than 20% of the demand. Road transport and farm pumps and tractors were the diesel guzzlers, he would insist. He turned his focus on users and what they could do to steer efficiencies of their own volition.

This led to a programme to drive home the point on energy use in the kitchen or good cooking habits. Little things like soaking dal or rice hours before you cook or cutting vegetables more finely so that you use less heat or using wide-bottomed vessels, so you make most of the heat from the stove, or turning the stove to simmer mode, or covering open vessels with a lid were all part of such efforts. An advertising agency that worked with us translated these ideas into a crisp copy. I recall a group of over 300 women at a gathering in Ahmedabad listening with rapt attention to a list of the little things that make a big difference in reducing kerosene and cooking gas use in any household. With a nationwide newspaper campaign, the message of petroleum conservation in homes, in transport, in industry and in farms began to form legs and then moved along speedily.

The interest among the public to seek information on effective conservation practices was simply overwhelming. I recall an early PCRA advertisement in a daily that invited readers to mail a filled-in coupon indicating their preference for information on oil conservation. What followed was the unexpected spectacle of bags of mail that inundated the post office at the capital's Parliament Street and made their way into our office in Connaught Place, a stone's throw away. Needless to add that our usual work came to a screeching halt for a couple of weeks due to this unanticipated turn of events. With all hands on deck, as it were, we geared to respond to the deluge of requests for information from consumers from every nook and corner of the country! Henceforth, the management decided, this work would be passed on to an off-site contractor much to the relief of the employees and, I guess, the post office, too. The message was clear. The Indian consumer was typically thrift-conscious, sought information and was prepared to introduce efficient measures and practices that would save fuel.

The seventies in India saw little learning from the West or the world outside. Statist policies of self-reliance kept the country largely insulated from outside influences. Two journals, *Plant Engineering* and *Power Magazine*, both from the US, were awaited every month, and devoured hungrily, for we had little information coming to us otherwise. A brochure from the US automaker General Motors on a campaign they ran to get motor car drivers to become fuel efficient startled us. They were talking of the same things that we had shaped here at a time when we had little contact with the world outside. It was nice to know that a bunch of us working in India on shoestring budgets could actually produce stuff that matched General Motors' research quality!

During those months, I got to know Raghu well. His approach to work, incisive mind and tendency to quickly dive into what the market needed left a strong impression on me. His rare talent for sifting thc vital few from the trivial many, and yet working on both with the same intensity of purpose, was incredible. Moreover, his programmes and ideas always aimed for a national reach. In fact, once he turned to the driver instructors of the Indian Army for help. He saw that they were disciplined, high on operation and maintenance (O&M) and drove well.

In the summer of 1980, I accompanied him to Srinagar for his meetings with Army officials. At one of the meetings, he found that the Army's overzealous O&M led to inefficiencies. The oil filters were being changed every three months though they were built to last for at least two years. These filters typically take two to four months and 1,000 km to become properly efficient, but in this case, they were being replaced just after they attained this efficiency.

Later, we met with civilians at the Jammu & Kashmir Road Transport Corporation for some answers to a nagging question. Earlier, as was his wont, poring over a sheaf of diesel consumption statistics by various state road transport corporations in the country, Raghu stumbled upon some surprising data. The state bus fleet had some of the lowest diesel economy numbers or average fleet passenger kilometres per litre. *What was the reason?* We asked ourselves. We would soon find out. The officials explained that they had a quota system that incentivized drivers to save diesel by following PCRA's list of good driving habits. The diesel saved by a driver from the quota allotted was his to use or sell. Many sold it in the open market and made some money. The corporation gained because the quota was not exceeded, and more importantly, it benefited the passenger too, since the fare was affordable and not frequently raised.

We seized the opportunity in front of us.

Raghu invited the Army's driver instructors to work with PCRA in different regions. The programme that he conceived for the bus drivers of various state road transport corporations was simple. A passenger bus was fitted with a makeshift calibrated jerry can that was connected to the diesel fuel system of the bus and placed next to the driver. On the first day of the training programme, a group of 10–15 drivers were required to drive the bus along a pre-chosen route of about fifteen kilometres traversing both the city and its outer limits. Before heading out, the driver noted the level of diesel in the jerry can and did so again when he completed the trip. Mileage per litre of diesel consumption was computed for each driver whose driving habits were watched with an eagle eye by the Army instructors. The next day was all classroom lectures with the instructors tutoring the participants on good driving habits such as avoiding overspeeding, changing gears at the right speed, anticipating stops, avoiding stomping on the brakes, switching off the engine while idling and so on. On the third and the last day, the drivers were asked to follow the first day's routine and traverse the same route. Fresh from the previous day's lectures, the drivers were careful and drove cautiously with an eye on the jerry can. At the end of the journey, each driver noted with anticipation the mileage achieved and were pleasantly surprised at the reduction in diesel consumption brought about by good driving practices.

I was asked to be a part of a similar training stint for Bharat

Electronics Ltd in Bangalore, which had a fleet of buses to transport employees from home to work and back. There, we saw a drop of at least 25%–30% in the use of diesel with simple and cost-effective expedients. This diesel conservation driver training programme continues to be conducted in many of the country's road transport corporations and private bus and lorry fleets, and of course, in the Army. It has also been emulated by others in the world.

Innovative Ideas, Dynamic Leadership

After a successful stint at PCRA, Raghu went on to do a master's at the Massachusetts Institute of Technology, following which he returned to India as Joint Advisor (Petroleum) at the Indian Planning Commission before heading IOC's Eastern region out of Kolkata. It was no surprise, years later in 1994, when he was selected to join Reliance Petroleum after a national search for a candidate to head their strategic planning and marketing wing. This was months before Reliance Petroleum's Jamnagar refinery was set up.

The striking story of his work with Reliance illustrates what governments could do if only they were quick with their decisions is worth the telling.

In mid-1994, a few months before Raghu joined Reliance Petroleum, he was invited by its management for consultations on a report by Arthur D. Little, a global consultancy firm. The report was on a detailed study of the Indian petroleum sector conducted by the company and advocated a strategy and plan to reform both the upstream and downstream sectors of the industry. Rumours were swirling that the government intended to implement some of the report's suggestions, specifically on the downstream side. In essence, the 'petro-nationalism' of the past, when more than 95% of the refining capacity of the country lay with the public sector, was likely to change by enlarging the participation of the private sector. Reliance was interested and began exploring opportunities in crude oil refining. A nine-million-tonne capacity refinery was on the anvil for which a manufacturing licence was imminent. They were not the only ones – several other private groups were clamouring to join the bandwagon.

On a humid, wet afternoon in June 1994, Raghu dropped by Reliance's offices in Makers Tower in downtown Mumbai. He was quickly ushered into a private room. In there was the Reliance patriarch, the legendary Dhirubhai Ambani and his sons, Mukesh and Anil. He was asked pointed questions on the oil import scenario unfolding globally and in India. India was importing two-thirds of its petroleum products at the time. This would not change for the next twenty years was the prognosis Raghu offered. From 40 million tonnes of total demand for crude with no more than 8 million tonnes that were produced internally in 1994. The figure was set to jump to 100 million tonnes by 2000. That import figure has been hovering around 83% as per the data released in 2019.

But the elder Ambani had other ideas – a global vision far beyond India's domestic needs. This was a recurring theme and the team of senior advisors and management was egged on to think big. There was an acute shortage of petroleum products like aviation turbine fuel (ATF), naphtha, petrol and diesel and the local refining capacity shortfall was in excess of thirty million tonnes. Dhirubhai Ambani zeroed in on this point and inquired whether the proposed refinery capacity at Jamnagar could be stepped up to meet the global demand. It did not seem plausible to Raghu at that time, since the cost of refined products would not be competitive for the Far East markets of China and Japan or Western EU or North American markets. Wedged between the sophisticated and efficient oil export infrastructure of Singapore and the Middle East, petroleum product export from India did not appear cost-competitive. The reason: oil product transport. Oil is normally transported in small tankers and, unlike the very large crude carriers (VLCCs), have higher transshipment costs since the economy of scale does not work in its favour. Raghu asked for a week to study the problem and get back with firmer numbers to strengthen his argument. Ambani was kind but impatient. He wanted immediate answers and suggested a meeting the following morning. Raghu arrived the next day armed with some more back-of-the-envelope numbers that buttressed his earlier argument. Ambani probed deeper. He wanted to 'shrink the distance' between the Jamnagar refinery and global oil markets of the East and the West. Reduction in the cost of oil product transportation was critical. Raghu pointed out that tankers are divided into two types: the product 'white oil' tanker and the crude 'black oil' tanker. The product tanker, designed to ferry cargo like refined oil products like diesel or gasoline from refineries to markets, is smaller than the crude tanker which is typically a very large crude carrier capable of carrying upwards of 250,000 tonnes in a single shipment. Given this and the unfavourable economics of smaller-sized product shipment costs, 'shrinking the distance' was well-nigh impossible. The meeting concluded with nary a solution in sight.

Raghu returned the next day to continue the meeting with the father and sons. And this time, he was a witness to a brilliant brainwave by the Ambani patriarch. It was such extraordinary insights that made him the numero uno Indian businessman of the time. *Why not transport the finished products in large white oil tankers that could dock at Jamnagar port?* The equations and calculations changed with the strategic use of Jamanagar's natural deep harbour, and the decision to set up a refinery with a capacity of twenty-two million tonnes was swiftly taken. Raghu was taken aback by the figure. At the end of the meeting, he turned to Mukesh Ambani and asked, 'Does this mean that we go ahead with 22 million tonnes?' Mukesh grinned at him, 'Did you not hear Papa say it? That decision is final. We will have to get the team to work out the figures and the technical feasibility all over again, and present it to him.' Some months later, Raghu recounted the story to me, and added, 'What the Planning Commission would have taken five years to decide was settled in less than forty-five minutes in that room.'

And there was more to come.

The largest single-stream refinery in the world moved quickly from the drawing board to the open field. More innovative ideas from the Reliance patriarch followed, all of which was anchored in one simple axiom – drive costs down to the lowest possible level. And to achieve this, hitherto untried measures and steps in the construction history of independent India – perhaps the world – were implemented. These included, but were not limited to, round-the-clock work to erect the plant and the machinery aided by an array of floodlights at night, prefabricated and preassembled refinery equipment shipped by global vendors and unloaded on site and concrete poured over pre-existing civil structures such as foundations, columns and tiers. Labour was procured from far-off states like Bihar, supported with intense hands-on training in civil, mechanical and electrical construction at training centres at the site before being absorbed in the workforce. Project management and execution at an unprecedented scale to coordinate a complex supply chain of global vendors, plant builders, designers, architects and engineers was underway in this small town of Jamnagar, tucked away on the western coast of India.

And so, the world's largest refinery came on stream within three years – the fastest ever in the history of the petroleum refining sector in the world. In 1999, the 22 million tonne refinery came on stream as planned. Its capacity over a period of time was incrementally increased to 27 million tonnes in 2002 and 30 million tonnes in 2005. In 2021, it is around 35 million tonnes. Today, with product tankers upwards of 90,000 tonnes available in a single shipment, the distance to distant markets has irrevocably shrunk.

For Raghavendran, coming as he did from the stultifying environs of the public sector, the speed of the decision-making and execution was awe-inspiring. In the early 2000s, several years after he had joined Reliance Petroleum, his ideas became even more relevant and were given wider acceptance with talks of decontrol and deregulation in the air. He enticed more truck drivers to drive into petrol and diesel stations selling Reliance products with the simple expedient of installing a pump automation system that tracked 'every molecule of fuel' – from the oil tanker that delivered the fuel to the station to the nozzle of the pump that transferred it into the customer's oil tank. The assurance of good quantity and quality fuel was a major relief to customers who were accustomed to being short-changed by unscrupulous dealers who occasionally tampered with the meters and were not above occasionally adulterating the fuel that they sold. This also did away with the traditional time-consuming custom of appointing a roving set of inspectors who did surprise checks on fuel quality and the efficacy of the fuel-dispensing system.

These measures paid off. In just a year, Reliance captured 15% of the all-India diesel market.

It was not as if the public sector or the government in its various echelons did not have inventive minds capable of such audacious thinking. It needs to be acknowledged how a lot of the work Raghu and his fellow officials did to set the foundation of marketing in the 1980s has served IOC to this day. The massive marketing campaign driven by IOC is not widely understood or appreciated. Old-timers often talk about the marketing innovations they had to introduce when they were promoting the use of LPG when it was first introduced in the late sixties in India. Safety was a concern, and consumers were shy and had to be persuaded to switch from kerosene, which used to be the staple fuel. The architecture of distribution is massive, and responsive to customer requirements of reliable and timely supply of fuels to industry, farms and homes. But the public sector did not have the liberating and aggressive ecosystem, where a decision could be made without the fetters of consensus and the labyrinths of a bureaucracy, that an Ambani could create.

For over four decades, I have witnessed the inability of most senior bureaucrats in the government and CEOs of public-sector companies to respond with the panache and agility that the private-sector leaders often display. Leaders like Raghavendran do exist in large numbers across tiers of management in the public sector. Can they be given the latitude to fully unlock their talent and capacity? If the future of India's energy sector has to be efficient on both sides of the supply and demand divide, the agility of leadership as embodied by Raghu, combined with decisions informed by forethought and clarity of vision, has to be ushered in.

CHAPTER THREE

Hard Thinking, Soft Solutions, 1985–90

Venturing Forth

It was the winter of 1985. I had spent nearly a decade between NPC in Delhi, a short stint in Italy on advanced industrial energy efficiency technologies and a spell in Chennai at NPC's training institute. A personal change was in the air. I made a career switch to the USAID as its energy program officer. Since 1951, under President Eisenhower's administration, USAID, Washington (henceforth, AID/Washington), the development arm of the US government, had been a bilateral partner and donor supporting India's efforts to address growing challenges in health, education, agriculture, clean energy and water. Over the past seven decades, the US has leveraged India's growing human and financial resources through partnerships that catalyze institutional and human-capacity development and innovation to deliver and solve its energy problems.

As I, for the first time, walked into the now-familiar offices of USAID on Shantipath in New Delhi's Chanakyapuri, I carried with me a sense of expectation. A big draw at my new office was the well-lit and congenial atmosphere.

Indira Gandhi had been assassinated the previous year and Rajiv Gandhi was about to step in as the prime minister of India with an unprecedented parliamentary majority. But my work kept me insulated from the buffets of the political changes. I was ready to put into use the industry-oriented skills I had picked up under the tutelage of PRS at NPC.

Development and Energy

Until about the time I joined USAID, its energy programmes were largely centred around scientific and technological solutions for the rural poor. These were advanced through collaborative science-to-science research projects between US universities, national laboratories and Indian academic and research institutions. Amulya Reddy, the legendary socio-economist from the Indian Institute of Science, Bangalore, whose work on Indian rural energy planning had made an abiding impression on USAID, whose officials were exploring deeper engagement with rural India – or as some might call it, Bharat. This was a front that was somewhat alien to me who had spent a decade working on the urban India of industry.

My understanding of rural energy borne more out of my personal reading than any professional work was that India's villages had gained considerably from the Green Revolution that began in 1967. For twenty long years after Independence, India had struggled with food shortages that refused to go away until the focus shifted to farm production and expansion of agricultural produce in Punjab, Uttar Pradesh, Haryana, and parts of Gujarat and Maharashtra. Interventions of the state and central governments at the village panchayat level increased with the aid (provided in part by USAID under the PL 480 programme that helped usher in the Green Revolution) and subsidies for fertilizers, pesticides and research-based hybrid varieties of seeds. Village governance, training and capacity building that had, for ages, been in the hands of the panchayats were redefined forever.

By the mid-1960s, the push from Jawaharlal Nehru and

his government for creating a massive infrastructure of dams, hydroelectric power and irrigated network of canals had increased both the generation of electricity and its consumption. In a sense, Nehru was heeding to the resonating call of Mahatma Gandhi on how India's soul rests in her villages when he gave his unique imprimatur to the vision of development he had crafted in the 1950s with Prasant Chandra Mahalanobis through the Industrial Policy of 1956 (considered to be the economic constitution of India).

P. C. Mahalanobis was perhaps the most important individual in directing Indian development planning. He was the chief advisor to the Planning Commission from 1955. Acknowledged as the father of modern statistics in India, he also founded the Indian Statistical Institute (ISI) in Kolkata. He had his foibles, as J. B. S. Haldane (who spent four years at the ISI and helped the institute develop in biometrics) describes elegantly how the 'journeyings of [their] director define a novel random vector', complaining of the frequent travels and absence of Mahalanobis from work.[1] But history would judge him for the work he rendered in defining the trajectory of India's economic growth during those early years. The Mahalanobis model advocated rapid industrialization with a focus on heavy industries and capital goods.

The Mahalanobis plan was, in a way, an invocation of the spirit of swadeshi or self-reliance.

The 'temples of modern India' rose with hope harboured in the hearts of millions of Indians who gave their lands for dams, and for the industrial behemoths that India set up for manufacturing steel. Industrialists were led by Nehru's call and the first flush of such generation and consumption rode the country. The first three Five-Year Plans offered less focus on agriculture. The second Five-Year Plan and the Industrial Policy Resolution of 1956 paved the way for the development of the public sector and ushered in the Licence Raj. The third Five-Year Plan came in 1958 after the Mahalanobis model was accepted. The quest to quickly industrialize had caused a large reallocation of funds away from the farm sector.

Agriculture outlay was nearly halved to 14% in the second plan. Food shortages worsened and inflation spiked. Imports of food grains depleted precious foreign exchange reserves. With diminished attention, agriculture saw a deceleration every year by at least 1% in overall food grains production.

Political Overhang

It did not help India when the Chinese aggression in October 1962 was sprung as a surprise, bled the exchequer and damaged the country's morale so badly that it took years to recover from it. The severe diplomatic setback broke Nehru's heart as he saw the unwarranted Chinese attack as the undoing of so many painstaking years spent in building amity among the nations in the developing world. He never recovered from the shock of his own failure on the external front and passed away three years later.

After Nehru, who? was a question on every Indian's lips, for the country had seen Nehru striding as a gentle colossus for seventeen years since independence.

Less than two weeks after Nehru died on 27 May 1964, Lal Bahadur Shastri was chosen to be the prime minister, post a very short interlude that saw Gulzari Lal Nanda as the interim head. This was a time when India was hobbling on its finances in the aftermath of the Sino-Indian War but the diminutive Shastri was in the saddle quickly.

For nearly the entire first half of the 1960s, India had been beleaguered by a financial crisis, a foreign exchange crisis and a food crisis. At every public function, Shastri shared his concern on the chronic food shortages afflicting India. The new prime minister exhorted India's masses across districts and cities to voluntarily give up one meal weekly, suggesting that the food thus saved could be distributed among the less privileged. He led the way with his own family skipping a meal for the cause. The response was overwhelming. Even restaurants and eateries downed the shutters on Monday evenings. Many parts of the country observed the 'Shastri Vrat'.

In September 1965, a year after he came to power, war broke out with Pakistan. A month later, on 19 October 1965, Shastri gave the clarion call – 'Jai Jawan, Jai Kisan' – at a meeting near Allahabad. This meant support in equal measure for both defence and farming and in turn, laid the seeds for the Green Revolution. The revolution was meant for the larger good of farmers and farm produce, but it was also an instrument of potent political influence as we saw in later decades that slowly debilitated the strength of self-governance in our villages.

Shastri ushered in major economic shifts that made a significant impact on the country in the fifty years that followed them. In the process of laying the foundations for growth in agricultural production, the energy imbalance grew with demand outstripping supply but also brought about food self-sufficiency. He had the distinct disadvantage of succeeding the charismatic Nehru and seemed an unlikely person to face up to the crises that India had been bequeathed. Shastri wore no ideological blinkers; he saw facts as they were in all their starkness. Chronic food shortages made him shift investment from basic industries to agriculture. Roaring black markets persuaded him to make a relative shift from controls to incentives, and the glaring inefficiency of the public sector made him agree to a larger role for the private sector and foreign investment. He also took measures to shift the locus of economic decision-making from the Planning Commission to the ministries and from the centre to the states.

Four months after he took charge as the prime minister in June 1964, Shastri visited the town of Anand in Gujarat. He was intrigued by the success of the Kaira District Co-operative Milk Producers' Union Ltd (or what is better known today as Amul) and wanted to know more. He stayed overnight with farmers in a village and even had dinner with a farmer's family. He intuitively understood this model could be scaled and replicated in other parts of the country to help farmers enhance incomes.

In early 1965, the National Dairy Development Board was established. This marked the beginning of the White Revolution, and today, India continues to be the world's largest producer of milk, responsible for a quarter of all milk produced. What is not often understood is the safety standards that India has mastered despite the high hygiene risks of energy-heavy processes like refrigeration, transportation and distribution. Very few countries in the world have the luxury of buying milk in a sachet, most live by milk powder.

The person who conceived, developed and ushered in the White Revolution was Varghese Kurien, a service officer from Kerala, posted in Gujarat. In 2004, while passing through Anand, the headquarters of the dairy board, I sought an audience with Kurien, who had by then relinquished his position as its chairman and become the chairman of the Institute of Rural Management in the town. When I asked him what had prompted his interest in milk cooperatives, he replied with a chuckle, 'I was planning on setting up an energy (electricity) cooperative at first ...' His reason, exaggerated for effect, for wanting to set up a power cooperative was even more startling. 'The Indian farmer loves to steal from the government but not from his neighbour.' I could not help but reflect on the profound impact such a cooperative of household energy generation would have had if Kurien could have managed it on the scale he achieved on the milk front.

It is useful to remember that this was in the harsh years of the Cold War and Perestroika would not be on the horizon for at least five more years. India's relations with the US had remained icy, with George Fernandes in 1978 as part of the Janata Party's regime having driven Coca Cola and IBM out of India under the pretext of the FERA norm of a minimum of 40% investment from an Indian partner. Fernandes, a firebrand trade union leader was a native of Mangalore. Initially on the path to become a priest, he had a change of heart and decided to commit to the socialist cause in India. In 1949, he moved to Bombay, where he joined the socialist trade union movement and emerged as a formidable trade union leader. He acquired legendary status during the Emergency of 1975 when he challenged the government for imposing an emergency, but the following year, he was arrested and tried in the infamous Baroda dynamite case.[2] In 1977, after the Emergency had been lifted, Fernandes won the Muzaffarpur seat in Bihar in absentia and was appointed as the union minister for Industries. It was during this tenure in the government that he ordered the American multinationals to leave the country for investment violations.

Even well-meaning American initiatives to help India were treated guardedly. It was a period when those in development were learning to design constructive approaches to address India's unique challenges.

Winds of Change

Our work at USAID remained mostly unaffected by the winds of political changes and clashes. To some of us, working on the mission to bring any and every model of energy development as we explored a whole new world of analyses and conceptual understanding was a thrilling experience.

USAID's energy programmes for India in the early eighties

were at a crossroads. The era of funding some of the large hydro and thermal power projects of the late 50s and 60s – the workhorses of the then Indian power sector – was over. The accent in the early 1980s turned to fostering scientific energy research collaboration between the two countries. Driven by an agenda that was largely set by American and Indian scientists, R&D projects were piloted in frontier areas of innovation – bio-gasification, solar drying, solar thermal heat and power conversions and integrated rural energy systems. These projects were classified in 1982 under an Indo-US bilateral programme called Technologies for the Rural Poor. This was the first donor-supported programme supported by the USAID and administered by the Government of India's Commission on Additional Sources of Energy. In 1986, it was upgraded to a department, the forerunner to the current Ministry of New and Renewable Energy Sources (MoNRE).

Though the pilots were successful, they were ahead of their time and the markets were neither ready, nor excited.

In the mid-1980s, USAID began to grapple with the challenge of energy supply to meet India's growing demand, led by its institutional models for economic development despite the beleaguering setbacks of the previous two decades. Discussions with many of its earnest officers revealed the depth of insights they brought into economic as well as development perspectives. A remarkable American of Indian origin with the curious name of David Jhirad (he had abbreviated Jhiradkar, a small town in the interiors of Maharashtra, for his surname) was one such custodian of USAID's energy programme directions and strategies for India.

Manner of Thinking

I crossed paths with David Jhirad in January 1986, who was visiting India after long years. He was part of a visiting design team from AID/Washington tasked with assisting the India mission. The subsequent spell of meetings with him was the beginning of a professional and personal association that greatly influenced my thinking on strategic energy efficiency programme design and development over the two long decades that followed, well into the 2000s.

When I first met David, my reaction was that of discomfort for I felt I did not match up to the calibre that the visiting team expected from me. David and the rest of the team did all they could to put me at ease and treated me as nothing but an equal. The element of unease gradually diminished as I worked with them to support and create the enabling policy environment USAID had visualized for India. But I'm getting ahead of the story.

A brilliant nuclear physicist, David had a Maharashtrian father and an English mother. His father, an Indian Civil Service officer in pre-Independence India, hailed from a small village called Jhiradkar in interior Maharashtra, home to one of this country's early Bene Israel community. David had spent his early formative years in Shimla, graduated from St Stephen's College in Delhi, proceeded to Cambridge University in England and obtained his doctorate in Applied Physics in 1972 from Harvard University in the US. After a stint at national government labs in the US in late 1984, he joined AID/Washington as a senior energy advisor.

The setting was tailor-made for him to re-acquaint with the country of his birth as an energy expert. As he once told me, 'When I left India in the early sixties, it was at a nascent stage in the evolution of its energy sector. When I returned in the mid-1980s, the sector was well into adolescence, grappling with the gigantic task of supplying reliable power to its 600 million citizens, 80% of whom were living in villages and eking a living out of farming. The progression to adulthood was imminent and so was the exciting possibility of introducing innovations in the Indian power sector. I was excited to be part of India's march towards energy development and security.'

David was an amiable and articulate professional with an air of sophistication about him. His rendering of the broad canvas of issues confronting the Indian energy sector was a classic example of brevity and astuteness. As he often said by way of introduction, the Indian energy sector was facing a 'triple-bind problem' of availability and reliability of supply, cost-efficient technological choices and scarcity of capital. This, he would urge, required a 'triple-bind solution' that combined innovations in policies and regulations, technological solutions and governance. He would almost always plunge artfully into analyzing and applying solutions that left his audience spellbound.

David supplied intellectual rigour to USAID's ambitious Program for the Acceleration of Commercial Energy Research, or PACER, aimed at creating market-driven institutional alliances between academia, enterprise and financial institutions to help move and scale basic and applied research from laboratories to the commercial marketplace. Today, this idea is a central theme of many climate change-related programmes in India and elsewhere. He brought the same edge to his other initiatives such as SPEED-India or Smart Power for Environmentally and Economically Sound Development Program. It was a novel approach to provide renewable energy to Indian villages whose inhabitants were either unserved or underserved. The programme develops and supports off-grid renewable power supply to mobile cell towers as well as to the rural community in the vicinity of the cell towers. By using the cell tower as the anchor load, the electricity generation system was designed to produce and deliver additional power to the adjoining communities.

He understood the importance of critically examining ideas before considering them to be worthy of implementation. He never said it in as many words over the long years I knew him, but the message was clear: always seek evidence, closely examine every reasoning and assumption, analyze basic concepts and trace the implications not just of what is said but also of what is done.

This is a lesson for every Indian professional, for our schools and institutions for higher education rarely teach analytical reasoning as a discipline. Critical thinking, analysis and deductive approach are crucial skills that ought to be a part of the curriculum.

Bureaucratic Receptivity

A large part of our lament on the lack of governance had also to do with the paucity of readiness and methodology. We asked ourselves, 'Is the civil bureaucracy sufficiently informed about climate change and the steps needed to address the environmental impact of energy development from a governance perspective? Are they familiar with the design and decision-making criteria of energy efficiency programmes?'

Such questions led me to an interesting episode that taught me a valuable lesson in preparedness in a complex country like India.

It was the summer of 2001. Seeking an answer to these questions took me and my colleague Richard Edwards to Lal Bahadur Shastri National Academy of Administration, the mecca for training IAS aspirants. Set amidst the scenic Himalayan foothills in Mussoorie in Uttarakhand, the academy provides just the right ambience for tutoring young probationary officers in administrative governance subjects before they are posted to the state and central bureaucracies across the length and breadth of this vast land.

We met with the academy's director, Wajahat Habibullah, an eminent IAS officer who would go on to become the first Chief Information Commissioner of India in 2005. Later, he also stepped in as the chairperson of the National Commission for Minorities. Sensing Habibullah's interest in introducing energy efficiency and climate change into the syllabus, we presented him with a hastily prepared outline in the hope of a happy outcome. He gave us a classic response. Honed by experience and a deep understanding of the responsibilities and travails of IAS officers, he shrugged off the offer. A pre-packaged training menu was not what he was looking for. He countered, 'Can you consult with a few senior officials in the civil service energy departments and prepare a curriculum that reflects the real needs on the ground?'

Chastened, we agreed to work according to his suggestion because we realized that he was making a valid point. He offered to host the consultative meeting at the academy. Three months later, in early August, we met with a group of India's senior-most officials heading central and state government energy ministries and departments for a two-day workshop at the academy. The outcome of this distinctive meeting with the aforementioned veterans was an energy management syllabus that was much more precise in its scope than the first version. We returned a few months later and conducted a successful pilot IAS probationary officer's training programme on clean energy, efficiency and climate change with the help of the academy's teaching staff. This programme found its place in the official curricula after being approved by the academic council.

This experience was a valuable reminder about doing one's homework. Nearly every American I have worked with at senior levels across New Delhi and Washington, has displayed this willingness to put in the requisite amount of time and work when conceptualizing their ideas. Unlearning previously held convictions and methodologies I had picked up during my time with Indian institutions took some time, but I gradually adopted the rigour of my American colleagues to my own approaches to solutions for the developing world. I have come to realize that with the nudge that American corporations offer Indian professionals, they can catapult themselves into the higher echelons of management in no time. One only needs to take a glance at the Fortune 500 lists published in recent years which include the names of many Indians who have moved from the lower rungs to head global corporations, and a lot of their success, they admit, is owed to what they learnt from people like David Jhirad.

CHAPTER FOUR

Tiruchy, Tennessee and Technology, 1986–2010

History advances insights and comprehension that enable nations to correct past errors while chalking out a new path. The economic compulsions gradually built over the three decades of the sixties through the eighties drove the decision to liberalize the Indian economy. India's economic liberalization of 1991 was triggered in part by an increase in world crude oil prices from $21 per barrel to a peak of $46 per barrel following the invasion of Kuwait by Saddam Hussain's forces.[1] Government finances became progressively unsustainable. The underlying fiscal crisis was worsening with the country having to mortgage its gold reserves.

The post-liberalization era was marked by innovation, initiative and change in India. The doctrines of the past were being challenged by major reforms which pushed the socialist, state-managed enterprises into an open, competitive and liberal economy. During those years of economic independence ushered in by the then Finance Minister Manmohan Singh and his aides, under the leadership of Prime Minister Narasimha Rao, Indian industry was stirred into action. The New Industrial Policy of 1991, that had been in the making during the two short-lived regimes of prime ministers Chandra Shekar and V. P. Singh, was brought to its logical culmination through deregulation, delicensing and competition by the Narasimha Rao regime.

Indian Coals: A Predicament

While liberalization was on its course, a quiet revolution that had originated in the early eighties was bearing fruit through one of the manufacturing plants of public-sector behemoth Bharat Heavy Electricals Ltd, Tiruchy – or BHEL Tiruchy for short. This revolution had aimed to develop indigenous technology to address the poor performance of India's coal-fired power plants. Electricity throughout India was mostly generated from the combustion of semi-bituminous coal, along with a smaller share from lignite in the south (Tamil Nadu) and the west (Gujarat, Rajasthan). Boiler operators in power utilities had to continuously learn to adjust and refine operating procedures to obtain maximum heat from the coal used and to minimize the environmental impact of poor fuel combustion efficiency. It was an uphill battle.

The root of the problem lay in the high ash content of Indian coal, ranging from 35% to 50% by weight. By way of comparison, coals in North America have a much lower ash content at around 10-15%. Its principal components are silica, alumina, iron oxide and calcium, with varying amounts of carbon. Ash is an undesirable residue left after coal combustion as it increases maintenance cost and reduces plant reliability. It does not provide any heat, adds weight to the fuel, and increases shipping and disposal costs. The theatrical question often posed about the nature of Indian coals was: 'Is it about ash in coal or is it coal in ash?' The output of ash in a conventional power plant in India was more than double the ash produced in its US counterpart.

The imported technology used in the power plants did not perform well while firing India's high-ash coals. And plants using indigenous technology did not fare any better since they were not designed to efficiently burn the inferior-quality coal either. The challenge, as was well known to discerning professionals, was the high inefficiency of combustion and poor reliability of the boilers. The problem was acute with power plants operating at barely 45% of their installed capacity compared to the average international norm of 75% and higher. Power-sector engineers frustrated with these issues sought answers to the following questions: *How do we manage the high ash content generated by the grade of coal we use? Are there ways of reducing ash generated in power plants? Could we turn this into an advantage by commoditizing fly ash into a by-product of some economic value?* It was clear that India needed to develop new and efficient coal-based power technologies to burn their unique brand of coal and dispose of the ash.

India-US Partnership

USAID eyed the prospect of working with the power sector's key players, knowing well that one needed to steer tactfully through the shoals of sensitive hierarchy within a core sector company like BHEL. However, the odds were in our favour. The government was willing to lend an ear and open India's windows to ideas and strategies, as long as they would not blow the house away, as Gandhiji had phrased it lucidly. BHEL's Tiruchy plant was the site of India's largest supplier of utility power boilers and the onus for developing indigenous coal-fired boiler technologies was squarely on them. And as an alumnus of the 1970s of the neighbouring engineering college located adjacent, I was familiar with the ancient temple town and BHEL's sprawling campus at Thiruverambur on the outskirts of Tiruchy.

We also chose to work with BHEL because they had been collaborating with Combustion Engineering, a US-based multinational company that primarily designed and built utility boilers, for technical knowhow. The US vendor's designs adapted by BHEL did not take into total consideration the poor grades of coal used in Indian plants. The solution lay in helping BHEL's boiler designers and engineers understand the local variety of coals better. The journey that began then has now led to nearly all thermal power plants in India operating at plant capacity factors as high as 75% and higher, in comparison to the dismal 45% of the past.

So, how did India take this leap in the mid-1980s? Several laudable and indigenous efforts by leading research institutions and laboratories such as the Central Fuel Research Institute and national agencies such as the Central Electricity Authority played a stellar role in this transformation. The nearly three-decade-long (1983–2011) period that followed was also marked by fruitful partnerships involving more than a hundred Indian and US organizations. The collaboration between key Indian organizations – BHEL and the National Thermal Power Corporation (NTPC) – and the US Department of Energy's National Energy Technology Laboratory (DoE/NETL) was steadfastly supported by four consecutive US-India bilateral programmes.[2]

A comparison between the US and India on the power-coal front here is relevant since it provides the rationale for their collaboration. Between 1983 and 2011, India's coal-fired generation capacity more than quadrupled from 24 GW to 106 GW and coal's share of total installed power generation capacity remained unchanged at 57%. During the same period, American coal generation capacity increased marginally from 277 GW to 338 GW and coal's share dropped from 45% to 31%. As a result of a rich history of developing efficient, clean coal technologies, environmental regulations and the availability of shale gas, the growth curve of US coal-fired power generation was flattening and the converse was happening in India. The situation was ripe for a partnership between the two nations for the transfer of experiences and technologies.

A Maven Appears

In 1986, my search for scientific talent for supporting BHEL's clean coal programme took me to Dr Radha P. Krishnan – or Krish, as he was popularly known – at the Oak Ridge National Laboratory in Tennessee. His doctoral research and his then professional work revolved around coal, in particular its particle movement and combustion. Krish was a devout Hindu who was as committed to his religious pursuits as he was to his professional ones. My conversation with Krish had him excited about what he could do back home in India. Though having no professional contacts in India made him apprehensive, he was happy to fly over to meet with the top brass at BHEL's Tiruchy facility. This was followed by a series of meetings with Krish which whetted their appetite to learn more. They agreed to set up a coal R&D centre and Krish committed to guiding them with the execution strategy.

As a south Indian from the deep interiors of Kerala who relished his filter coffee, Tiruchy was the perfect work location for Krish. He was fascinated by the Tiruchy temples and the spiritual resonance he found there. He would often spare a few hours from work and visit the temples for the serenity they offered him.

As I got to know Krish better, I realized he had a charming side to him which he often put into use to get his Indian counterparts to accept new ideas. Krish once reflected that his visit to India with the US design team in 1985 was supposed to be a quick visit, and he had been planning to return to his routine in Oak Ridge in no time. When I introduced him to BHEL, it opened an inflection for him that lasted a lifetime of steadfast, focused dedication. He lived a sparse life in Tiruchy. His guest house bills totalled no more than $25 a month, much to the bemusement of my colleagues in Delhi and Washington. After moving to the Soviet Union for his studies, he left mid-way to pursue his master's and a doctorate in the US in the early 1960s. Through the programmes he led, he had trained over a few hundred engineers – no mean feat – on the nuances of power plant design and operations. Krish would at once be suave in the American world while being his effusive Indian self when at work. He kept the American visitors to BHEL in great humour and ensured the Indian hosts did the little things that made the difference in terms of the warmth of hospitality. One of Krish's strengths was that he could draw people out and have them respond to what was needed at the moment. It is a combination of the unquantifiable with devotion to a purpose that is single-minded that can make such change possible.

The latter half of the 1980s saw Krish and the team from the National Energy Technology Laboratory (NETL), Pittsburgh, work with engineers at BHEL at a very technical level to shape their design approaches with empirical data derived from experimentation and testing. Much of their success, however, was derived directly from the extensive capacity-building training and demonstrations of best practices for operations, maintenance and overhauling that took place in both Indian and US power plants and classrooms with many partner organizations from both countries. Lasting impressions were formed and long-distance relations were built and maintained.

Scott Smouse, a young engineer from United States Department of Energy (USDoE) who accompanied Krish to Tiruchy, is today, three decades later, the senior energy advisor at the Office of Clean Coal and Carbon Management. When asked about the legacy of these early programmes with BHEL, Scott had this to say: 'We discussed with our Indian counterparts many technical firsts, in terms of introducing technologies and best practices and their impact, but what impressed me the most was the decades of partnerships involving more than hundred organizations from both countries. Our legacy is one of partnerships first because without them, there would have been no accomplishments.'

The many firsts accomplished at BHEL through USAID's

energy programmes included a fuel evaluation test facility that enabled Indian engineers to evaluate the combustion performance of high-ash coals and solve operational problems in existing power plants as well as improve the design of newer plants. Another key outcome were the studies arising out of the assessment of remaining life conducted at an Indian state utility's coal-fired power plant that enabled renovations and modernization options to extend its life by fifteen years. Such comprehensive remaining life assessment studies are routinely conducted today by specialist firms at coal-fired power plants in the country.

Apart from the transfer of technology and knowhow, this partnership also enabled the import of state-of-the-art instrumentation and data acquisition systems not readily available in the country at the time. It also enabled certain commonplace processes in the US to be adopted in India. My favourite example is a simple yet telling one. While the test facility was being readied for operation, finely pulverized coal had to be fed to the burners. BHEL workers used to do this by hoisting barrels of powdered coal onto hoppers from where they would be gravity-fed to the burners. Our American team members looked at this labour-intensive process incredulously and clicked photos. Bemused, I asked them why they were doing so. They said that they wanted to make the Indian team see how this clumsy process could be bettered. And that happened a few weeks later when the Indian engineers visited the USDoE's facilities in Pittsburgh. Their jaws dropped when they saw a vacuum pump transfer the coal powder to the hoppers in just one hour, a process which took BHEL workers two or more days to accomplish!

Krish continued to introduce new ideas and establish processes at BHEL for many years. What had started as a small step in the mid-1980s with my visit to Oak Ridge to first meet Krish, led to him to spend nearly a decade on BHEL projects.

But the best was yet to come.

Expanding Frontiers of Efficiency

Our other major partner was NTPC, a giant Indian public-sector organization and the largest coal power producer in the country. In 1994, NTPC, with a generation capacity of around 25 GW (now 90 GW), was in the process of erecting super thermal power plants with boiler unit sizes of 210 MW and 500 MW. It was apparent to several of us that the battle for advancing clean coal technologies had to shift from vendors like BHEL to major coal users like NTPC. The technology insights that the DoE-BHEL programme offered were something that NTPC needed at the apex of the value chain in the power sector. Besides, the corporation had realized they could not leave the development and adoption of clean coal technologies and practices to BHEL and other vendors but had to learn the ropes themselves.

BHEL's success in achieving improved performance with their newly designed and manufactured utility boilers did not go unnoticed. NTPC had discovered that USAID had initiated it and that Krish and the DoE/NETL team were driving the BHEL programme. By the early 1990s, Krish sold the idea of setting up a research centre dedicated to improving the efficiency of India's thermal power plants to NTPC. With the support of R. V. Shahi, the corporation's technical director, who went on to head the Indian power sector as the power secretary, Krish made a persuasive case for the setting up of a centre of top-notch engineers who would act as in-house auditors of all the NTPC power plants and improve operational and technical performance (referred to as 'heat rate improvement') with better testing, analysis and execution. The USAID funding support was forthcoming for this novel idea under the newly designed Greenhouse Gas Emissions Prevention Program, or GEP, in 1995.

Concurrently, the Clinton administration of the early

nineties had a passionate and eloquent energy secretary in Hazel O'Leary. Recognizing the business opportunities that India could provide by opening its private power market, Secretary O'Leary and a bunch of US officials and business leaders chartered a plane and flew to Delhi. She was briefed on the potential collaboration with NTPC under GEP. In a town hall meeting on a hot summer day in June that year, O'Leary announced, in the presence of Indian and US officials, the establishment of the Centre for Power Efficiency and Environmental Protection (CenPEEP) in partnership with NTPC. Soon thereafter, the work began.

In 1996, two years after the announcement, CenPEEP was launched in Noida, along with two other regional centres at NTPC's super thermal power plants at Korba and Singrauli. CenPEEP was conceptualized as a national facility with the aim of introducing innovative technology and providing training on how to improve the efficiency of existing coal-fired power plants and reduce emissions of greenhouse gases. These three centres were also outfitted with various state-of-the-art diagnostic equipment and instruments commonly used by the US power-generating community.

CenPEEP brought to India's power sector scientific techniques to improve heat rate (a measure of energy efficiency) and documented guidelines and best practices in the operation and maintenance of coal-fired power plants including non-destructive testing methods for monitoring the condition of critical power plant components like infrared thermography. A few years later, CenPEEP dramatically expanded to designing and testing technologies like water-fogging and sodium conditioning to reduce particulate emissions and introduce risk-based plant management concepts to prioritize replacement of critical coal-fired power plant components using financial risk optimization software.

Today, CenPEEP has engineers – many of them trained in the US – working in different areas of thermal power plant practice, with a part of its operations shifted to Raipur in Chhattisgarh. NTPC's Dadri power station near Delhi was among the first to introduce the innovations developed by CenPEEP's technical staff. With that, Dadri became a magnet for visitors from the US. Adjacent to the facility is a mountain of coal ash dotted with saplings and trees planted by visitors from India and the US. This horticultural marvel was nicknamed Mount Ashmore.

The story that Krish scripted at BHEL and later at NTPC laid the foundations of supply-side energy efficiency in two of the country's premier public-sector institutions. Scott Smouse once affirmed, 'Without Krish, I can say, without a doubt, that we wouldn't have had a legacy because he was not only the catalyst for our partnerships but also the glue that sustained them. He was undoubtedly Indian, but passionately American, and deftly bridged both cultures to build lasting relationships.'[3]

For Krish, CenPEEP was a cherished dream. Later, when musing aloud about his work in India, he said, 'Of my thirty-year involvement in USAID's energy programmes in India, I am most proud of my contribution to the establishment of CenPEEP and the partnerships forged at all levels between India and the United States. These partnerships have introduced US technologies and best practices for power plant efficiency improvement to Indian utilities, which have been widely adopted, resulting in the avoidance of many millions of tonnes of carbon emissions.'

In conclusion, I cannot help but make an observation. The universal science of efficient fuel combustion is centered around three T's: Time, Temperature and Turbulence. Coincidentally, in a manner of speaking, India's journey on the path to more efficient coal combustion was also centered on three T's: Tiruchy, Tennessee and Technology.

CHAPTER FIVE

Energy Options and Hobson's Choice, 1986–97

The Evolution of Efficiency

In hindsight, one can claim that all national movements have decisive moments where a fork in the road dictates a directional choice and a destination. India's energy journey was dotted with such choices, big and small, that influenced its ability to address varied challenges. From about the early 1970s when energy efficiency challenges first began to acquire the attention of the Indian government, there have been four broad phases.

The first phase, after the 1973 oil shock, was a turgid, state-led one, imbued with idealism and altruism. 'Save Fuel, Save the Nation' was how people and industry were exhorted into doing their bit towards energy savings. Then began the second phase around the mid-1980s, during which primarily large energy-intensive industry was assisted by employing technology solutions and operational efficiencies that sought to make them more competitive. While there was no net reduction in the oil import bill for India, given the demand growth rate, it can be argued that in the absence of industry-led conservation efforts, the country's oil bill would have been somewhat higher.

The third was a phase of consolidation. From 2000 onwards, the business and services sector in urban India, especially buildings, were grabbing attention for the savings and health advantages that a green, clean building could offer. The fourth and current phase which began around 2015 is one in which climate change, global warming and international commitments are all pushing for initiatives and technologies on a new scale – beyond process efficiencies – and for a step change in energy productivity in industry and enhanced resilience in urban living. As value addition by industry through diversification and modernization is increasing, so are instances of communities promoting sustainable practices in natural resource use. The production of alloy steel to create precision machine tools is an example of industrial value addition and recycling wastewater in urban communities is a classic example of current trends in water-saving or sustainable practices.

For the past fifty years, institutions like NPC and PCRA have been consistent and unremitting in their focus on energy efficiency. Over the years, they have been joined by others in this national endeavour, industry associations such as the Confederation of Indian Industry (CII) and the Federation of Indian Chambers of Commerce and Industry (FICCI) and research institutions like The Energy Resources Institute (TERI). With the launch of the Bureau of Energy Efficiency (BEE) as part of the Ministry of Power in March 2002 under the provisions of the Energy Conservation Act, 2001, national efforts for sustainable energy resource utilization were considerably broadened. BEE's Perform, Achieve and Trade programme enjoined designated industry consumers to meet prescribed energy savings targets. A nationwide cadre of BEE-certified energy auditors employed by private firms provided technical and advisory support to this cause.

Through those five decades, the partnerships forged in every phase among donors such as the Asian Development Bank (ADB), the World Bank (WB), German development agency (GIZ), UK's Department for International Development (DFID), United Nations Development Programme (UNDP) and USAID to drive clean energy programmes remained strong. If the local partners chosen for an innovation initiative are equipped well enough for the management and execution strategies, encouraging results would follow.

A Bilateral Donor

Support towards the country's energy development was slowly yet perceptibly changing in the early eighties. The era of grant funding of infrastructural power projects such as large hydro and thermal power projects of the late fifties and eighties – the workhorses of the then Indian power sector – was over. USAID chose to step away from funding large infrastructural power projects and instead focused on fostering scientific energy research collaboration between the two countries. While this resulted in a few promising research partnerships, the technological innovations tended to remain within the confines of laboratories with little or no relevance to the needs of the Indian marketplace. What was needed were programmes that incentivized the movement of basic and applied research from the laboratory to the marketplace.

What crucially changed things was the appetite for risk-taking with innovations that USAID, as an external catalyst, could offer. A donor could afford to experiment and even fail, the Government of India could not. This simple truism helped launch several bold energy programmes that pushed the frontiers of innovation.

The approach had a pattern: bring in the ability to accept greater risk than any government agency could; seek partners who could bring innovative products, business models and processes; pilot solutions through support from enterprise, academia or social entrepreneurs; validate and document it as well as we could; and share the results through outreach programmes. This offered the hope of scaling up, and therefore, the most bang for the buck. At the centre of this approach was the promise of the business potential to replicate market-driven initiatives that would acquire a life of their own. USAID also didn't lose sight of the intent to create peer-to-peer relationships with Indian partners. Mutuality of interest was paramount and perseverance paid off.

Today, India has elegantly grown from a traditional donor-recipient model of the past to a position of strategic partnerships that mobilize resources and solutions from a broad range of new development actors. Says a recent USAID website, 'Building on India's talent for innovation, a vibrant private sector, and an engaged diaspora, USAID is unlocking opportunities to leverage finance and technology for greater development impact. This will ensure that India can take ownership of its own development solutions and accelerate its journey to self-reliance.'[1] This could well have been said in the 1990s too, when clean energy initiatives were being nurtured and leveraged through institutional alliances and partnerships.

Indian institutions are rarely monolithic and often differ in structure and intent from state to state and region to region. Foreigners visiting India typically picked their mosaic of pictures (read impressions) on the country's energy scenario from those whom they met in Delhi or one of the other metros or from newspapers or journal articles or other predictable sources. This would often lead them to a blind alley. So, foreign donors needed interlocutors and partners to be effective agents of change. In effect, every developmental programme, be it in energy or any other sector, needs a catalytic process to create institutional alliances between the world of finance, business and research to advance technologies, products and best practices into the marketplace.

For a donor which attempts to independently play each role runs the risk of being blindsided.

A Programme Unfolds

One story of the creation of institutional alliances and collaborative platforms from my early days at USAID is worth sharing here. The story, like always, began with an effort to attract a range of private and public partners, and then leverage the initial, often small, financial contribution and the impact one made as enablers of a development initiative.

It was January 1986. A team from Washington on an India energy mission was in Delhi and I was invited to participate in their discussions on designing an innovative energy programme for India through synergies among the institutional domains of technology, enterprise and finance. Jim Sullivan, director of the Office of Energy in AID/Washington's erstwhile Science and Technology Bureau headed the team. The untiring strategist David Jhirad who also came in with the team from Washington, sat through every animated discussion with a sharp, sensitive ear. The Indian economy under Prime Minister Rajiv Gandhi was at the early stages of shedding its socialistic image and beginning to slowly pivot towards much needed reforms to accelerate growth. It was clear that economic growth under every conceivable scenario of sectoral reforms would have to be accompanied with a massive rise in energy demand. That apart, the financial picture was fraught with impending gloom with oil imports accounting for 80% of the consumption.

The Americans, understandably, weren't quite aware of the spectrum of home-grown technology development solutions available in Indian labs. A burning question engaging energy policymakers in India during those times was: Which energy technologies do we choose to develop indigenously and how do we help scale and commercialize these? Most such labs in India spent chunks of money on basic research and some field testing but made little effort, if at all, to align with the demands of the marketplace.

I suggested we meet officials at the government's Department of Non-conventional Energy Sources (DNES). It was then a tiny department, not the large, thriving ministerial office that it is today. Dr J. Gururaja, who was the department's advisor and had been associated with energy projects carried out by NPC, I knew, would lend a receptive ear to our questions. He had been my professor at the Indian Institute of Science, Bangalore and had worked with PRS earlier when both were faculty members at the institute.

During the meeting was a moment when Gururaja said, 'We are bureaucrats. Someone comes through the door and claims the best thing is solar energy. Another comes in and says wind energy, someone else says biomass. What should I do? Wish it were Hobson's choice since we don't have a system that suggests what kind of projects one should be supporting.' The last bit was accompanied by a sigh of resignation. When we returned to base, David had a gleam in his eye. 'Guru has defined our programme,' he declared with a quiet conviction. We spent the next few days identifying the triad of enterprise, finance and technology. India had a plethora of development institutions, R&D labs, financial institutions and enterprises working in isolation. They were like ships passing by silently in the night. We had to get them to talk to each other.

It must be said that right now as India moves into challenges of the next three decades through 2050, the question that Gururaja asked remains as poignantly relevant.

We chose to ask, 'What is the nature of energy R&D pursued in Indian labs and what is its link with industry, enterprise and finance?' We decided to pitch our idea to TERI. David Jhirad and R. K. Pachauri, notable environmentalist and former head of TERI who passed away in early 2020, were schoolmates. While they went about discussing it, we paused to look into a developmental institution that could act as a catalyst for the success of our idea.

The Industrial Credit and Investment Corporation of India Ltd (ICICI) was founded in 1955, not as a bank but as a leading developmental financial institution. ICICI played a vital role in the economy for over forty years until 1994, when it transformed into a bank. It was started as a joint venture by the World Bank, India's public-sector banks and public-sector insurance companies to provide project financing to Indian industry. Its respectable chairman, Narayanan Vaghul had enthusiastically endorsed and chaired the governing board of another USAID programme, Indo-US Partnership to Advance Commercial Technologies. This programme, which explored disparate areas from intense mushroom farming to health devices, was beginning to make waves among US and Indian private-sector companies engaged in joint technology development and commercialization. ICICI had caught our eyes as a possible partner.

I had read something about Vaghul and his intrepid ways of spearheading innovative financial mechanisms. Under his early stewardship, ICICI had begun to address problems of industrial development holistically and became more deeply involved in the economic and social conditions of its borrowers. It diversified its sources of funding, drawing from a growing number of bilateral and multilateral sources. The strengthening of the ICICI research staff stimulated interaction with the academic and enterprise community and allowed it to claim the role of an intellectual leader in development matters in India. Later, he pioneered the Universal Banking Model that laid the foundation of a new era in Indian banking, launched the first venture capital company in India, set up ICICI Securities – an investment banking business – and introduced the concept of credit rating in the country.

Lab to Markets

The autonomy and clout I enjoyed as a USAID representative made it is easy to walk into just about any CEO's chambers. I asked David to accompany me to a meeting with Vaghul in Bombay in early June in 1986. We had impressed Vaghul with our compelling and powerful vision for India. He was interested in the process of exploring energy technology development and connecting it with enterprise. One man who sat quietly through the meeting in Bombay that humid afternoon, was Suresh Shripad Betrabet, a long-serving hand at ICICI. They asked us two pertinent questions: How do we move energy technologies from R&D to the marketplace and how can we oil the wheels with finance? I informed them that DNES had signed on. With that assurance, ICICI was willing to jump on board. David and I returned to Delhi after successfully completing our mission. Our next task was to get research stakeholders and invite them to be key players on a programme that would revolutionize the manner in which the triad of enterprise, finance and technology would move energy R&D from Indian labs to the commercial marketplace.

An idea was born.

The programme was initially called Energy Research and Enterprise, acronymed ERE. Owen Cylke, the ingenious USAID mission director who constantly egged the design team to be creative, did not like the sound of it. David came up with a new name: Program for Acceleration of Commercial Energy Research, or PACER.

We were ready to kick-start the programme.

The project papers were prepared, and we were on top of fulfilling the formalities specified by the Government of India. Along the way, I realized we had to have someone who could steer the programme. ICICI, with its corporate mien and outlook, seemed like the natural choice. But I was sceptical.

How do we ensure objectivity in the long run, I wondered. We couldn't offer complete autonomy to ICICI without risking the government's authority and influence. The programme, after all, had to ensure that the research money was spent on the basis of objective assessments and thereby act as a model for all future energy R&D investments. A senior USAID colleague, K. C. Kapoor put it succinctly, 'The programme's glory is that of the government's but the reins and consequently, the hard work, should be with ICICI.'[2]

After this, we returned to DNES advisor Gururaja who agreed to chair the PACER board. This allowed us to bring policy alignment and objectivity to our national programme. Institutions seeking such collaborative platforms on bilateral programmes would want to remember this crucial requirement. There was another lesson here as well.

PACER was driven by the market, and hence, did not distinguish between energy efficiency or renewable energy or clean coal projects. It was meant to be technology-agnostic. We told ourselves that we should ideally work with the Ministry of Power since the grant funding size was large enough for leveraging commercial loans and governmental outlays. DNES was not a line ministry. We did not know how wrong we could be. We went to meet with a joint secretary at the power ministry. The officer was a sharp lady and a trifle impatient to find out what we had in mind. We shared that the size of the grant that USAID was offering was 20 million dollars. She replied brusquely, 'The Ministry of Power works only with proposals that are over 300 million dollars and more. If you want to play with toys, you could go to DNES.'

This happened when the World Bank was financing India's super thermal power projects by lending it hundreds of million dollars. India's borrowing was more than that of many countries combined!

After we had decided to collaborate with DNES, Jim Sullivan went back to Washington. David returned, too. Now it was up to us at the India mission to get the plan moving. This was when the Cold War was on. As a consequence of India's nuclear explosion at Pokhran in 1974, the US delayed shipments of enriched fuel supplies to the Tarapur Atomic Power Station to pressurize India to sign the Nuclear Proliferation Treaty, which India refused to do on account of its discriminatory nature. This controversy deepened further with the possibility that the USA might abrogate its obligation to supply enriched uranium for the entire lifetime of the power plant, that is up to 1993.[3] The US and its agencies were never taken too seriously in Delhi's corridors and mainstream areas of the power sector were declared out of bounds for them as impinging upon India's perceived national security interests. While this did not directly affect PACER's preparatory work, it did cast a shadow on US-India energy relations of that era. A US official once graphically described the situation during one of our project meetings as '... a camel flying in the sky with the rare possibility of crashing down on a poor, lone goat tethered to the ground' – the camel being the nuclear fuel controversy and the goat being USAID's PACER.

We had to figure out a way out of obligating the $20 million grant fund for PACER before the deadline on 30 September as the US government required federal funds to be obligated before the end of the fiscal year, failing which, the funds would be returned to the US Treasury. It was already early September. David supported me from Washington, advising me not to stress over the deadline. Gururaja at DNES could not push beyond a point. Since this was seen as a 'scientific project' that would not raise hackles as being inimical to broader 'security' concerns, Gururaja was willing to pilot it through the bureaucracy. In order to ensure that the government would not raise any red flag, it was promoted as an innovation project – which in any case, it was.

Meanwhile without my knowledge, ICICI helped move the programme unwittingly. They had got wind of it from the Department of Economic Affairs under the Ministry of Finance and lobbied gently to seek an engagement which helped us get the proposal signed by the union government well before the deadline that we were up against. Though this may sound like the detritus of every bureaucratic wheel, it finds its place in these pages, for the larger vision of any effort that one seeks to initiate is often stuck in the trivia of procedures. If we plodded along reasonably successfully through those years in the 1980s, it was because of such positive manoeuvring that was unavoidable if we had to get things going.

We put together a project committee of experts and the process of solicitation of new projects for PACER began. The sense of anticipation within the team was palpable. The ICICI at Bombay had established a PACER secretariat headed by a very resourceful individual, P. H. Vaidya, who reported directly to Suresh Shripad Betrabet. Vaidya and his team at the PACER secretariat were up to the task. They built trust among partners through transparent and candid communication and frequently travelled to Delhi and proactively reached out to the PACER project committee. Before we knew it, we had ended up crafting a successful partnership between a private-sector finance entity and a department of the government along with a host of technical research institutions in the US and in India. A non-intrusive yet wholesome plan to work on India's energy R&D needs was put into motion. Now, we needed project proposals from interested consortiums to test our developmental hypothesis.

We had defined the larger intent and our message was crystal clear: Go out and get proposals, but you have to do all the hard work and offer the credit and glory to the ministry.

The Consortia Fit

We got down to the business at hand. But how were we to go about identifying technology development projects for PACER? Given the lack of coordination between manufacturers, end users, academia/labs and financial institutions, we agreed that a consortium of these four stakeholder groups needed to be stitched together.

'Consortia Fit' was what Betrabet called it, and soon, Vaidya and the PACER team at ICICI were on this task scouring the country's industrial and R&D landscape for potential project opportunities and participants. The incentive of a grant fund to support half the cost of such projects, with the rest funded by promoters and developers, could pave the way for manufacturing companies to want to come on board. We set the maximum threshold for PACER grant funding at $3 million per project. At about ₹30 to the dollar, a $6 million investment in the 1990s was a tidy sum at about ₹18 crore with half of this (₹9 crore or $3 million) coming by way of grant from USAID. ICICI led by proactively seeking consortiums of partners while scouting for innovative ideas for developing energy efficient technologies.

At this point, an interesting twist came about thanks to ICICI's financial savvy. While drafting the grant fund agreement for every project, Betrabet and Vaidya worked in an ingenuous covenant that obligated the grantee companies to return the grant fund with a matching amount, if the project succeeded. If the project failed for any reason, both PACER and the promoters/developers lost. If it succeeded, the conditional grant ensured that the profits gained by the consortium through the market sale of the technologies constituted the reflows.

We looked for projects across India. I scanned the industry landscape and chose to meet Rohinton Aga, who headed Thermax. Aga was also chair of an energy subcommittee at CII, and therefore was a key industry representative.

When I flew down to Pune to meet him, Aga first acknowledged and thanked me, as an NPC alumnus, for the D. V. Kapoor Committee report[4] from a few years ago. The recommendations of the report had given Thermax a firm toehold in the campaign to displace the Lancashire variety with their packaged boilers. I was glad that the D. V. Kapoor Report and the initiatives that followed it in the mid-1980s were gradually beginning to pay off. In-house energy management cells and investments in energy efficiency created by energy-intensive industry were now a part of corporate strategy. The savings for the country was significant and enduring, thanks to not just legislative intervention but also markets accepting the idea.

Thermax lost no time. They brought in Trinity Forge Private Ltd, another company based in Pune, to jointly develop a regenerative oil burner, a fuel-burning device that works on heat recovered from the furnace stack and is more efficient than conventional burners. The device was to be installed in their factory if it worked. The project appraised in 1988 cost $25,000 (₹7.5 lakh).The challenge was to develop a low-cost system. With the reduction in costs and paybacks of less than a year, other companies committed to the project without hesitation. Over the next few years, PACER supported several consortium-led projects, including solid polymer electrolyte fuel cell, industrial waste heat recovery systems, fluidized bed furnaces, advanced low-cost combustion control systems, 500 kW biomass gasifier operating on rice husk and woody biomass, pinch technology for chemical process integration, coal beneficiation and coal gasification systems.

Financing Risks, Developing Technologies

By 1997, nearly a decade later, PACER had spent $16 million over twenty-nine projects as conditional grants. A USAID project activity completion report published in September 1998 noted, 'The PACER project helped overcome the energy constraints on India's economic development by promoting the development of new or innovative products or processes relevant to the Indian energy sector … the potential impact of PACER funded projects likely to see commercialization in India is very significant. It is estimated to be ₹7,300 crore [$2.4 billion in 1998] on an annualized basis, for the twelve projects that were successfully commercialized. This speaks volumes for the national benefit of the PACER program.'[5]

The surplus funds were put away into a corpus accessible by both ICICI and USAID to finance other innovation projects that drove energy efficiency according to market-driven principles. In the current context, with green equity financing taking wing in the new decade of the millennium, the structure we put together in the early 1990s continues to be relevant.

Reflows into ICICI began to increase. They did not belong to either of the players – ICICI or USAID. We agreed to support certain activities in consultation with ICICI. The formula was simple: the grant doubles and reflows to the ICICI-USAID kitty if a project succeeds. And several of them did succeed. The diligence mechanism had been mentored well and ICICI played the executive role competently. An Indian green business centre (GBC) crafted around 2001 (see Chapter Eight) is one of our success stories which was initially funded by this ICICI 'reflow'. It was not as though there was no risk at the initial stages of each of these forays in innovation. But the blend of partnerships with institutions and individuals who championed the purpose with insight, hard work, determination and diligence made things work.

With PACER, the historical disconnect between science, enterprise and finance was gradually being bridged.

CHAPTER SIX

The Deep South Shows the Way on Cogeneration, 1992–95

Laws of Efficiency

In thermodynamics, the first law of efficiency gains importance in light of the second law. The first law compares energy in terms of enthalpy; so much energy in and so much out, and one divided by the other offers you the efficiency coefficient of conversion. It doesn't distinguish between the quality of energy, which the second law does. The energy of the highest quality for doing 'work' – as James Prescott Joule, the English mathematician, physicist and brewer described it – is high-grade heat that can be used for low-grade processes after it has produced mechanical power or work. And so, heat and work can be simultaneously combined in a single facility to deliver energy services. This conclusion breathed life into the Total Energy Systems Concept.

I had developed, from my learning with the genius that PRS was, a working understanding of what he termed the Total Energy Systems Concept.[1] In any enterprise, you have parallel inputs of energy to meet end-use needs, such as cooling, lighting, power for motors and heat. Using a single source of energy to supply these parallel needs will bring the highest energy conversion efficiency values. This was an elegant way of presenting the prospect: use a single source – oil or coal – burn it in a boiler to generate the highest level of steam pressure and temperature, expand the steam across a turbine to generate power and divert a part of the steam for process heat. One could use the process steam in absorption refrigeration for cooling, drying, distillation, evaporation or simply heating. This is closest to the ideal energy system in an industry or commercial building which can secure freedom from the utility grid. It would serve both process and power demand, a concept known as cogeneration or the combined generation of power and heat in a single facility.

Combined Heat and Power

It was President Jimmy Carter who made cogeneration a national campaign in the US. His administration passed the PURPA (Public Utility Regulatory Policies Act) under the US National Energy Act of 1978. The law set their energy industry on the road to reform and restructuring. PURPA was originally passed to conserve electrical energy. It was subsequently extended to encourage increasing efficiency by making use of cogeneration in facilities, making retail rates for electric consumers fair, speeding up the creation of hydroelectric energy production at small dams and conserving natural gas.

The main vehicle that the PURPA law used to try and accomplish these goals, specifically cogeneration, was by creating a new class of electricity generation facilities called 'qualifying facilities or QFs'. PURPA gave QFs special rate and regulatory treatment. This helped mainstream it in the US marketplace. *Could this be emulated in India?* This question crossed the minds of some both outside and at USAID. A short background here might provide a better sense of the events that unfolded hereon.

Industrial cogeneration had been the subject of considerable interest and inquiry in India since the late sixties. The main arguments for it were centered on two compelling needs of that era. The first was to augment the supply of power in a regime of endemic power shortages, and secondly, to promote energy conversion efficiency and thereby conserve scarce fossil fuels. It was hardly a surprise, therefore, that until then cogeneration in India had been restricted to the production of electrical energy for self-use by industry and had been viewed as a way to meet on-site heat and power demands independent of the grid. Industries such as pulp and paper, sugar and textiles have been 'cogenerating' electricity and steam for many years. The location of these industries in regions removed from the grid (for example, sugar mills and paper plants), the availability of by-product fuels (such as bagasse and black liquor) and the steam requirements from the industrial process involved were in favour of in-plant cogeneration. Beginning from the mid-seventies, the number of industries favouring cogeneration had grown to include chemical producers, oil refiners and fertilizer manufacturers. These industries have large and simultaneous steam and power demands and had installed cogeneration units to insulate themselves from the unreliability of utility supplies.

Many industrial 'smokestacks' in India, especially textile and paper mills, have a large steam base with much of the steam generated at low pressures in boilers. And yet these companies were buying power from the grid. We wondered: Why can't such companies produce their own power through cogeneration by generating steam in high pressure boilers and using the excess heat for process requirements?

An earlier NPC report had attempted to answer this question and also provided a technical and theoretical estimate of 1,800 MW of cogeneration potential from the total steam base in about 300 process industries in the country.[2] While this might be a relatively small number in today's terms, it amounted to 7.2% of the total generation capacity in India, which was around 25 GW in 1978. This report was subsequently strengthened by a USAID-sponsored study conducted by

Hagler Bailly Inc. – based in Washington, DC – on Gujarat and Maharashtra in 1986. The report recommended a PURPA-like regulatory intervention. Initially, the findings were met with some resistance by the Ministry of Power which mistook the study to be an endorsement of privatization of power generation – an idea that did not find favour with the political ideology of those times. A change in the report title to 'Non-utility Power Generation' found greater acceptance.

Cogeneration – Beyond the Fence

The report on non-utility power generation in India had underscored the need to explore cogeneration opportunities in Indian sugar mills. The argument made to support this contention was simply thus: India as the world's largest producer of sugar with over 800 sugar mills presented an opportunity to generate electricity using bagasse as fuel and feed excess power to the electricity grid. Given that sugar mills are located in rural areas where access to electricity was a challenge, this would accelerate economic development and improve the living standards of people in the villages. The Indian sugar industry had to shed its traditional system design of 'within the fence' cogeneration and instead adopt the modern practices of sugar mills in Hawaii and the rest of the world, namely, supplying power to the central electricity grid.

The first step was to prepare a business case for sugar cogeneration with exportable power to the grid. The Energy Policy Innovation and Commercialization (EPIC) programme of AID/Washington, with its strong support for the concept and the opportunity to execute a project design and development activity, was our launch pad. We needed partners and I was becoming familiar with the formula too. Find research and private business institutions and involve the government. Thus unfolded another Thermax story with its chairman, Rohinton Aga, visiting Washington for the launch of the project.

In early 1992, the National Press Club in Washington was organizing a seminar two blocks from the White House at the National Press Building and wanted a speaker from India to talk about energy efficiency and the dynamics of India's economic growth. I was asked for recommendations and I suggested Aga's name. He readily accepted the invitation and flew in for the seminar. He spoke extremely well. He was an economist and a peer of ex-Prime Minister Manmohan Singh at Oxford and now the scholar was the country's finance minister. Aga was a Parsi and hailed from a family which was in the business of manufacturing sterilizers and baby boilers for hospitals in Pune in the fifties. From such a small beginning, it was now India's leading industrial boiler manufacturer. The setting seemed propitious.

Aga came to Washington post riding high on the package boiler transformation in the previous decade. Sensing that it was an opportune moment, we broached the subject of cogeneration in the sugar industry and the project development study that we had envisaged in India with him. Aga was interested and offered Thermax's support as a partner. A private manufacturer becoming a partner of USAID made sense since this was not a theoretical or academic study.

It was going to be a hands-on project development exercise for which we needed help from experts. David offered me a free hand. I looked to my friend, John Kadyszeisky, who was with Winrock International (WI), one of the partners for the EPIC programme at AID/Washington. On John's advice, I picked a six-member team, three from WI, two sugar industry professionals from Hawaii and the remaining one from the among the 'beltway consultants' in Washington. The team of George St John and Felix Ah Kee from Hawaii came highly recommended by John. George was an acknowledged expert on power agreements involving utilities and sugar mills, while

Felix was a hands-on sugar industry professional with a deep understanding of its processes. The third expert was Arun Sanghvi, a highly reputed economist from Hagler Bailly who later went on to join the World Bank as a power pricing and utility economics expert. I also roped in John's colleagues at WI, Don Hertzmark, a financial analyst; Brad Holloman, an energy analyst familiar with biomass systems; and Ken Langer, a market business development expert who had previously lived and worked in India.

Prior to the field mission to India, a pre-qualification survey to identify candidate sugar mills for the techno-economic study was undertaken by Thermax. Led by Harish Bhargava and P. K. Sen, directors of Thermax, and supported by their technical staff, eight sugar mills in Tamil Nadu and Maharashtra were screened and evaluated. Three mills were finally chosen, two in Tamil Nadu and one in Maharashtra.

I landed with my newly constituted team in Pune for a meeting at Thermax's office. We decided to focus on Tamil Nadu first and then Maharashtra. This was mid-1992. We visited Thiru Arooran Sugars at Thirumandangudi in the deep south of India. Thermax had sized it at 19 MW, including the potential for 5 MW sale to the state utility, Tamil Nadu State Electricity Board (TNEB). The other mill was Aruna Sugars at Pennadam, South Arcot District. Both were private mills unlike the third mill – VSSK Ltd – in Maharashtra, which was a farmer's cooperative mill located in Sangli, a district near Pune.[3]

Selling power to the grid was important; cogenerating power 'within the fence' was not enough. India did not have any example of a local energy producer synchronizing the supply of power to the grid. However, that was the least of our problems.

There was a genuine concern shared by the sugar mills about how the sale of power to the utility might not be honoured by the state utility and the mills might be better off banking power with the state grid and withdrawing it as and when needed, subject to certain conditions. Another option was to wheel the power through the grid and sell it to a third party for a mutually acceptable tariff rate. Banking plus wheeling is a variant drawn from the concept of banking in which the payback of the banked energy involves supplying it to a delivery point different from the point of injection.

For George, who was an expert on power purchase contracts, this was unchartered territory. In sugar mills in Hawaii and elsewhere, the typical contractual agreement covered only the purchase of power by a utility from a cogenerator. Wheeling and banking was an unfamiliar and perhaps outlandish idea for him. The model contract draft he had first developed assumed that the mill was a willing seller and TNEB a willing buyer. When he realized that it was not the case, he went back to the drawing board. The subsequent draft was a sterling example of a flexible yet stable long-term contract that amply addressed the issue of security of payment to the sugar mill in a cogeneration system and the reliance of the utility on exportable cogenerated power. The primary focus of the contract was the operational considerations. The key provision was the obligation on the part of the state utility to accept all the energy made available by the sugar mill for sale, via banking or wheeling. Furthermore, a unique provision of direct bank payment at the request of the sugar mill was included to prevent a default by the state utility on the payment front.

The contract drawn by George soon became a standard model for contractual provisions for formulating cogeneration power purchase agreements in India. Beyond the legal originalities contributed by George, several other innovations were brought into the country. Key measures for power maximization and flexibility of operational conditions were introduced in the Indian sugar industry for the first time.

The methodology for pricing cogenerated power was another novelty. Arun's skills in establishing a pricing framework for power sales to utilities was fully tested. Efficient power purchase for direct sale to the utility grid is relatively easier to establish than tariff for other transactions such as wheeling and banking. A direct sale to the grid comprised almost every transaction in established power markets and was based upon economic principles and methods that pricing experts like Arun were intimately aware of. In contrast, setting wheeling and banking tariffs generated much discussion and debate in the team. Arun provided the breakthrough. 'Given the prevailing institutional and operating environment in India's power sector,' he argued, 'a case can be made for all of the power transactions for reasons other than economic efficiency. For the sugar cogeneration market to develop, it is necessary for state utilities like TNEB to encourage prospective suppliers. If such suppliers are not forthcoming under a direct sale transaction but [were] available [for] some other type of transaction structure such as wheeling and banking, then specific pricing principles should be applicable.' Arun went on to develop a robust methodology for the pricing of cogenerated power based on estimated 'avoided cost' for generation and transmission and distribution network of the state utility with wheeling and banking in mind.

There were challenges on the technical side too. One of these was the low steam pressure generated by the boilers at the mills. The average steam pressures were in the range of 10 to 21 atmosphere (ata) with a trend towards higher pressures in some mills up to 42 ata. The study recommended a dramatic increase to 63 ata, which was unprecedented in India at the time. The choice of going in for such high-pressure systems was based on two significant issues, namely, the level of confidence of mill managers and employees when it came to operating and maintaining high-pressure systems, and the need to install more advanced water treatment systems like demineralizers. There was also the issue of the steam turbines. The typical turbine technology used in the sugar industry worked on the conventional back-pressure systems, in the range of 1–5 MW operating at low to medium steam throttle pressures. These turbines, usually single or multistage axial, have poor conversion efficiencies, from 55% to 65%. Felix Ah Kee, the technical expert in the team, was simply unimpressed by these turbines. In one of the team meetings, the generally taciturn expert was animated in his opposition. 'The back-pressure turbine is clearly unsuited for the purpose of power maximization and flexibility in performance,' he said, 'the extraction condensing turbine is more satisfactory for this purpose and can be operated during off-season periods with steam generated by surplus bagasse and expanded through the condensing section of the turbine.' There were other advantages as well. And so we proposed the change to Ram Tyagarajan, the chairman of Thiru Arooran Sugars. Young, dynamic and determined to be the country's first sugar mill to establish a modern high-steam cogeneration plant with exportable surplus power to the grid, he gave his assent. And Thiru Arooran Sugars became one of the first mills in India to have a cogeneration system that supplied power year-round.

But I am getting ahead of the story.

The TNEB officials were not too enthusiastic, nor did they understand what it meant to the grid and the country's energy future. Stirring them out of their comfort zone needed a whip from higher up. Chief Secretary T. V. Venkataraman, the highest-ranking civil servant in the state, had to be convinced. I knew him from the days he headed the Tamil Nadu Energy Development Authority.

I took the entire team to Fort St George. Founded in 1964,

it is the first English fortress in India and had been built for the colonial administration and defense of the city of Madras. It now housed the state administration that included the office of the chief secretary. His office was crowded with people waiting for an audience with him to present a petition or complaint or simply seek a favour. It was late evening by the time we were ushered into his presence and he was a trifle tired. But when I shared the reason behind our visit with him, there was a visible change in his countenance. I had his full attention. His interest in biomass and biogas worked in our favour. He turned to his officials and bellowed, 'Anyone from TNEB here?' The answer was a no. He picked up the phone and directed the chairman of TNEB to come over in thirty minutes. Without reading the elaborate report that my team had prepared, he quickly cut into questions about pricing, economics, technology and operational challenges. It took us more than by surprise; his questions were discerning. It was obvious that he had been on the field for this. The team from Washington responded to the volley of questions well enough. We informed him that the model would not be complete without the electricity board consenting to an arrangement of wheeling and banking based on a reasonable power tariff. A legally enforceable power purchase agreement was of paramount importance.

Venkatraman turned from us to the TNEB chairman, who had arrived as instructed. Without demur, the man said yes. He promised to have his officials examine the proposal. The stage was set. It took no more than twenty-four months for the Thiru Arooran sugar mill to install its cogeneration plant with a capacity of 19 MW at the cost of ₹45 crore at Thirumandagudi, with surplus power being fed into the state grid.

Triggering the Cogeneration Market

A succession of sugar industry cogeneration projects for exportable power followed in the state and its neighbour Karnataka followed by Maharashtra and Uttar Pradesh. Commercial banks like Industrial Development Bank of India (IDBI) and ICICI provided loans on a concessional basis for the projects. A national biomass cogeneration programme was launched by DNES – MoNRE's predecessor – which provided a capital subsidy to eligible plants through its financing arm, the Indian Renewable Development Agency. Within three years of our study, Indian sugar cogeneration capacity had reached 350 MWs and was still growing.

It was an era of innovative ideas. One of them was an initiative by the Uttar Pradesh Non-conventional Energy Development Agency (UPNEDA). Despite UP being the state with the largest share of exportable power through sugar cogeneration, project development remained uneven and halting. Most of the development had taken place in private mills with little progress underway in the state's federation and corporation mills.

At a business meet organized in Lucknow by UPNEDA in association with the UP Sugar Federation Corporation and USAID in early 2005 on 'Green Power Development in UP', an interesting idea was making the rounds. 'Can we route green power from sugar mill cogenerators to save the Taj Mahal?' asked a participant. Air quality in and around the city of Agra in UP, home to one of the seven wonders of the world, the Taj Mahal, had steadily deteriorated due to the pollutants released by small foundries, transport, captive diesel generating plants and a petroleum refinery upstream from the monument. A study by the Clean Technology Initiative programme of USAID had confirmed that the large-scale usage of standby diesel was a key reason for the pollution. The fear was that the pollutants would subject the monument's pristine marble to acid attack. This had prompted environmental activists to pressurize the state government to designate the Taj Trapezium Zone as a 'no power cut' area to ensure an uninterrupted supply of power and eliminate the use of captive diesel power generators by shopkeepers, industry and hotels and restaurants. A corollary to this was that exportable power from the state's sugar mills would provide a corridor of firm, stable power to the state grid for distribution to the power-beleaguered city.

'Green power to save the Taj' was the clarion call. Sugar mills rose to the challenge.

The progress of sugar cogeneration continues even today. In December 2019, the installed capacity of sugar cogeneration in the country was 9,131 MW, of which 3,000 MW was exported. As a sugar mill owner once remarked, tongue in cheek, 'Power sales is a profitable enterprise for us with sugar production as a by-product.'

I cannot help but reflect on its beginnings over two decades ago. On one end, it took a bold decision by an astute bureaucrat like Venkatraman to cut through red tape and sugar mills in the country's deep south to develop business partnerships, and on the other, out-of-the-box ideas by environmental activists in north India to protect India's heritage monuments.

Turns out, it takes many to tango!

CHAPTER SEVEN

Power, Pelf and Pandemonium, 1991–2000

Private Power

Another major landmark in this energy story had its origins in a relatively insignificant meeting in 1991. I was working with a small consultancy firm, International Development Energy Associates Inc in Washington, DC, on EPIC, which is AID/Washington's policy programme under its Office of Energy. Back home in India, the economy was reopening and liberalization was on the horizon. Both the ever-vigilant David Jhirad and I anticipated some change in the state of affairs. Officials in the Ministry of Power had persuaded the reform team led by Manmohan Singh to take cognizance of the yawning deficit in the country's power generation capacities and the inability of central and state resources to finance the much-needed expansion and future growth of the power sector.

The only way, they argued, while taking up the case with the Cabinet Secretary Naresh Chandra, was to enlarge the role of the private sector. Until then, only the metros of Bombay, Calcutta and Ahmedabad had seen private-sector participation in the generation and distribution of electricity since 1947. These private players were licensees of the state electricity boards and saddled with a plethora of regulatory constraints that inhibited their growth. They needed to be reviewed, the officials had argued, and their views were later communicated to Prime

Minister Narasimha Rao and Finance Minister Manmohan Singh.

The question before the political leadership was: How could they privatize India's power sector and see some of its projects to fruition within the time a political regime has? Narasimha Rao's was a coalition government, so pushing through such a reform took courage. With the nod of the PM, a small group of power sector officials led by Secretary of the Ministry of Power R. Vasudevan and Joint Secretary N. Ramji began a consultative process that led to the preparation of a White Paper outlining measures to incentivize international and domestic developers and investors to invest in the country's power sector.

Ramji – erudite, sharp and driven – was eager to present his Ministry's proposal to an international audience of potential investors and developers. Across the world in Washington, DC, the EPIC programme was on the lookout for opportunities in the Indian power sector. Policy and financing innovations were part of the programmatic mandate and the recent moves encouraging the participation of the private sector had caught our attention.

During one of my visits to Delhi, I sought a meeting with Ramji. David was present as well. The bureaucrat asked us whether AID/Washington could help them organize meetings in the US with some federal government and private power company leaders. We saw great potential in their proposal. On our return to Washington, DC, I got to talking to some of the mainline US power companies, developers, investors and consultants while keeping the conversation going with Ramji, who was busy assembling an Indian team. We agreed that besides government officials, the team should include the chiefs of three private power companies in India. The rationale being that their presence would lend weight and credibility to the government's proposition of encouraging private-sector participation.

A Historical Trip

A couple of months later, a first-of-its-kind delegation descended on Washington. It was a formidable powerhouse of officials, including Finance Secretary K. P. Geethakrishnan, Power Secretary R. Vasudevan and the heads of the Calcutta Electric Supply Co., Bombay-based Tata Power and Ahmedabad Electricity Company led by Cabinet Secretary Naresh Chandra. This was altogether strange since the cabinet secretary is rarely engaged in any international endeavour. Apparently, Prime Minister Rao thought the situation called for this deviation from the norm and sent his top-most bureaucrat to signal his government's strong mandate and commitment. The meeting at the Watergate Hotel in Washington saw a strong contingent of leaders from American power companies, investment houses, developers, consultants and the country's departments of Commerce, Energy and State, including AID/Washington.

The Indian team had a broad idea of the steps they needed to take to bring about power sector reforms in India. Their presentation largely drew from the government's White Paper on private power, which included a package of financial incentives that prescribed allowable debt, equity ratios, permissible return on investments, power purchase policy, fuel supply and obligations of the private power licensee. They declared to their audience at the outset that sovereign guarantees were off the table.

The questions posed by the US company heads were not something the Indian delegation was prepared for. Someone asked about 'bandhs' in Calcutta, a local term for worker strikes that could shut down economic activity in a city, state or region, and how it impacts the finances of the state utilities. Another CEO asked about coal quality and supply and the challenges of railroad transportation. A third wondered about the absence of independent regulatory commissions, remarking, 'It seems the government is the operator and the regulator.' And rubbing salt to the wound, a few questioned the process of determining the tariffs and inquired whether the rates were based on economic pricing principles or political considerations. Someone among the invitees declared in conclusion that the issues discussed were potential risks and unless these were addressed appropriately, it would be difficult to justify any investment on their part.

Finance Secretary Geethakrishnan turned around to David, a trifle bewildered, and said, 'They seem to be only listing the risks.' David looked him in the eye, and said, 'Welcome to the real world. Power sector reforms are not about scratching the surface but about radical policy, governance, institutional and regulatory changes.'

Though the seed for power sector reforms had been planted, the Indian delegation realized that they had a lot more to do.

In later years, with the assistance of multilateral development banks like the World Bank and the Asian Development Bank as well as donors like DFID, reforms were initiated by the state. The Indian Electricity Act, 1910 was modified and the Indian Power Reform Act was promulgated. It was beyond my field of work at the EPIC programme in AID/Washington and I had not joined the World Bank yet. But that's another story, a snippet of which is covered in Chapter Nine. Soon, I got a call from Enron Inc., a leading American power company which had attended the recent parleys with the Indian delegation in Washington, DC. A cheerful senior official expressed their interest in pursuing the conversation beyond the meetings. When we met in person, he was accompanied by a young mid-level official, now somewhat infamous, Rebecca Mark. At that time, I had no inkling that she would go on to become the subject of front-page news in India for her role in furthering her company's business interests in the country. I recall her quietly listening, barely participating in the discussions and taking down notes. Enron wanted to know which would be the best state to set up a power plant. I suggested Maharashtra and Andhra Pradesh (AP) and told them to meet officials in Delhi to find out more. I further recommended that they get insights straight from the horse's mouth – Joint Secretary Ramji, who now headed the Ministry's Private Power Cell, established soon after the Indian delegation had returned home. They went back to Houston to work on an engagement strategy with the Indian power sector and a business plan which they presented to their board for approval. A fortnight later, they called to let me know that their board had concurred with their proposal. I called Ramji and learnt that he was more than happy to spend time with them and enable meetings with the relevant offices in Delhi and the two states.

The Enron Saga

Rebecca was a member of the team that arrived in Delhi to meet officials and so was Enron CEO Kenneth Lay. This was a clear sign that they meant business. The Government of India was looking at one private-sector project that could be fast-tracked. The timing was perfect. Their internal diligence had helped them zero in on Maharashtra as the site for the power plant. In 1992, Enron approached the Maharashtra government with the idea of setting up a 2,184 MW liquefied natural gas (LNG) powered plant at an estimated cost of $2.8 billion at Dabhol, Ratnagiri. Dabhol, a small town 100 miles south of Bombay, lay on the western coast overlooking the Arabian Sea. It was an ideal site. The plan was to sign a contract with Qatar for LNG and the ships could be docked near the plant. Moreover, the power generated could be evacuated to the massive load centre in the state capital. Thus, the foundation was laid for the Dabhol Power Company (DPC).

Enron went about the task with focus and precision. The

project was financed by Enron, Bechtel, General Electric and five major lenders, including IDBI. The state and central governments enthusiastically provided the requisite clearances and did their best to pave the path for smooth execution.

General Electric provided gas turbines to DPC, Bechtel was responsible for the construction and Enron was charged with managing the project through Enron International. The plant was to be set up in two phases. During the first phase, naphtha was to be burned to produce 740 MWs and help stabilize the local transmission grid. Though the construction had started in 1992, the plant began generating power only in 1999, two years behind schedule.

Problems plagued the project during Phase 1. In 1995, local villagers swarmed the project site to protest the potential displacement of locals. A riot broke out and subsequent actions by the security forces guarding DPC was criticized by Amnesty International for being excessive and Enron was blamed for being complicit. Later that summer, the political dispensation in the state changed and a new coalition government opposed to the project came to power in the state. The new government appointed a committee of state ministers – the Munde Sub-committee – chaired by the state's deputy chief minister, Gopinath Munde, to review the project. The committee's findings were a damning indictment of the project. On the issue of whether the Enron project was useful to the state of Maharashtra, the committee report was candid: '… the committee is of the view that such high-cost power as Enron envisages will, in the immediate future, and in the long run, adversely affect Maharashtra and the rapid industrialization of the state and its competitiveness'.[1] The report was damaging, and acting on it, the Maharashtra state government ordered the project to be halted because of 'lack of transparency, alleged padded costs and environmental hazards'.

By then, Enron had invested about $300 million into the project and entered into arbitration to seek compensation. The state government, in turn, filed a suit to void the agreement, alleging fraud and misrepresentation. US officials, including Energy Secretary Hazel O'Leary, under whose watch the Enron project received US government backing, cautioned the Indian central government that its action would discourage foreign investment. The central government expressed its inability to interfere since electricity, a subject under the concurrent list of the Indian constitution, was under the jurisdiction of state governments.

And then, a ray of hope emerged. Backchannel discussions between Enron and the state's political parties set the stage for a meeting between Rebecca Mark, now head of Enron International, and Bal Thackeray, the charismatic leader and founder of the Shiv Sena, the key political party in the state. Journalists from that era still recall how the senior Enron executive persuaded Thackeray to let the project continue.

Post the breakthrough, negotiations followed between Enron and the state government and a revised agreement was signed. Finally, in May 1999, Dabhol Phase 1 was commissioned and began generating and selling power to the Maharashtra State Electricity Board (MSEB) only to run into a hurdle barely eighteen months later, in January 2001. The snag was caused by power purchase tariffs.

The issue of poor project economics had already been sounded eight years back in 1993 by the World Bank, when it was approached by Enron to help finance the project. The bank had predicted the project's inherent weaknesses and refused to give a loan. In a letter written to the then economic affairs secretary, M. S. Ahluwalia, a senior bank official had said that they had 'examined the proposed Dabhol Power Project of Enron Power Development Corporation to which [they] were requested to consider World Bank financing. [Their] analysis indicates that the LNG-based project as presently formulated is not economically viable' and that in their assessment, 'the proposed 2015 MW project is too large for base-load operation in the MSEB system'. They observed that the 'project design is inflexible and would result in uneconomic plant dispatch, as already existing lower variable cost coal power would be replaced by the higher cost LNG power'. The letter went on to state '... given the standing which the companies sponsoring the proposed Dabhol Power Project enjoy in their field of business, it would appear worthwhile for you to explore possible ways to sustain their interest in investing in India's energy sector, in particular, to see whether it would be economically viable to reshape the project to serve higher value intermediate load in the Western Region'.[2]

So, it was hardly surprising when, in 2000, it came to light that MSEB was purchasing power from DPC at ₹4.14 (approx. 10¢) per kWh while it was charging an average of ₹1.89 per unit from its retail consumers. The tariff paid by MSEB to DPC was almost double the average local cost of producing electricity and more than three times as much as the cheapest producer. Furthermore, the price of Enron's energy was slated to rise to ₹13.3 (33¢) per kWh by 2017! Given the precarious financial position of MSEB, it stopped paying. Since the power purchase agreement between the two had a clause that required MSEB to pay whether DPC generates or not, the state sought to cancel the power purchase agreement. The cycle once more began with Enron beginning arbitration proceedings and the US Secretary of State Colin Powell raising Enron's problems regarding Dabhol with his Indian counterpart. Finally, in May 2001, DPC ceased Phase 1 operations of the plant and halted Phase 2 which was 90% complete (1,444 MW).

In the meantime, another high-powered committee headed

by a senior ex-government bureaucrat, Madhav Godbole, and four other eminent citizens released its report. The report recommended a judicial probe into the entire Enron power project deal saying it signified 'the failure of governance that seems to have characterized almost every step of the decision-making process relating to the Dabhol power project'.[3] It proved to be the proverbial last straw that broke the camel's back. On the heels of the snowballing controversy generated by the Godbole Committee Report, which reverberated in the state legislature, the Indian parliament and media, came another unexpected development. Enron Inc. in the US spectacularly collapsed in 2001 (this had nothing to do with DPC) sending almost all top executives of the company to prison. Not much was heard about Rebecca Marks after that.

Eventually, Enron's stake in DPC was bought by GE and Bechtel, and the tangle of agreements between various state agencies had the project mothballed for nearly five years. After many twists and turns, the erstwhile DPC was renamed Ratnagiri Gas and Power Pvt. Ltd. It started operation in May 2006 under restructured and reconstituted ownership and management. The new management, too, had its own set of problems with the plant having to shut down in July 2006 due to a lack of naphtha supply only to restart operations a year later, when the Qatar-based RasGas Company Ltd started supplying LNG to Ratnagiri. The private power utility's debt estimated at ₹10,500 crore ($1.3 billion) in 2015 continued to grow. In a bid to revive the loss-making plant, the company was split into two, one responsible for power generation and the other for LNG import. In 2019, after twenty-two years of legal battles, the Supreme Court closed the cases of alleged corruption against it. Dabhol continues to hobble and stands out as a painful testimony to the Narasimha Rao regime's earnest but unsuccessful effort to privatise the power sector.

Its failure was thanks to hubris and the little men who tend to cripple an enterprise even before it has started because of their greed for ill-gotten gains.

We had no role to play in the cataclysmic events that followed the first meeting in 1991 that we had initiated. Thereupon the partners shaped their destiny. But I remember meeting Rebbeca Mark at the Indian ambassador's home in Washington, DC, in the autumn of 1997. This was around the time Enron had hit an impasse during Phase 1, but things had not completely fallen apart. My presence was graciously acknowledged by Rebecca who admitted that the company's foray into India would not have happened without our support and the introduction we had engineered.

An Object Lesson

The aftermath of the drive to privatise the power sector was not very encouraging. The mid-1990s saw a virtual stampede of American brokers and power companies seeking meetings with officials of various state governments. On a trip to Hyderabad to meet senior officials at the erstwhile unified Andhra Pradesh State Electricity Board, I discovered they too had received many proposals from the US. Indian state utilities were not prepared for the deluge of interest. Odisha was looking at similar initiatives and facing similar roadblocks. Power purchase agreements were not refined yet and Indian officials were clueless about the clauses and covenants. They lacked the professional ability to carry out due diligence for the verification of credentials. In a sense, it was good that many of these suitors from the US went back without cutting a deal.

The Enron debacle was an eye-opener and a watershed moment for the power sector in India. The lessons learned have paved the way for many admirable adjustments and modifications in government policies and approach. Perhaps the most important of them has been the establishment of a competitive and transparent bidding process overseen by an independent regulatory authority to select potential private power generators. The evolutionary reform process to attract private investors has involved 'learning by doing'. Today, there is a battery of trained consultants and firms who have the requisite legal and technical expertise. Most importantly, India has substantially overcome the challenge of providing competent governance and leadership and realized that the power sector should not be treated as a source of political patronage.

CHAPTER EIGHT

Greening Buildings and Urban Habitats, 2000–2010

Post the crisis brought about by OPEC's embargo in 1973, happy accidents of life had taken me to some of the finest thinkers and strategists of the time like G. R. Dalvi, D. V. Kapoor, R. K. Pachauri, T. L. Sankar, Kirit Parekh and P. R. Srinivasan, to name a few. Though a few are unsung and forgotten, their influence over how India shaped its policy and directions on energy efficiency in government, industry and other sectors was powerful.

My work for over nearly twenty-five years till 2000 had been anchored around industry. The path-finding work we did on clean coal, cogeneration, electricity distribution reforms and the water-energy nexus, brought forth innovative practices which are today the norm in the power, industry and agricultural sectors. But there was one area that had escaped my attention: cities and buildings that consumed energy.

At the turn of the millennium, Indian cities were still manageable – water, energy and waste challenges had yet not assumed the serious proportions they have today. India was still a few years away from the building frenzy that would dominate the next two decades. I must confess that most early studies and official documents from the seventies up to the late nineties were silent on the need for energy efficiency in buildings. This changed, however, with an innovative US-India bilateral programme, Energy Conservation and Commercialization (ECO) Program which rolled out in three phases over ten long years. The energy conservation codes promulgated by the government had already set the stage for ECO Phase 1 to advance energy efficiency in buildings. Again, the mantra was putting in a regulatory and market-driven foundational effort that yielded energy efficiency on a significant scale, with the potential for replication.

Strategic partnership with the Indian private sector, as this chapter recounts, helped trigger the Green Building Movement which became a nationwide crusade. India now ranks only second to the US in terms of the size of its green building footprint with nearly eight billion square feet of certified green buildings.[1]

To appreciate India's monumental progress, it is important to delve briefly into the past.

India's spiritual past, from the Vedic ages, had been interwoven with sustainable living in total harmony with nature. This is reflected in the design of its ancient monuments and habitats that dot the country's landscape and serve as reminders of a glorious past. Green buildings have been an integral part of the country's 5000-year-old rich heritage with its endless array of sustainable techniques for building construction. Traditional Indian architecture is a storehouse of rich psychological insights and nuances of processes and constructs. A presentation at a Green Building Congress event in Pittsburgh, US, in 2003 brought this home in an inimitable manner.

The speaker, an Indian architect whose green antecedents were well known, addressed a largely Western audience about a succession of ancient townships, monuments, forts and palaces from the Mohenjo Daro and Harappan civilizations of 2500 BC through the Mughal empire (15th–18th century AD) to buildings in current-day India. Each edifice was given a 'LEED' (Leadership in Energy and Environmental Design) rating. The audience was flabbergasted to hear that if these ancient structures were to be assessed today for their environmental and resource-efficient design, they would all be rated as Platinum – the highest rating! It was an example of environmental stewardship and responsibility exercised by an ancient civilization, conveyed subtly and elegantly.

Planting the Seed

When did the Green Building Movement in India actually begin? It is difficult in cases like this to point one's finger to a specific date or occasion. But it would not be a travesty of the truth if one were to say that it began in 2001 on the day a few of us at CII, the state government of Andhra Pradesh and USAID took the collective decision that India's premier green business centre would be housed in a green building in Hyderabad. But let me circle back to the events that led to this 'leap of faith' decision.

It was mid-January 2000, and I had just relocated with my family to New Delhi a month ago to work with USAID, having obtained a two-year leave of absence from the World Bank. The President of the United States (POTUS) Bill Clinton was slated to visit India in early March. I received a call from a senior ex-colleague and energy advisor to CII, V. Raghuraman. He wanted to know whether there was a way, in my opinion, that would strengthen the case for getting President Clinton to visit Hyderabad. On being asked about the context, he explained how at the World Economic Summit in Davos, Switzerland, the chief minister of AP, Chandrababu Naidu, had asked his boss and head of CII, Tarun Das, for help in orchestrating a POTUS visit to his state, during his stay in India in March that year. The case for a POTUS visit to AP had to be very compelling for it to interest the Americans. Tarun had seized upon the idea for he saw an opportunity for CII to do something significant that would leave a lasting footprint. He promptly turned to his senior staff, including Raghuraman, for ideas. That's when Raghuraman decided to reach out to me.

I sat in my office, long after the call, on that cold evening with a gentle patter of winter rain on the window, turning over the idea. I was intrigued by the call from Raghuraman. I did not know how to respond. But I, too, had sensed the opportunity to launch an initiative in India that would be impressive enough to stir the interest of Indian industry and government as well as the White House. The challenge was real: any such state visit by the POTUS would be packed with competing schedules and agendas; to squeeze in something that made it to the Government of India and the White House shortlist had to be really dramatic and of interest to both nations. There wasn't much time, for Clinton's itinerary was close to being finalized. I was idly riffling through a *Newsweek* magazine and the term 'Green Business' in a two-page feature caught my eye. I wondered: Would a joint endeavour to set up a green business centre (GBC) in Hyderabad fit the bill?

I spoke to my USAID office chief, Richard Edwards (Dick), about his thought on my idea. He was supportive as long as the request emanated from India, which would have more impact on the White House planners. I called Raghuraman the next morning and asked him how he felt about a green business centre in Hyderabad. We knew that climate change was high on the list of Clinton's presidential priorities, and a joint statement on the US-India clean energy partnership was on the POTUS visit agenda.

Neither Raghuraman nor Tarun Das had heard of a GBC before. I told them it would be a centre that would look at sustainability, energy efficiency, renewables and so on to help Indian businesses become more energy-efficient and thus, improve the bottom line. I told them about USAID's plans for the ECO, and how such a centre could perhaps offer a slew of services, including training for business leaders and managers in India.

CII asked for an explanatory note and I sent it over that weekend. A revised version moved to the Indian Ministry of External Affairs. They found it interesting enough to want to include it in the India agenda for the presidential visit and sent it to Washington. The note had a prominent reference to climate change, so it drew the attention of Jeff Seabright, a senior White House aide presiding over the White House Task Force on Climate Change. He called me up and said, 'I heard India has asked for an initiative on green business centres.' I confessed that the idea had emanated from my desk and urged him to include it in their agenda. Jeff galvanized to action. An advance team including Jeff was to visit India the following week and they made time to meet Dick and me at the USAID office. Pleased with the meeting, Jeff pushed for the GBC to be included in the POTUS agenda.

Clinton's Hyderabad itinerary was IT-centric, for Chief Minister Naidu was set on turning the state capital into a tech city. A reformist leader who was technologically adroit, Naidu was different from most politicians of his era in India. Often referred to as the 'CEO of Andhra Pradesh', he ran the affairs of his state like an astute businessman. In Clinton, he had a friend. President Clinton had a packed schedule but took some time out to announce the launch of a green business centre, with Naidu doing his bit by announcing the allocation of a piece of land in an emerging industry hub called the HITEC City. The next day, newspapers carried President Clinton's stirring message that India has the potential to grow its economy and reduce carbon emissions at the same time. Green businesses were going to enable us to do that.

After the president had left, the head of CII walked up to me – thankful and relieved that the first leg of the mission was behind us – and said, 'We have asked our Chennai office to track this from here.' That was when S. Raghupathy, a slim man in his forties at CII's Chennai office stepped in. I would later realize that concealed behind that amiable visage was a sharp and organized mind. He was an expert chess player but had given it up for a career at CII.

But the CII team as a whole needed some guidance before they could execute their plans. During one of my meetings with the team, a question about their thoughts on the functions of the GBC they were working on left them confused. The meeting left me unsatisfied. Something was missing. Dick suggested that USAID could sponsor a strategic study to determine the centre's mission, goals, structure and road map. CII readily agreed. We approached an international energy and environment consultancy firm in Washington, DC, which had on its rolls an energy efficiency expert named John Armstrong. John was my ex-colleague at Hagler Bailly and had visited India several times before. His understanding of the country's situation and needs was sophisticated and informed. At our request, he paid another visit to the subcontinent in connection with the proposed study.

John put together a fairly comprehensive outline of what a GBC ought to be doing, in terms of its constitution, structure and activity. I looked at it and felt that the report carried the risk of gathering dust in an attic if we did not put a spin to it and give it a practical edge. We needed to secure buy-in from the Indian partners, CII and the Government of AP. At the same time, the CII team needed to have a better understanding of the parallels that existed in the US. To this end, we agreed to sponsor the visit of an Indian team to the US and enable meetings with people who were in the know.

A Historic Visit

In December 2000, a USAID-sponsored team – including Raghupathy and S. Srinivas from CII, architect Karan Grover, Chairman of the Andhra Pradesh State Electricity Board Ramakant Reddy and me – landed in the US capital. The green centre in Minneapolis, which impressed us with its emphasis on natural lighting, was one of the sites we intended to visit. We then visited an energy education centre in Tulare, California, run by Southern California Edison that looked at water and energy issues in agricultural farms. Houston's industrial hubs were part of this tour as well before we headed back to Washington. There, meetings at the World Bank and the USAID headquarters were followed by a visit, at John Armstrong's suggestion, to the office of the United States Green Building Council (USGBC) on L Street.

It was a cold, blustery morning when a few of us, not very appropriately bundled for the freezing weather, entered the premises of the USGBC office. We were not exactly sure what to expect. It was the last stop of our week-long whistle-stop tour of the US.

The vice chair of the USGBC board at the time was Kath Williams, who took us through a lovely virtual presentation of their LEED rating system and what it took to construct a building rated platinum, gold or silver. USGBC, launched in 1987, was at the time about twelve years old. They were still sharpening their professional spurs. During the meeting, a staff member of the council, Donna McIntyre, mentioned that the Chesapeake Bay Foundation headquarters at Annapolis in Maryland was the first and only platinum LEED-rated building in the US. There were none outside the US, she said and volunteered to set up a visit. The effervescent Karan blurted, 'We will put together the first platinum-rated building in India with rating offered by USGBC.' I held my breath, not sure what he meant and how the Americans would respond to it. Kath politely offered to help but did not seem very convinced.

Nevertheless, the idea that a similar system could be devised for India and it could be the first platinum-rated building of the country had been seeded in our minds. Karan Grover was excited by the prospect, though I must confess I preferred to tread with caution. Back at the Holiday Inn, where the team was staying, Karan shut himself up in his room and drew on a large sheet of paper the first scratch of what would eventually be the GBC's headquarters in Hyderabad that today stands on an acre of the five acres Chief Minister Naidu had granted to CII. The structure was circular, and his ingenious brush strokes had got the team excited. It served as an anchor for the other meetings. He slapped the drawing on the wall, and we discussed it in some detail, not sure whether there would be a green building in India and who would build and own it.

The next day, we drove to Annapolis to see the LEED platinum building that Donna had told us about. We later learnt that she was one of its principal architects. We were quite taken by the extent of detail reflected in the building's features – its passive architectural design, the use of natural ventilation and water conservation and recycling systems. Could we match this? No one voiced their apprehensions, if not misgivings, about how things would pan out.

Origins of Green Building

On our return to Delhi, Tarun was briefed about the visit and Karan presented his sketch. The CII head lost no time in suggesting that they had to find a corporate partner. He had someone in mind. A corporate leader with a strong environmental record: Jamshyd Godrej. He was a senior CII member and the scion of Godrej Industries. As a business leader who firmly believed in 'planet before profit', Godrej was known for his commitment to environmental sustainability. The Godrej Group, under his stewardship, has dedicated itself to managing 2,000 acres of mangroves in Vikhroli, a suburb of Mumbai, providing much-needed lung space to the beleaguered city. A week later, Dick and I travelled to Mumbai for a meeting with the man. Godrej liked the idea and offered his company's support for the initiative while we reciprocated by offering to support the software side of training, institutional capacity building and certification process with LEED. A few years later, CII-GBC broadened its programme to establish an independent entity, the Indian Green Building Council (IGBC) whose partnership with USGBC was fostered by USAID.

In the meantime, I reached out to Kath Williams and asked if she would visit India to lend second wind to the discussions we had had in Washington. She was planning a visit to Singapore and said that she could swing by Delhi for a stopover of sorts. Though not lacking in enthusiasm, unlike the first time we met her, she had some misgivings about travelling to India, which was a large country in a part of the world that she had never visited before. But she made it to Delhi in early 2001. I met her, along with Karan, a few architects and a couple of building industry professionals. They requested her for another meeting a couple of months later during which they wished to present a series of training programmes supported by USAID.

The multicity tour she and her colleague Donna McIntyre – including Delhi, Bombay and Chennai – had left them deeply impressed, particularly the enthusiasm of the industry professionals and particularly the architects they had interacted with. By the end of the tour, Kath was convinced that India could be fertile soil for seeding the Green Building Movement. Years later, reminiscing about the tour, Kath shared, 'We did the multicity tour explaining green building and LEED as a tool. I pushed that LEED was adaptable for India, not a US standard alone. The tour was sponsored by Indian industry, which was unusual for that time period. Most of the LEED tours were sponsored around the world by governments or NGOs.'[2]

This visit had set in motion the movement which has expanded today to nearly 6,300 registered green buildings (as of March 2021) and made India the country with the second-largest green building footprint in the world. Kath went on to help grow USGBC and build her own consultancy firm out of Montana, and Donna became a sustainability leader at the US State Department.

To get this bilateral project off the ground, we had to obtain the formal consent of the Government of India. Shashi Sekhar, then head of the fledgling BEE, was happy to sign off. We had met Shashi Sekhar a few times around the time we had launched ECO. Shashi was glad that USAID was willing to support the initiative with the Indian private sector to build a GBC with resource experts from the US and a bit of funding for the capacity building capsule. Thanks to my colleagues, we devised a way to tap into some of the funds that were residing with ICICI. This old partner of USAID had been handling the reflow of money earned from our successful PACER projects. ICICI officials visited the CII office and worked out a memorandum of understanding that committed funding support to the latter for the nationwide development of their GBC initiative. Godrej chipped in to fund the 'hardware' – the construction of the building Karan had sketched.

Thereafter, CII assembled a team of professionals to lead the GBC. The team moved to Hyderabad, into a modest office as the new headquarters was not ready yet. The headquarters was to be a green building. So, the GBC team reached out to the AP government for support, while Karan was in touch with Kath and her team for guidance on the LEED rating system and the design features that would win them rating points.

India's First LEED Platinum

The GBC headquarters earned the LEED Platinum rating – the first building outside of the US to do so – in September 2003. I recall a late-night call from Kath Williams who was travelling from her hometown in Montana to Australia, during which she shared the decision of the USGBC assessment committee with me. Her voice was laced with joy and emotion when she confided that the GBC building had been awarded the highest rating.

The building was formally inaugurated by President A. P. J. Abdul Kalam in July 2004. Later that year, I accompanied the GBC team to Pittsburgh for the World Green Building Congress where the platinum award was conferred formally to this 20,000-square-foot green building. The building and its activities were now formally christened the CII–Sohrabji Godrej Green Business Centre, or CII–GBC for short. The centre went on to host an annual series of Indian Green Building Congress events in Hyderabad; there were events held elsewhere in India as well. The Congress's growth each year was impressive. From a modest beginning of 100 participants to over 1,500 who were unable to fit them inside the symposium hall. Seating had to be arranged outside for people to view the proceedings on large video screens. This GBC marked the birth of a new era in Indian industry. And it also signalled the procession of USGBC American professionals coming to India with their ambitious ideas of energy-efficient buildings.

At the time, I had thought the creation of the green building for the CII green business centre was a distraction. That hardware is not as important as the development of the software of capacity (training, capacity building and outreach programmes) in the country for enhancing energy efficiency in all sectors, including buildings. How mistaken I was! In retrospect, I can see how the construction of that building helped everyone get to mission mode right from the start. It set professionals at the GBC on a path that was closely aligned to what Dick and I and others like John Armstrong and Kath Williams had hoped for – the making of a national centre of excellence in energy efficiency and management. At the time of writing this book, the centre, over a long and fruitful journey of over twenty years, has staged many energy efficiency events and launched several initiatives. A new era of resource efficiency in Indian businesses had begun under Jamshyd Godrej's and Raghupathy's leadership. In the years to come, the GBC would prove instrumental in pushing the business ecosystem in Indian industry to broaden and deepen its approach to energy efficiency to include green ratings for industry, green power, water and waste management.

Formative Green Years

The early years of the Green Building Movement were not exactly a smooth ride. Not sure of its economics or its efficacy, few Indian corporates showed interest. ITC Ltd, one of India's largest private-sector conglomerates, decided that its corporate office for the hotel division in Gurgaon, near Delhi, would be a green one. Their green story is worth recounting.

I received an invitation from the Niranjan Khatri – general manager of Sustainability Initiatives for ITC Hotels – to attend ITC Hotels' board meeting in early 2003 as a special invitee. The plan to build a corporate office in Gurgaon was under discussion and Niranjan and his colleague, H. S. Kumaraswamy, were aiming to make it a green building. They needed the board's permission to do so since a cost overrun of ₹7 crore was expected. Niranjan wanted me to weigh in with my recommendations. 'An outsider's opinion might help,' he said, 'and if we go ahead we would like to be guided by USGBC to obtain LEED certification.' I agreed to attending the meeting.

Though the board was supportive, there we hit a snag. ITC was a large Indian conglomerate with business interests in a number of areas such as agriculture, paper, leather, fashion and, more importantly, tobacco. ITC stood for India Tobacco Company, although over the years, as its other business interests surged forward, its cigarette manufacturing business had begun to plateau. But green buildings were smoke-free environments. 'What message would ITC be sending out if their affiliate companies were to endorse a ban on the use of one of their main products?' wondered a few board members. The decision was deferred until further consultation and approval by the ITC chairman's office in Kolkata.

Chairman Y. C. Deveshwar was quick with his response. It was a no, but with a rider.

He challenged the team to think of a way that smoking could be permitted without compromising on the principles of maintaining the high standards of indoor air quality of a green building. That was classic Deveshwar, always pushing his team to excel in all that they did. YCD, as he was popularly referred to in corporate circles, had joined ITC right after graduating from the Indian Institute of Technology, Delhi. Sixteen years down the line, in 1984, he became a member of the board. He was subsequently appointed the chief executive and chairman in 1996. He was not just the youngest chairman of a frontline conglomerate in India but also the longest-serving one – for twenty-three years. Under his leadership, the Kolkata-based company transformed from a cigarette maker to a conglomerate with interests in sectors such as fast-moving consumer goods, hotels, paper and packaging and agri-business. His name had been synonymous with ITC Ltd until he passed away in 2019.

YCD's challenge spurred Kumaraswamy and his team to

think of alternatives. They went back to the drawing board and consulted with Kath and her USGBC colleagues during one of her visits to India. Kumaraswamy also took stock of the green buildings in the US and held consultations with their architects. The plan they formulated post their research was simple and elegant. Each floor of the ITC Hotels corporate building would have a smoker's chamber. Each of these would have an exhaust which would allow smoke to be evacuated into a central duct that would run up and through the individual chambers located on each of the five floors before being let out into the atmosphere. The draft in each chamber would be controlled with precision to ensure that while infiltration of outside air would take place, there would be no ex-filtration of smoke into the corridors and rooms outside the chamber. USGBC's LEED assessment team was convinced. In July 2008, the building received the LEED Platinum rating.

A year later, in June 2009, when US Secretary of State Hillary Clinton visited the office, she offered to make a statement on climate change cooperation with India against the 'green' backdrop. ITC Hotels went on to become the first hotel chain to embrace sustainability and green building concepts in their existing and new hotels. Some of them – ITC Gardenia in Bangalore, ITC Grand Chola in Chennai and ITC Sonar in Kolkata – even received LEED Platinum ratings. ITC was also the first hotel chain in India and the world to claim the distinction of receiving the highest LEED rating.

Until 2006, the Indian Green Building Council (IGBC) and CII had been working together. In order to steer clear of the obvious conflict of interest, since training and certification were being offered by the same entity, IGBC was separated from CII. Over the years, its growth has been phenomenal. Under the leadership of IGBC's founding chairman, S. ParasuRaman (Parasu), the awareness of green buildings saw a slow and steady rise, beginning with well-meaning corporates and professionals. Parasu's early stewardship of the Green Building Movement helped build its solid foundation. The council's logo designed by him is recognized by architects the world over as the symbol of green buildings in India. In recognition of our contributions to the movement, IGBC bestowed the Hall of Fame Award to Kath, Parasu and me in 2013.

Following Parasu, who relinquished his position in 2009, IGBC's leadership was passed on to Prem Jain, an icon and the undisputed leader of the HVAC&R (heating, ventilation, air conditioning and refrigeration) industry in India. Known as the 'father of air conditioning in India', Prem was a legend in the country's building industry having started ASHRAE India. He had played a key role in the drafting of the HVAC section in the country's National Building Code. A warm and charismatic person, Prem's stewardship of IGBC took it to great heights. His extraordinary vision, which helped IGBC become a global leader, was an exercise in simplicity and directness. His clarion call – 'Every person in India, that is Bharat, should contribute one square foot of registered green footprint' – took the scoreboard of the registered green footprint under IGBC from a tottering 13 million sq ft in 2009 to 1 billion sq ft by 2015. As of March 2021, the number stands at 7.75 billion sq ft and the target for 2022 is 10 billion sq ft. Following his unfortunate demise in late 2018, the baton was passed to V. Suresh, a doyen of the country's building industry, who continues to provide exemplary leadership.

Back in 2000, there was a collective sense in USAID that India was moving from a traditional donor–beneficiary relation to a peer-to-peer one. The USAID mission was able to leverage this as a massive advantage for its energy efficiency agenda in India with very little investment of time and of money, thanks to the competence of CII. It was a tribute to CII's vision as well. A complementary effort in designing and introducing the Energy Conservation Building Code for compliance by state and central governments in partnership with BEE under the bilateral ECO project provided an additional fillip to the Green Building Movement.

It is heartwarming to see how that one small step – a meeting in Washington, DC – led to the beginning of this crucial movement in India. Many significant milestones have been achieved over the past two decades. These include 28 IGBC green building ratings that cover all building types; 1,870 member organizations in over 20 regional offices; 4,950 qualified IGBC-accredited green building professionals and over 250 student chapters at various architectural and engineering colleges across the country.

This work assumes far greater relevance as India moves into the third decade of the millennium, battling the gap between growth and ecological crisis. As I look back, I realize it is time for the GBC as well as IGBC to reinvent their roles and lead a second-generation shift in thinking and direction for the future.

Consolidation and Growth

The market for green buildings has consolidated well. IGBC's move towards certified energy-efficient buildings is expected to expand to about 60–80 billion sq ft of green footprint by 2030–35. But the built-up area in India has been growing at an alarming rate. In 2000, the total built-up area in the country was no more than 60 billion sq ft. In the two decades that followed, it rose to 50 billion sq ft of residential, commercial and other building typologies adding to the challenges faced by local city and town authorities to provide affordable and reliable electricity, water and transportation services to its inhabitants. By 2030, we will be looking at a whopping 160 million sq ft!

Urban India hosts nearly 8,000 towns and cities, spread

over 1,40,000 sq km, occupying no more than 3% of India's landmass. Nearly 400 million people occupy this small percentage of land and consume 75% of natural resource while feeding off the forest ecosystems of the remaining 60% of the population. We owe it to our future generations to accelerate the pace and scale of sustainable buildings and habitats.

The GBC has acquired a life of its own and has become a world leader within a decade, just like IGBC. With its newfound authority, IGBC has developed its own rating and certification systems and examination for the accreditation of green building assessors. Ever since its inception, American companies, suppliers and architects have been willing to consider it seriously and be involved in supporting India's Green Building Movement. An ecosystem was created with initiatives on both sides with the private sector driving it, not the governments. Only by nurturing private-sector endeavour and with the support of technological expertise and benign support from the government, can sustainable, resource-efficient services be institutionalized.

CHAPTER NINE

Last-mile Distribution, 2002–2010

The Umbilical Cord

In October 1993, at a World Bank conference in Jaipur, in the presence of several state and central ministers and officials, an idea permeated the air. The need to reform the Indian power sector to make it more competitive and efficient and reduce the burden on the public exchequer was being discussed threadbare by those present. As one state government official put it, 'It was time to sever the umbilical cord between the state electricity boards and the state governments.' The million-dollar question was how it would be done and who would be the guinea pig. This issue was soon put to rest at the conference itself when Biju Patnaik, the bold and intrepid chief minister of Odisha, volunteered to work with the World Bank on a power sector reform programme in his state. Soon thereafter, a World Bank mission visited Bhubaneswar, the capital of Odisha, in preparation for the work ahead.

While Odisha prepared for the programme, in the summer of 1984, I joined the Asia Alternate Energy Unit (ASTAE) as a demand-side management specialist. ASTAE is a unit within the World Bank and worked in a broad theatre of action that spanned Southeast Asia and South Asia, extending from China to the Philippines, to Indonesia and Malaysia, and as far as India and Sri Lanka. Its mandate was to assist operations managers in the bank's power sector in Asia to promote, identify and prepare investment strategies for renewable energy and energy efficiency projects. The primary work was on scaling-up strategies for renewable energy, cook stoves and other initiatives in these countries, impact assessments of mini and small hydropower generation plants, and so on. Interestingly, it also monitored progress on each country's energy front through impact indicators that covered renewable energy, energy efficiency and access to energy to underserved and unserved communities. ASTAE was supported by the Dutch and a few other trust funds deposited at the World Bank.

I was soon co-opted into the mission engaged in the ongoing Odisha power sector reform programme. The job was to scout for load management and energy efficiency projects among the customers of the Odisha utility.

Demand-side Strategy

ASTAE's plan to establish a presence in India and South Asia led them to reach out to my employers, Hagler Bailly Inc., in Washington who in turn recommended me to the World Bank unit in early 1994. I was working in Cairo on an energy conservation programme evaluation at the time. On my return, I was hired as a short-term consultant to assist ASTAE in preparing a demand-side management (DSM) strategy for their power sector reform programme in India.

I visited India with a team of senior bank officials led by Loretta Schaeffer. She was the manager of the ASTAE group; though not a subject expert, she was a task driver. As the consultant, I was tasked to set up meetings and provide subject-matter guidance to the team. A fortnight of travel took us to Delhi, Mumbai, Bangalore and Chennai where we met with state government officials, utility officials and energy experts. The flurry of meetings was productive.

I wrote a 100-page-long substantive report on DSM

strategies for India which was carefully reviewed by Loretta and her staff before it was passed on to World Bank's India energy chief, Francois Bauer. A meeting was called to discuss the report. I attended the meeting but was not expected to participate. The pecking order in such meetings usually meant that 'consultants' would not be addressed directly. Loretta was the focus of the chat. The energy chief was blunt. He said dismissively, 'All of this,' pointing to the report he held in his hands, 'is mere potential, a guesstimate of the energy savings possible, and therefore, of little practical relevance.' Someone else chipped in and expanded on the big picture of power sector reforms, and the conversation in the room veered off in another direction. I could see they did not know how to respond to the report. Perhaps they were looking for a concise note of no more than two pages! I chimed in, much to Loretta's consternation, by saying that the least they could do was to offer attention and time to the report and the complexities of bringing such change in India, given its diversity and other challenges.

As luck would have it, my indiscretion at that meeting helped them take the discussion forward. The chief saw that they could do well with an outspoken man on their side. And so began another journey as I was invited by ASTAE to join them on their mission for India.

I was tasked to organize a strategy meeting with a decent bunch of energy experts and economists. The team meant to work on demand-side projects in India. None of them had got under the skin of this odd beast called demand-side management – with respect to both last-mile supply distribution and energy demand in end use. The term was new, even in the West, and its coinage in India was rare and more so in state utilities.

So that's how I got to be a member of the Bank's state power sector reforms mission to Odisha.

A Peak Load Tale

The work expected of me seemed straightforward on paper. I was expected to identify and design energy efficiency and DSM programmes and projects among the utility's major electricity consumers which when implemented would result in reducing and/or shifting the growing peak electricity load that the utility was confronted with.

With this objective in mind, I set about my task to gather data and analyze at a fundamental level, which category of consumers and end-user applications contributed to the state's electricity load. I soon discovered that this data would be difficult to obtain. Ferreting data from old billing records was of little help in those days since consumer meters, if installed, were less than accurate. A visit to the load despatch station provided some information at a gross sector level but not at a sub-sector, end-use consumer application level. Disaggregated, fine end-user data which I needed for my analysis was simply non-existent.

Out of desperation, I requested a meeting with a few officials from the state electricity utility. At the meeting, I posed a straightforward question: Which end-use application, in their opinion, contributed most to the state grid's peak electricity load? Was it water pumping, lighting, air-conditioning or water heating or something else? The answer I received bewildered me further. No two officials agreed with each other, with each person suggesting a different end use. Perhaps, it is the electrical 'chakki' – a contraption used to grind corn – volunteered one. Another believed it was the continuous use of TVs in most homes. A third disdainfully dismissed the two and made a fervent plea that street lighting was the cause. None of this helped and I left, feeling a little dejected.

Walking back that evening to the hotel where I was staying, I passed a manned electricity distribution sub-station of the state utility. I decided to go in and talk to the officials there. They were gracious and welcoming. There, I noticed the needles of the ammeters that measured current flow were jerking forward. On asking the reason, I was informed that households in the city were preparing dinner using electric cookers. They explained that most households used locally manufactured electric cookers for cooking. Each cooker was of approximately 2 kW capacity and consisted of copper wires strung across a ceramic plate – a somewhat crude backyard design of a resistance-type cooker.

Later, based on sample household surveys I concluded that electric cookers – accounting for a fourth of the average electricity load and more than 50% of the evening peak – were perhaps one of the major contributors to peak load in that state. I estimated their share to be around 400 MW. A programme to substitute electric cookers appeared impossible at that time because of two major constraints. The first was the highly subsidized electricity tariffs offered to households by the government, and second, there was no alternative cooking fuel. The state did not have an LPG distribution network, kerosene was in short supply – and generally reserved for lighting hurricane lamps in rural areas – and firewood and coal were banned. I dropped the idea and instead, several other projects were identified, including municipal water pumping which appeared to be a good candidate for a pilot DSM demonstration project. But the electric cooker conundrum remained unresolved.

Five years later, in 2001, after I had moved back to Delhi. I met B. C. Jena, chairman of Grid Corporation of Odisha, who was visiting the city. I learned from him about an interesting turn of events. Power sector reforms had taken deep root in Odisha in the intervening years and several changes had taken place. Household tariffs had been revised upwards, LPG was freely available in the market and consequently, the state had seen a rapid shift from the inefficient electric resistance cookers to LPG stoves. This brought about a momentous change in the electricity grid. Peak load demand had perceptibly dropped by 400 MW or so compared to load demand figures five years earlier, when I had confronted the electric cooker puzzle. While feeling somewhat vindicated, I could not but help think that even the lack of data can unearth surprises.

Distribution Tidbits

Distribution reforms in the power sector had engaged my mind for a long time. While the Odisha situation provided an opportunity to address the issue of load management, I came across other compelling problems as well. It was the summer of 1997. A north Indian state was under pressure to improve the performance of its electricity distribution system. With state elections around the corner, they went on a media blitz to educate the public on the positive impact of their programmes. 'Power cuts have been lifted and power is available in rural areas 24x7,' screamed advertisements in the local press and political leaders of the ruling dispensation. Around the same time, I was part of a World Bank mission team visiting the state and accompanied by a few international energy experts to help design a demand-side programme for the state utility. The work required us to visit a rural power distribution circle outside the state capital and observe its operations. During the long drive back to the hotel that night, we passed through well-lit towns and villages. On the horizon, we could see the twinkling of distant lights. To us, it appeared that there was no evidence of a blackout, as alleged by a few. When one of the team members glanced back, he saw the lights gradually dim and go out. Trailing behind was a spectacle of total darkness in the villages we had just passed. In their quest to create a favourable impression, the utility officials had cut off power line feeders in a sequence that shadowed our travel along the road!

Improving customer relations was at the heart of a strategy to incentivize users to save energy. Simple measures yielded significant results. One such was an innovative idea introduced by an IAS officer, T. V. S. N. Prasad, the MD of the Andhra Pradesh Central Distribution Company Ltd (APDCL). A Haryana cadre officer Prasad was handpicked and deputed to serve at APDCL in early 1998. He did not disappoint. Soon after joining and realizing that customer trust was at a low ebb, Prasad went about addressing this situation. What could the utility do to raise the level of faith and conviction with the consumer, he wondered. He instinctively realized that repairing the relationship would prepare the ground for an honest exchange aimed at raising the service levels of power supply that could yield revenue dividends through the reduction of unpaid bills by customers. Realizing that continuity and reliability of power supply was crucial to customers during events such as weddings, festivals and parties at homes, he offered a pledge that the utility shall endeavour after having received prior notice of a community or home celebration, quality power supply during such occasions. The results were quite dramatic. Users saved money in not having to resort to costly back-up captive power generation, trust deepened and over a period of time, unpaid bills steadily declined and recovery rates improved.

Encouraged by the enthusiastic response, utility personnel pressed ahead to respond to customer grievances and emergencies at speeds hitherto not observed. An incident that I witnessed brought home to me this changed attitude.

On one of my visits to Hyderabad around that time, while in my hotel room, I glanced out the window and was startled by a bright arc of light followed by a plume of smoke. One of the distribution power cables had short-circuited, and shortly thereafter, supply to the neighbourhood was cut. 'It should take a day or two for power to be resumed, if we are fortunate', asserted the hotel lobby manager when I asked about resumption of supply. To me, this seemed a good opportunity to test the efficacy of the grievance addressal system that Prasad had put in place. A quick call to the customer service center helped register a complaint and in a matter of less than thirty minutes, a utility forklift truck with a repair crew pulled up in front of the accident spot and set about repairing the fault. Power supply resumed within the hour.

Prasad's initiatives also impacted favourably other areas of the company's business. Several other equally impactful schemes were launched during his tenure. The relationship repaired, mutual trust restored, paved the way for a number of demand response programmes aimed at reducing peak load and generating energy savings.

Beating the DRUM

The Odisha experience and later the AP experience taught us there are indeed solutions that can be explored. In early 2002, in the quest to understand how USAID could assist in designing implementable solutions in the country's power distribution, we sought a meeting with the union Ministry of Power. R. V. Shahi, former technical director at NTPC and ex-CEO of the country's private-sector utility, BSES in Bombay, before being co-opted by the Vajpayee administration to head the ministry, was one who offered a willing ear. I knew Shahi from my earlier days at the WB and my colleagues at USAID had worked closely with him on the CenPEEP project with NTPC (Chapter Four). He leaned forward towards the end of a meeting in his office at Shram Shakti Bhawan and said, memorably, 'Let us create a few Taj Mahals of excellence in distribution.' We went back, happy to have found an ally at the highest levels of India's civil bureaucracy.

With the decks laid out on the likely partners for a bilateral energy programme, our minds whirred with the possibilities.

The Distribution Reform, Upgrades and Management (DRUM) programme was born soon after, in 2003. This India-US bilateral energy project was developed by USAID, essentially to help electric power utilities be efficient in managing their distribution energy losses which were as high as 35%–50% in some cases. The design of the project did not take much time, thanks to the organized data that was already available. But an unanticipated problem cropped up that delayed the official sanction for the project by the two countries. The USAID mission staff were, for the most part, evacuated to Washington in view of the rising military tensions between India and Pakistan. On US State Department orders, I had to leave my post and our frequent meetings to plan and execute the preparatory work, for the programme was hampered. Thankfully this interruption was brief, and we were allowed to resume our work three months later. The following summer, with all clearances and approvals obtained and agreements signed, the project was ready to roll.

The pilot project component referred to as the 'centres of excellence' – or in Shahi's words the 'Taj Mahals of power distribution' to showcase best practices and technologies in the distribution sector – exceeded our expectations. Electricity losses in the three project sites in Maharashtra, Gujarat and Karnataka were reduced from an average of 53% to an average of 15%. Billing and collection shot up to 100% from an average of 65% and transformer failures plummeted to a historical low of 2% compared to 10% prior to DRUM. Customers, especially farmers, reported up to a 15% increase in their incomes as a result of receiving reliable and higher quality power supply. Recognizing the improvements made by the three distribution companies, or discoms, at the three sites, the project was recognized for innovation at the India Power Awards in 2010. At a national conference in February 2011 to mark the formal conclusion of the seven-year programme, a book on DRUM case studies was released by USAID. It is today accepted as a credible and authentic guide for utilities elsewhere in the country desirous of replicating the DRUM model.

Little did any of us know that besides successfully creating and demonstrating the 'Taj Mahals of last-mile distribution excellence', DRUM would make a lasting contribution in two other areas too.

Rural Electricity

Way back, during the Great Depression of the early 1930s, when Franklin Roosevelt was the US President, he launched with great fanfare the New Deal to provide succour and jobs to his country, which was reeling from an unprecedented and devastating economic crisis. A significant outcome in the decades that followed was the Rural Electrification Authority. In 1935, only 12% of the country's rural population received electricity services, but with the authority's efforts through rural cooperatives the figure increased to about 99% by 1970. There were settlements that preferred candles and hurricane lanterns and refused electrification, and they made up the remaining percentage. Over the years, the Rural Electrification Authority drove programmes that provided rural cooperatives with financing and technical support for electric power, civil infrastructure, water and waste treatment, electric power and health and telecommunications services. By 1994, these programmes were offered under the Rural Utilities Service (RUS). It was a fascinating story that got us hooked. The rural terrain in both US and India, while fundamentally different in the nature of their population and living standards, had some similarities. Both were vast and diverse with prospects for the potential of rural electricity cooperatives to own, operate and deliver electricity services.

In January 2005, I reached out to the head of the RUS at the US Department of Agriculture about establishing similar services in India. She was not too sure. 'We have never worked beyond the United States, with the exception of Mexico, and I haven't a clue of what India needs,' was her first plaintive response. But we had planted a seed. On returning to India, I went back to Shahi who agreed to meet with the RUS senior team in the US. Three months later, during this breakthrough meeting in Washington, DC, Shahi turned to us, visibly impressed, and whispered in Hindi, 'India's rural electrification programme can gain from RUS's experience; the solution partially lies here.' As a visionary himself, he saw the potential in this initiative. But many others didn't. This was one of the many hurdles we would have to cross during this journey.

The first was the internal bureaucracy. The deadline for hiring DRUM consultants was fast approaching. If RUS continued to drag their feet and not agree quickly, the alternative was to offer the rural electrification component of the programme to some other organization. I was hesitant about this, knowing that the institutional involvement and presence of RUS was key. The deadline given to me was mere forty-eight hours away. Out of desperation, I called the director of RUS. A sleepy voice answered. It was a little after midnight. In my hurry, I had forgotten that she was in a different time zone. I apologized profusely. Having woken her up, I thought that I might as well tell her about our predicament. She interrupted me midway. 'I have instructed my officials to write you a letter that RUS is interested and is on board.' Unknown to me at that time, a colleague had met her the previous evening and had made a strong pitch. He had explained that RUS's engagement would be that of a benign partner to handhold and guide

Indian counterparts on the finer aspects and intricacies of creating and managing rural electric cooperatives. She saw that all that was needed was to get Indian engineers and experts to understand the operating landscape of an efficient rural utility.

In Delhi, among the many quasi-government institutions under the Ministry of Power was the Rural Electrification Corporation (REC). The post of the chairman – a sinecure – was held by an IAS officer posted temporarily until a more senior position was available elsewhere in the bureaucracy. REC's aim was to work with state governments to finance and implement programmes to electrify rural towns and villages. We had found a kind of local counterpart for RUS to work with. Soon thereafter, an RUS team visited India. It included seasoned veterans Howard Barnes and Larry Beluzzo, who had spent decades in establishing rural electric cooperatives in states like Colorado and Florida.

Though the initial meetings with REC went well, soon we ran into a wall of resistance. The problem lay in the emphasis that REC put on the electrification of agricultural pump sets over rural homes and municipal services like street lighting. The fact that REC's definition at that time for village electrification appeared a bit bizarre to the RUS team did not help much either. A village was deemed electrified if an electric pole within its revenue jurisdiction was connected to the grid and received electricity. RUS's emphasis, therefore, on ensuring power supply to individual homes was, though interesting, not a key REC objective. It became apparent that we needed to find an alternative partner who would comply with RUS's best operational and managerial practices. We had to find a way.

The search was on. Several contenders were considered. We chose to go directly to the electricity boards of the concerned states, specifically the state distribution companies. Sanjay Bhatia, chairman of Maharashtra State Electricity Distribution

Company Ltd (MSPGCL), was interested in a partnership with RUS. Bangalore Electricity Supply Company, with whom we had an ongoing programme under DRUM, was another organization that saw value in such a collaboration with the Americans. We set up a meeting with key officials from both parties.

The RUS experience in delivering electricity services to rural America provided a glimmer of hope in both Indian utilities as well as in the Ministry of Power, who were wrestling with this contentious issue here in India. Surprisingly, it turned out to be a two-way street with both the Indian and US sides drawing valuable lessons.

Rural America had one kilometre of distribution cables to serve one to five customers, while in India for every kilometre of power lines we had anywhere between a hundred to five hundred farmers and other rural consumers – a hundred-fold increase! The team of officers from RUS were excited, for they saw in it an opportunity to learn how to manage power supply to such a dense population with ease. The Indians were flummoxed by this happy turn of events and were more than glad to share insights on the nuances of rural distribution network design, operation of rural feeders, metering, flat-rate billing and security protocols that India had evolved over years to avoid theft and tampering of meters – things that were strange and bewildering to the Americans. In turn, the Indian engineers were keen on learning from their US counterparts about how to bring down their losses from 25%–35% to 2%. The safety of linesmen was another problem for which the Indian side eagerly turned to their US partners for solutions. The RUS engineers were happy to share insights on such efficiency that was par for the course in their well-oiled grid distribution mechanism. As part of this, the US safety manuals were studied and texts translated to local Indian languages.

In a subsequent exchange visit programme to the US, the Indians were taken aback by the level of standardization they witnessed in the country's electrification front. As one official later said to me, 'Even the colour coding and the location of items on the shelves storing utility equipment and spare parts across cooperatives in states as far apart as Florida and Colorado were identical.' Considering the wealth of knowledge and experience that was gained from this exchange programme, we knew that our efforts had paid off.

Human Capacity Development

R. V. Shahi threw another interesting challenge at us. From our conversations with the engineers from Jaipur's state distribution company at a workshop in that city in May 2006, we had learnt how distribution was hardly ever given enough attention but generation always occupied the centre stage for the planning satraps in the utility and the state and central governments. Even worse, the management and operation of the low voltage distribution system was completely left to linesmen. With a few exceptions, the last-mile distribution was in shambles, with high technical and commercial losses. This situation earned the sobriquet of T&D losses: a term used by electrical engineers to refer to energy losses in transmission and distribution of electricity. It could be more appropriately termed as 'theft and dacoity' losses.

The head of the Ministry of Power said to us, 'Help me put together a cadre of about 200 distribution managers who are MBAs for all of India, and I will work on bringing best commercial practices into distribution.' He was rueing the fact that in the eighty-odd electricity distribution firms in the country, one could hardly find qualified people at the helm with exposure to modern management practices.

It took us no time to connect with the Management Development Institute near Delhi. Dr Pritam Singh, the institute's director, and his deputy, Professor Atmanand, were happy to create competent courseware for officers of distribution utilities across India. So began a one-year executive MBA programme on power distribution management at the institute's Gurgaon campus. It was another first in the country. In three years, 150 engineers were trained for senior positions in the country's distribution utilities. The discoms gained significantly on simple inflections in management at the distribution end of the power grid that paid rich dividends.

A few years ago, an internal reshuffle at the Management Development Institute led to the decision to merge the programme with the broader one-year National Management Programme with power-sector distribution management offered as an elective. Sadly, a chunk of those trained professionals was offered the opportunity to work in the Middle East, where they found their ability better utilized and rewarded.

Apart from the MBA programme, over 36,000 distribution personnel in virtually every state and private distribution utility in the country were provided short-term training on efficient system operation and maintenance. The training was delivered through a network of twenty partner training institutes spread across the country totalling twenty-four training modules on nineteen subjects that covered the entire gamut of power distribution. This training was later institutionalized under the central government's Accelerated Power Development and Reforms Program. DRUM became a byword in the corridors of the power sector in the country's state and central governments. The short-term programme is today a staple for all public and private utilities. However, the MBA programme was a cherry on top of that DRUM cake. Looking back, I cannot help but marvel at how a chance meeting with a few disgruntled officials in Jaipur set us on this road.

After my association with the DRUM chapter of India's energy story, I turned to the persistent challenge that efficient and reliable power supply to agriculture posed. And thus was born WENEXA.

CHAPTER TEN

The Water–Energy Nexus: A Silent Passage, 2003–2010

A Farmer's Dilemma

Raj Kumar, who works a small farm in Doddaballapur, a village on the outskirts of Bangalore in the southern Indian state of Karnataka, looks anxious. His brow is creased with worry as he scans the sky, desperately looking for rain-laden clouds. His rice fields are getting dry and parched, and if the rains fail, he fears his crops will perish. Groundwater, the succour of farmers like Kumar, has failed him too because the water levels have dropped precariously. The power supply is irregular, which means his pumps are never operational when the need for water is the greatest. Moreover, the poor quality of the power delivered makes pumping a risk since the motors are likely to burn out. The cost of rewinding burned-out motor coils because of low supply voltage conditions is an additional expense that Kumar can ill afford.

A similar scenario plays out across several regions of India, where struggling farmers like Kumar are held hostage to the lack of power availability, poor power quality and reliability, rapidly receding groundwater levels and the vagaries of the monsoon. Nowhere is the link between water, energy and poverty as stark as in these regions, where it creates a cycle that often spins out of control. But I am getting ahead of myself. Let me take you through the tortuous decade-long journey in search of a solution to this grave problem.

A Formidable Challenge

It was in 1996 in Uttar Pradesh, India's largest and most populous state, that we first confronted a problem that was more widespread than we had imagined. We had discovered that commercial energy losses, a euphemism for theft and technical losses, were being masked as power consumed in agricultural operations such as irrigation water pumping. A simple back of the envelope calculation showed that, if the data was true, all the irrigation pumps in the state would be working around the clock! But the reality on the ground was different. Farmers whom we talked to said that they hardly received two to three hours of electricity during the day and that too, in some cases, at night. I soon realized that power supply to agriculture was among the most intricate problems fraught with social, political, economic and technical challenges. Trying to solve it was immensely difficult since a solution that favoured farmers and their patrons invariably did not find favour with the utility and vice versa. It was the six-hundred-pound-gorilla in the room whenever and wherever power sector reforms were discussed in predominantly agricultural states.

From my vantage, addressing the problem from an energy efficiency and demand management point of view was both a professional and intellectual challenge. Indeed as T. L. Sankar, a doyen of the Indian power sector, once famously said, 'The fate of the Indian power sector is linked to the power supply to agriculture and how water is used, priced and managed.'[1]

Farm Water Use

It is important to discuss briefly some basic facts that underscore the critical issues concerning agriculture in India. The country's landmass extends to nearly 3.3 million sq km. Over half of it, about 1.85 million sq km, is under agriculture. Of this, about 145 million hectares are under sown areas of cultivation.

In 2013–14, only about 36.7% of total agricultural land in India was reliably irrigated, and the remaining two-thirds is dependent on monsoons. Irrigation in India includes a network of major and minor canals from Indian rivers, groundwater-based systems, tanks and rainwater harvesting projects. Of these, the groundwater system is the largest. At 39 million hectares (67% of the total irrigated area), India has the world's largest groundwater irrigation system (China with 19 million hectares is the second largest and the USA with 17 million hectares is the third).

The agricultural sector uses 85% of the available freshwater, around half of which is groundwater. Groundwater withdrawal is an energy-intensive operation performed throughout the agricultural sector resulting in a fourth of the power consumption in the country being used for roughly 50% of the national irrigation water consumption. More reliable groundwater delivery and declining extraction costs due to advances in technology and, most importantly, government subsidies for power and installation of groundwater structures (like irrigation pump sets) have contributed to this growth. With about twenty-one million electrical pump sets and an additional nine million diesel operated pump sets throughout the country, India has more than four times the number of irrigation structures of China, Iran, Mexico and the US combined.[2]

Access to groundwater is the most crucial factor determining the reliability of irrigation, which in turn is key to the complete 'green revolution' package of fertilizers, seeds and other inputs. Without a reliable water resource, the risk associated with other investments in agricultural production is high because variations in precipitation can lead to heavy losses, forcing small and medium farmers into poverty. Since groundwater availability is relatively independent of fluctuations in rainfall there is often substantial interannual storage which means a farmer's access to water is rarely threatened by climate changes – at least on a short-term basis. This gives groundwater irrigation a substantial advantage over surface irrigation with respect to poverty alleviation. But the amount of water a farmer requires necessitates the use of tube well pump, therefore, farmers are wholly dependent on the availability and reliability of the power supply. Due to uncertain power availability, farmers tend to pump when power is available rather than when crops need water. The use of high-capacity pumps to reach deeper levels leads to overextraction of groundwater and evaporation loss, and eventually, lower water table.

The highly subsidized tariffs for farmers in most states and free power in some have contributed to the indiscriminate extraction of groundwater. The following story from Andhra Pradesh dating back to the Green Revolution in the late sixties might be relevant here. Farmers were urged by state and central government authorities to use fertilizers, pesticides and seeds together with the electrification of pump sets for pumping groundwater to irrigate their fields in a quest to increase food production. The pumps were metered, and utility personnel came by every month to note the meter readings. Soon the AP utility realized that it took a large chunk of their manpower to carry this out and record the readings in a ledger for their accountants to eventually bill the farmers. It was a tedious, time-consuming and labour-intensive manual operation that was not at all cost-effective. This went on for some time until a junior official had a brainwave. 'Why not,' he suggested to his superiors, 'introduce a flat-rate metering system, where farmers would have to pay a fixed monthly cost based on the horsepower of their pump? That way there will be no need for meters nor meter readers.' The suggestion was acted upon in various districts of the state, and eventually, in other states as well.

The arrangement worked well for a good many year until the late eighties when the number of pump sets used in the country began to skyrocket. As long as it was in the low hundred thousand, as in the early years of the Green Revolution, the financial impact to the utility was marginal. With the rising use, utilities had to resort increasingly to cross-subsidization by increasing industrial and commercial tariffs. And when these tariffs threatened to get out of hand and industry decided to go off the grid and resort to captive generation, the states invariably stepped in with a direct subsidy to the utility to cover their losses. The trends in power tariffs across India during the period 2008–09 is revealing. While the average cost of supply was ₹3.4/kWh, the agricultural tariff was ₹1.94/kWh – less than two-thirds of the cost of supply.[3] The total all-India state power subsidy in 2008–09 was estimated at around ₹50,000 crore ($6.6 billion). This represented more than 20% of the total all-India state fiscal deficit in that year. To put these numbers in perspective, the ₹50,000 crore power subsidy was comparable to the country's annual expenditure for education and more than double its expenditure for health in 2008–09.

Coping with Uncertainties

There were other unintended consequences as well. With flat-rate tariffs, the marginal cost of pumping water was zero. In other words, it cost the same to the farmer if he pumped one or ten kilolitres of water or if he operated his pump for a few hours, or for as long as power was available. Indeed, the watering habits of farmers took on a characteristic that was wasteful. A commonly observed tactic was to keep the motor starter switch in the 'on' position all the time. And when power was available, water gradually flooded the fields until the power supply was switched off. Irregular timings forced the farmers to resort to different ways to alert themselves of when grid power became available. A common practice was to have a tall delivery pipe from which water would gush forth at a height visible to the farmer from his hut located at the far edge of his field.

Such coping strategies in the face of uncertain power supply began to exact a heavy toll on groundwater levels in the country. Many regions in India are witnessing shortages in water supply, with groundwater levels falling as much as one metre every three years – to the point where they are 15–25 m below the levels fifty years ago. In Coimbatore, a tranquil city in the state of Tamil Nadu, surrounded by the Western Ghats, groundwater levels have precipitously fallen to below a thousand feet. Farmers in adjoining areas have resorted to what is euphemistically termed as 'competitive drilling'. When a farmer sinks his borewell to a depth to tap groundwater, a neighbour drills further down to access the same pool of water from the aquifer that serves them both. And the cycle continues till the well is bone dry signalling them to move further afield. In many parts of Mehsana district in the west Indian state of Gujarat and most of Rajasthan, the horsepower of electric motors have undergone a sea change – a 5 HP motor-pump system has been replaced by 15 HP and higher capacities. Approximately 12% of all aquifers are severely overdrawn, and the problem is exacerbated by the runoff of surface water. As of 2020, the Central Ground Water Board has estimated overexploitation of groundwater in over 800 industrial projects and 162 areas, deemed as critical, across the country.

As one speaker at an energy conference eloquently put it, 'If you visualize India as one gigantic well, we have reached a stage where the current level of groundwater extraction is exceeding recharge and is therefore unsustainable.'[4] While three states, Punjab, Haryana (the breadbaskets of India) and Rajasthan have already reached this stage, three other states – Tamil Nadu, Gujarat and Uttar Pradesh – are not far behind.

Suboptimal energy and water pricing policies are also a significant contributor to India's growing carbon emissions (estimated at 1–1.5%) as considerable energy is required to extract water from aquifers that have not been mined for millions of years. In addition to this, the lack of effective groundwater management strategies, such as aquifer recharge, and the loss of topsoil due to commercial exploitation of forests, has led to the widespread use of poor-quality groundwater which can cause potentially serious long-term health problems because of the fluoride in it, increased salinity and microbiological contamination.

Quest for Solutions

Our quest for a solution to this egregious and elusive water-energy nexus problem took us to Dr Palaniswamy, a hydrologist at the Tamil Nadu Agricultural University, Coimbatore. Palaniswamy was cordial and believed that the problem required an integrated approach encompassing watershed management and farm-level water conservation techniques such as drip irrigation, water harvesting structures and bunds. This was also consistent with the views of researchers from the International Water Management Institute of the likes of Tushar Shah, the famed scientist whose work on water resource management in India was legendary.

After taking into consideration the work of these eminent scientists, we felt that a piece of the jigsaw puzzle was still missing. This was prompted by the observation of a senior ex-IAS bureaucrat and World Bank advisor, K. C. Sivaramakrishnan, whom I approached for guidance. His missive was penetrative as was its wisdom. 'The water and energy sectors,' he observed, while we were chatting in the bank's canteen, 'in most countries in South Asia, are like ships passing silently in the night. One needs to get them to talk to one another for solutions to emerge.'

So we continued with our search. Soon we discovered that under a DFID project Dr M. V. Krishna Rao who headed the electricity distribution department of the AP state utility in Hyderabad was the man behind the improvement in power supply to Nalgonda, an agricultural district on the outskirts of the city.

Our next stop was Hyderabad. Sharp, astute Krishna Rao brought tremendous understanding and passion to our mission for change and innovation. In graphic detail, he described the vicious cycle in action. 'It all begins,' he explained when we met him in his office with his table crammed with files and charts on the wall, 'with the underinvestment by most utilities in the rural electric network.' He went on to elaborate how poor electric network design results in long electric distribution cables (low tension lines) that convey low voltage electricity from the transformer typically set up in the middle of a village. Snaking through the village and across farms, the electric lines are connected to motors that operate the irrigation pump sets placed by the side of the borewell. Good network design calls for a ratio of 1:2 between the length of a high tension line and a low tension line. But in actuality, this ratio could be much higher, 1:8 or 1:10.

The fundamentals of electrical engineering tell us that the longer the low voltage line is, the higher is the energy loss as well as the drop in line voltage at the terminals of the motor. Typically, a three-phase AC induction motor is designed to operate at a line voltage of 220 V ± 10%, receives power at a low voltage of 120–180 V. This causes an onrush of current in the windings of the motor and results in a rise in temperature in the motor armature causing it to burn out and fail. In order to protect the motors from failing frequently, the farmers installed motors with thicker copper windings that could withstand higher temperatures. The hallmark of these motors were their higher inefficiencies and non-standardized components. Such motors were easily available at roadside motor rewinding shops that dotted the countryside.

A recurrent joke was that in irrigation pump manufacturing hubs like Rajkot in Gujarat or Coimbatore, the dealer had only one question to ask of the purchaser, 'Which part of the country or district do you hail from?' The shopkeeper would then present the customer with a motor that was customized for the power quality of that place! These makeshift motors were generally of a higher capacity than the ones they replaced since the farmer wanted to be assured that it would pump water even with low voltage supply. The use of these pumps created a ripple effect which often overloaded the local distribution transformer leading it to blow out and be replaced by a higher capacity transformer. And everything would spiral out of control. 'This vicious cycle,' Dr Rao concluded with a flourish of his hand, 'had to be replaced by a virtuous cycle.'

Under the DFID-supported Nalgonda programme, Rao nursed a project to replace irrigation pumps in a defined geographic area. Power supply for these high-impedance, heavy-duty pumps were being supplied with three-phase power. Rao thought differently. He believed a switch to single-phase motors to drive the irrigation pumps would reduce energy losses and ease the pressure on the grid. He held many discussions with the farmers in the area and persuaded them to make the change. As he went about the process, much to his own (and our) disappointment, he realized that in any distribution sub-grid, if even one farmer chose not to comply with the switch to single-phase motors the project would fail. All farmers would have to comply. For those who did not, the existing three-phase power supply would have to be made available, complicating the switch further. Though the power supply quality did improve in Nalgonda because of Dr Rao's efforts, what he feared came to pass and the project had to be aborted.

Dr Rao had his heart in the right place but was misplaced in his approach to solutions. He had not taken recourse to arriving at a broader consensus with the farmers that would have helped him identify the risk before embarking on the mission. There was much learning for us from him for he was among the few who empathized and ran with the idea that reforms on the distribution side of the power equation were vital if we wanted the power supply problem in agriculture to be addressed in wholesome ways.

In our search for solutions, we turned to international experts. Tilting at windmills, the experts had little to offer by way of solutions since the complex sociopolitical context of India generally eluded them. But this did not stop the ceaseless flow of reports describing the problem in vivid terms. 'Race to the bottom,' said one expressive report describing the relentless fall in groundwater levels due to indiscriminate pumping. Another report argued in detail why irrigation pumps should be the preferred mode of irrigation for alleviating poverty but was silent on how to address the problem of efficiency and sustainability. 'Here is yet another Shakespearean report,' we would declare to one another after perusing its lyrical contents. We were at our wit's end looking for a demonstrable pilot project that would be a win-win situation for all the stakeholders.

A Solution Emerges

Meanwhile, our team had expanded with the arrival of Chinmaya Acharya, an energy analyst who had worked previously with a leading social institution, Xavier Institute of Management, in rural Odisha. And it began to pay dividends. The brain trust of my colleagues at work hammered out a possible solution. This was further refined with the assistance of Jim Hogan, a consultant working on the DRUM project. I was sceptical at first but agreed that we could at least float the idea. The plan was to incentivize electricity distribution companies, farmers and energy efficiency service providers to come together as partners under a utility-driven DSM programme. In simple terms, a water energy service company (WESCO) would be selected through competitive bidding to invest in pump set replacement and modernization including irrigation efficiency and would be paid out of the energy savings under a performance contract. The farmers would be enlisted to participate and cooperate but not required to invest. The discom would retain a part of the savings and sell the saved power to the higher paying industrial and commercial consumers.

Shortly thereafter, we met with K. Jairaj, Karnataka's additional chief secretary (Energy) to discuss the partnership. On his suggestion, we followed up with the state's principal distribution utility, BESCOM. We prepared a project report and prepared bidding documents. Eventually, Enzen Global Pvt. Ltd was selected as the WESCO partner. The site identified for the country's first WENEXA (Water-Energy Nexus in Agriculture) pilot was Doddaballapur Taluk, a rural district in the outskirts of Bangalore that had a significant groundwater problem.

Doddaballapur was where we met Raj Kumar, the farmer featured in the beginning of this chapter. Hundreds of farmers like Raj Kumar were the intended beneficiaries of the WENEXA project. The question on all our minds was: Would WENEXA help turn around the vicious cycle we had identified into a virtuous cycle?

We had to wait for two years for a definitive answer.

The WENEXA Pilot

The agricultural site at Doddaballapur Taluk was spread over 11,000 acres with cultivated area amounting to 7,300 acres

(64%) of which 1,700 acres was irrigated by a combination of groundwater (23%) and rainfall (77%). The major produce from the lands irrigated by groundwater included grape and mulberry. These two accounted for almost 59% of the total groundwater consumption. There was in total 947 irrigation pump sets and the energy savings potential were estimated to be in the range of 25%–40%. An additional potential of 15%–25% was anticipated through the adoption of efficient irrigation methods like drip irrigation, construction of bunds and check dams.

The WENEXA interventions were site-based activities to identify projects that reduce both water and energy consumption while enhancing farm income. These interventions followed upon a year-long survey conducted by Enzen Global on all borewells to analyze, measure and record energy and water usage patterns as well as agricultural farming practices. While the Bangalore electricity distribution utility ensured that all the preconditions for the project – such as redesign of cables to reduce energy losses, installation of high voltage distribution system to minimize voltage drop and installation of distribution transformers – farmers received a brand new irrigation pump set free with an eighteen-month warranty. The WESCO company financed the investment required for the pumps and provided ongoing O&M support to farmers. As per the terms of the performance contract agreement, the company was allowed to recoup its investments through a shared energy savings agreement with the distribution utility.

The programme faced several challenges. Initially, the vast network, tough terrain and the reluctance of farmers to participate stood in our way as a stumbling block. This was further compounded by outdated consumer records, unplanned network extensions and lack of water-related data. The bidding process to select a WESCO had also been challenging since this was a novel project and perceived as risky by vendors and WESCOs. All these challenges were overcome along the way through dialogue with local NGOs who represented farmer interests and the development of a bankable business model that addressed the risk perception of the stakeholders.

The question we had posed to ourselves in the beginning of this quest for solution for the water-energy problem was answered resoundingly. The WENEXA programme had successfully uprooted the vicious cycle and replaced it with a sustainable outcome reflected by the better power supply quality, lower electricity and motor maintenance costs and rising levels of groundwater in borewells. Replacing 280 pump sets had resulted in energy savings of approximately 1.5 million kWh per annum (33% saving). This could power an additional 3,500 rural households in the state. In 2009, BESCOM won the India Power Awards in 2009 for its contributions to the WENEXA project. Later, the programme went on to win the Platt Award for Excellence in 2012.

Post WENEXA

The WENEXA story did not end there. When Uma Rajaratnam, the dynamic manager at Enzen Global, took up the cudgels for the project, other discoms decided to take a leaf out of the Doddaballapur experience and implemented similar programmes in Karnataka. In the Byadagi and Nippani sub-divisions of the Hubli distribution utility, 590 pump sets were replaced resulting in energy savings of approximately 3 million kWh per annum (36% saving) which, in turn, powered an additional 8,000 rural households in the state.

Beyond the state, different projects building on the core principles of WENEXA began to take root and surface. In the states of Maharashtra and Rajasthan, variations of the WENEXA programme were successfully implemented. The

BEE launched a nationwide agricultural DSM sensitization programme for utilities, NGOs and farmer associations. The Energy Efficiency Services Ltd offered a line of credit to finance agricultural DSM programmes that included the use of solar PV systems to power the pump sets. In response, MoNRE launched the Kusum scheme for solarization of farmer pump sets and setting up of decentralized, grid-connected solar power systems providing capital subsidy incentives for the hardware and feed-in tariffs for power sales to the grid. Among its other contributions, WENEXA's pioneering work on water reuse stands out.

Water Swapping

Water reuse is a practice as old as time, every time we take a drink, we're consuming water that has been used many times before. The water cycle guarantees that nature uses the same supply of water over and over again. Water reuse requires the use of treated wastewater for non-potable uses, thereby conserving potable water and energy used in its conveyance. Large scale planned water reuse is common in the US. By some estimates, the water in the Mississippi river is used seven times before it reaches New Orleans. As pointed out earlier, around 85% of India's freshwater is used for irrigation. Farm irrigation can be further supplied with groundwater through a 'swap' of reclaimed water for a portion of the freshwater currently used in other competing non-irrigation applications. While water reuse was not new to India, large-scale planned municipal water reuse was. And that was soon to change in 2015.

In early 2009, a chance meeting between USAID and the commissioner of the Nagpur Municipal Corporation set into motion a series of events that enabled the establishment of an economically feasible wastewater recycle and reuse project which benefited not only the city of Nagpur but also the state electricity, MSPGCL. Nagpur, the second capital of Maharashtra and the geographic centre of India, used to receive 124 million gallons per day (MGD) of freshwater from two rivers – Kanhan and Pench – and the Gorewada reservoir tank. The city also generated about 100 MGD of sewage that was partially treated and discharged into natural water bodies such as drains and lakes.

This narrative begins with MSPGCL, located about seven miles from the city centre, scouting for a secure source of water for its three upcoming 500 MW power units. The utility had been allocated 45,000 ac-ft/year (55 MCM/year) from the Pench river but that was inadequate for the additional water requirement of 47,000 ac-ft/year (58 MCM/year) for the new power units. Moreover, the Pench river also supplied water for irrigation, and thus, seeds were sown for an emerging conflict between farmers and the utility about the allocation of water and its socio-political ramifications. The state irrigation department which was responsible for the allocation of water resources was approached. They could not fully accommodate the electricity utility's request but were agreeable to meet 20% of the additional water requirements or 9,000 ac-ft/year (12 MCM/year) with a maximum of 15,000 ac-ft/year (20 MCM/year) or 32% of the additional water demand, albeit with a caveat. There was the possibility of a 10% variation in the supply due to force majeure. The shortfall of up to 80% in their additional water requirements forced MSPGCL to explore alternative sources of water.

To resolve the issue for the electricity utility, the WENEXA programme initiated a feasibility study that included water demand assessment and evaluation of alternate water sources including treated water from Nagpur city's wastewater plant.[5] The study also set up a pilot plant to showcase the quality of the treated water in order to secure the involvement of the two partners, the electricity utility and the municipality. The pilot test plant, designed and erected by an engineering firm, used advanced ultrafiltration technology to carry out tertiary water treatment for a slipstream of wastewater which had undergone secondary water treatment from one of the municipality sewage treatment plant.[6] The result of the pilot project published in 2019 was reassuring. Quality tests have shown that the reclaimed water can be used for several applications at the power plant, ranging from its use in draining out the ash in the utility's ash handling plant and as make-up water in the utility's cooling towers. The study helped estimate the total water reuse potential to be 69,000 ac-ft/yr (85 MCM/yr) – which was one and a half times the utility's requirement! But more importantly, it paved the way for an agreement between the Nagpur Municipal Corporation and MSPGCL to supply treated water from the latter's sewage treatment plant to meet the additional water demand of the electricity utility.

The cost of the reuse plant was estimated at ₹200 crore, which was to be invested by MSPGCL. This was the lowest cost option compared to the alternative solution of constructing a dam and pipeline to store and convey water from a freshwater source which would cost ₹350 crore. Furthermore, the municipality was able to access a government grant of ₹80 crore towards the project while also successfully negotiating a yearly royalty of ₹15 crore from the electricity utility for a period of fifteen years. This was truly a win-win situation for the partners which also reduced freshwater demand for non-potable applications and saved the energy which would have otherwise been lost to pump sets.

The story of WENEXA represents a major milestone in the country's energy efficiency journey on the demand side which has highlighted the need to bring energy and water independence to farmers. The success of this journey lies in the combination of higher yield, lower water use and lower energy use. This would require India to chart a strategic blend of water-efficient agricultural production; design watershed initiatives that yields two crops a year with the quantum of water they can harvest; propose water management which can protect the crops from damage owing to dew, moisture, excess heat, humidity and temperature rise; arrange proper systems for soil preparation, soil mechanics and testing, ploughing and furrowing, seeding, pruning and management of plants; and construct farmer-operated storage systems for water that are native to the region and cost-effective, bunds and revetments and surface water harvesting tanks. This is discussed in detail in Chapter Fifteen.

WENEXA and similar programmes have shown that such water and energy efficiencies in agriculture can bring resource savings that surpass the entire savings derived from industry and the urban sector.

CHAPTER ELEVEN

Energy Efficiency Centres of Excellence, 2006–2012

An Idea Surfaces

The US-India Energy Efficiency Technology Cooperation Conference held in May 2006 in New Delhi was attended by over 300 participants. That day, a simple question asked by a delegate from a southern Indian utility set USAID on the path to establishing centres of excellence across South Asia and the Indo-Pacific. His utility had launched a pilot project to enthuse household consumers to substitute their power-guzzling incandescent lamps with the more efficient compact fluorescent lamps (CFLs) – a technology that had just reached Indian shores. The pilot was being hampered by the lack of awareness of the advantages of this lighting technology among consumers. According to him, this was because of the absence of facilities to inform the public about efficient illumination technologies. 'Are there examples of centres in the US or elsewhere operated by utilities that serve as information and demonstration hubs?' he asked. At the end of the conference, it was the unanimous view of the delegates, sparked by the questioner, that actions to accelerate energy efficiency market transformation was critical and one of the means to do so was through the creation of regional centres of excellence and expertise in energy efficiency.

USAID had arrived at the same realization just the year before. In 2005, under ECO, we had designed a pilot project on illumination called the Bangalore Efficient Lighting Program (BELP). BELP incentivized domestic residents to trade their incandescent lamps for compact fluorescent bulbs with pre-selected traders who were paid by Bangalore's distribution utility. Customers paid back the utility in monthly instalments that cost them less than the electricity they saved. Since its inception, BELP had contributed to a 75% increase in the sales of these efficient lamps among participating suppliers in Bangalore city. This resulted in a system peak reduction of 19 MW and an annual energy savings of 25 million units.

One of the key lessons we learned from BELP was the same as pointed out by the delegate at the 2006 conference. The lack of information on energy-efficient lamps and a total absence of facilities promoting the advantages and use of these products. The concept of a functional, competent and efficient lighting centre in Bangalore was beginning to emerge. J. R. Meena, chairman of Karnataka Power Transmission Corporation Ltd, supported the idea and offered his help to set up a lighting museum in Bangalore which could disseminate information on lighting for citizens and promote BELP.

While we were planning how to execute this idea, I received a message from a professional contact at the USDoE. Would USAID mission in Delhi be interested in hosting a young professional as an intern, to assist us in realizing takeaways from the conference? And that's how Carolina Warfield joined us in October 2006 for a three-month internship. Her first task was to gather information from the US and elsewhere about such centres – what do they do, how are they managed and funded and do they deliver on their promise? Her research was revealing. Specialization in a narrow area had its advantages since it could bring deep technical expertise to its target audience. After an initial period of funding, most centres could become self-sufficient by providing services for a fee. As per

Carolina's research, there were no good or bad models. In the US, she had argued, most centres were either administered or operated by universities. In China, Eastern Europe and Russia, the centres worked to promote investments and were operated by government agencies. All in all, centres around the world had varied and broad scopes and included research on technology and policy, education, outreach, training and a variety of on-site and off-site services.

A promising lead that turned up in Carolina's work was the Lighting Research Center (LRC) at the Rensselaer Polytechnic Institute (RPI) in Albany, New York. The LRC – established in 1988 – is among the leading university-based organizations in the world devoted to lighting research and education. The director of Research and head of the Solid-State Lighting programme was the global expert on LEDs: Professor Narendran Nadarajah. He was credited with helping set up a formidable research programme and advanced testing and training facilities at the institute. I reached out to Hari Mamak, formerly with Philips Lighting (India) and the chairperson of Electrical Lamp and Component Manufacturers, India. 'Do you think it's a good idea to have Dr Narendran [Naren] over and have him advise us on a centre of excellence on efficient lighting?' He knew Naren well and was willing to find out whether this would be a plausible plan for the professor. The next day, Mamak called to convey that Naren was planning on visiting Seoul, South Korea and would be happy to drop by for a chat. With the plan for a lighting museum in the works, this turn of events seemed a godsend to us.

An Illuminating Concept

The meeting with Naren in March 2007 was an eventful one. His scintillating speech on the state-of-the-art efficient lighting technologies such as CFLs and the then-new and emerging

LEDs had the audience spellbound. The simple insights that he had shared captivated the audience. Because lighting systems operate to serve an application and the people using a particular space, the application itself is an important factor in the overall efficacy of light. Application efficacy refers to the amount of light delivered directly to the task itself. This is quite different from system efficacy, which considers just the amount of light coming out of the fixture per watt of energy, regardless of how much ultimately reaches the task surface. For example, an under-cabinet light fixture may have a good system efficacy, but is it directing enough light at the countertop to perform tasks, such as cooking and chopping fruits and vegetables? It was observations such as these that caused people to pause and ponder.

Soon after, Naren accompanied us to a meeting with the secretary of the Ministry of Power, Anil Razdan. Razdan was anxious to reduce the cost of compact fluorescent fixtures from ₹800 for a 40-watt lamp to less than ₹100. Naren had suggestions for aggregating the lighting market to reduce procurement costs. A subject of greater concern to him was the inclination of the government to focus on these lamps and their lack of adequate attention towards the emerging LED market. 'The CFL is being touted as a cure-all for the lighting energy problem. In general, this is true. It uses one-quarter to one-third of the wattage to produce the same amount of light as an incandescent lamp. They are now smaller and quieter than in years past and their price has also come down considerably in the last decade. But we need to be conscious of its drawbacks,' maintained Naren. He continued 'The colour quality of the light is one. Consumer research has found that this is a major complaint and a primary reason why some people refuse to buy them for their homes. Compact fluorescents also take time to "warm up". Unlike incandescent lamps, they do not put out all their light the instant the switch is flipped. Additionally, because all fluorescent lamps require a small amount of mercury to operate, their environmental impact is a matter of concern.'

The mercury paradox had drawn the attention of many the world over. A poor-quality CFL would have up to 10 mg of mercury while standard ones would have around 4–5 mg. Anil was nonplussed. Would India have to roll back its efficient lighting programme based on CFLs and opt for LEDs instead? Would they be cost-competitive? There were no easy answers, and by the time the meeting came to an end, a seed of doubt had been planted in everyone's minds. Except for Mamak. 'If cost reduction is the only consideration,' he declared, while returning from the meeting, in his baritone voice, 'we might be better off with incandescent.' The last bit with a twinkle in his eyes.

Next, Naren accompanied me to Bangalore to meet with Meena who had offered to support us in our endeavour to build a light museum. Meena and the team he had put together joined forces with us to plan the next steps. It was agreed that the Government of Karnataka in technical collaboration with USAID and others shall establish the Light Museum and Energy Centre (LIMEC) in Bangalore. A three-acre property near Hoodi Industrial Park at Whitefield, a fast-growing suburb of Bangalore, was proposed as the site. A quick visit to the site left us pleased about the location and the facilities it offered.

Meena's vision for LIMEC was identical to ours. We had agreed that it shall advance awareness about efficient lighting technologies, showcase and promote innovative designs and products, facilitate information sourcing, develop human resources and catalyze policy change. He began to reach out to others. Soon enough, several parties expressed their interest in partnering with LIMEC, including Electrical Lamp and

Component Manufacturers and BEE. On his suggestion, a design competition for LIMEC was organized for interested architects. The bid solicitation carried the following message.[1]

> Lighting is an expensive commodity with significant environmental impacts and the ability to produce social change far beyond mere convenience. In India, there is a dearth of accurate information on the merits of lighting. There is, therefore, a need to disseminate information on high-performance lighting applications and improved aesthetics. LIMEC would be a unique culmination of cutting-edge innovation in technology, art, architecture and design and would be a world-class exhibition of energy-efficient lighting products and systems operated in an interactive mode. The exhibition centre would showcase illumination technology that allows light to be used in diverse areas ranging from homes, offices, theatre, shops/malls, streets, industry, painting, photography, laser/light shows and holographic 3D images. It will cover Indian and international technologies designed to be of interest to lighting professionals as well as the general public.

Twist and Turn

The LIMEC project won favour with the Ministry of Power's joint secretary, Arvind Jadhav. He was an IAS officer from the Karnataka cadre and was familiar with Bangalore since he had earlier been posted there. He arranged for the Union Minister of Power, P. Shinde, to announce the launch of LIMEC during one of his visits to Bangalore in May 2007. With his seal of approval and blessing, we were ready to roll. But there was a sting in the proverbial tail, a last-minute hitch.

I received a call from Meena. He was in Delhi and was

wondering if I could meet him that evening, after office hours, at the Karnataka State guest house which was close to my office. 'Can we shift the location of the museum elsewhere out of Bangalore?' he asked. He suggested Mysore or Hubli or Dharwah, the other major urban towns in Karnataka. I was confused and wanted to know the reason. He explained that his board was reluctant to provide permission for the land in Hoodi for this cause since they believed that it could be employed for purposes that were more relevant to their power corporation's core business of power transmission. I demurred. The reason was simple. Over 50% and more of the lighting market was in Bangalore. Moreover, BELP had made major inroads among the residents of the city. Besides this, Bangalore was the state capital, an emerging global IT powerhouse and, therefore, would have visitors and tourists who would benefit from the museum being located there.

Disappointed with this turn of events, we began to examine other options.

Upali Dharanganama, an energy specialist and an additional secretary with the Sri Lankan government was an old friend of mine. During a meeting over drinks in Colombo, he gave me a tour d'horizon of the island country's energy situation. Upali explained that Sri Lanka had become increasingly dependent on imported oil for electricity generation, with more than 40% of its electricity being generated by oil-fired power plants. This resulted in high electricity prices and volatile oil prices, which was adversely affecting the competitiveness of local industry and, in general, the whole economy. About 41% of the grid-connected domestic electricity consumption was for lighting and the evening system peak was about 1,800 MW, half of which was contributed by the lighting load. He rightly surmised that lighting played a significant role in terms of both energy demand and the capacity requirement of the national grid.

Any cost-effective reduction in lighting demand would directly lower the demand for oil-based electricity generation and hence would have positive economic implications. 'Coming out, as it were, from the current militancy problem in the north, any post-conflict step to mitigate the situation through job creation, industrial and economic growth would be seen favourably by the government,' Upali averred when I shared with him the possibility of establishing a regional lighting centre.

Additionally, I gathered that although efficient lighting appliances like CFLs were fairly well known through the publicity efforts of the Ceylon Electricity Board and the Sri Lanka Sustainable Energy Authority (SLSEA), other methods and technologies like efficient reflectors, daylight usage and LEDs were not. Upali shared that efficient devices like LEDs would bring significant benefits to off-grid applications, such as solar PV power plants, due to their low power consumption. The new systems would also be smaller in size and would result in lower initial costs, and the existing systems would be able to accommodate more appliances or users. Hence, awareness creation and effective promotion of these new technologies was a critical need of the Sri Lankan electricity sector. The case for a lighting centre appeared promising for the country.

The next day, Upali took me to meet with Power and Energy Secretary M. M. C. Ferdinando. The meeting exceeded my expectations. Secretary Ferdinando was supportive and urged us to move quickly while assuring all support from the Sri Lankan government. As one of the senior-most civil servants, he was greatly respected and known to be influential in the higher echelons of the government. A courtesy call to US Ambassador Robert Blake who I had the privilege of knowing when he was the chargé d'affaires at the US Embassy at Delhi was very assuring. That evening, back at the hotel I called Naren who was in New York at the time to share the news with him. I also hinted at the possibility of his involvement. Naren was excited and jumped on board right away.

The Lighting Regional Center

Looking back, I can say that it was Naren and his colleague Russ Leslie who were responsible for the rapid progress we made after my Colombo visit. Russ Leslie was the associate director of LRC at the time and a leading architect who was the brain behind LRC's initial creation in 1988 supported and funded by the New York State Energy Research and Development Authority. It helped tremendously that Naren was of Sri Lankan origin and had family and friends in Sri Lanka. They were proud of him and saw him as one of their own. Naren, on the other hand, was excited about the rare opportunity to give back something to his motherland. Progress moved apace. The government directed a joint team from the Ceylon utility and SLSEA to create a state-of-the-art lighting hub – the Regional Centre for Lighting (RCL) in partnership with RPI's LRC in Troy, New York. As the knowledge partner, LRC was instrumental in developing education, research and testing programmes, as well as strategic research initiatives. A team of Sri Lankan officials, together with leading industrialists and university professors, visited Troy to acquaint themselves with the comprehensive capacity building programme that Naren had drawn up. The programme was taken up by a technical team from SLSEA and the utility who were deputed, after training at RPI's lighting laboratory to take up positions at the new 1,000 sq m facility in Colombo.

During the first couple of years, Naren and Russ Leslie visited Colombo and conducted several lighting educational programmes to elevate the knowledge of efficient lighting in stakeholders and emerging young professionals interested in energy conservation activities in Sri Lanka. Within two years of the start of the collaboration, the Colombo centre was operative with a well-equipped electrical and photometry laboratory, a demonstration centre with training facilities and a qualified team of lighting experts. An important development was the support received from the Asian Development Bank that enabled the centre to expand its lighting product testing and quality control services.

Naren in a quiet and determined manner, with the support of Upali and their respective colleagues, drove the initial growth and development. In December 2010, his dream of setting up a first-of-its-kind LED-testing facility with a photometry lab and off-grid lighting test bench was realized. Today, these facilities cater to the needs of manufacturers, dealers, users and policymakers in Sri Lanka and South Asia. They support much-needed evaluation of the quality of various programmes to ensure compliance with standards. An agreement with the Sri Lankan University of Moratuwa led to the creation of formal educational courses on lighting and a library and the RCL information centre. After the initial success, Naren encouraged the RCL to make an effort to move its services beyond Sri Lanka, to the other countries in the region. With USAID sponsorship, the effort reached a milestone when global lighting manufacturers, world finance and development organizations, and leading government representatives met to develop a regional lighting technology road map at the first South Asia Lighting Transformation Forum in January 2011 in Male, in Maldives. The forum was designed to create the framework for a five-year, step-by-step guide to establish the widespread use of sustainable lighting through LEDs.

The Launch of WISER

Progress of the RCL in Sri Lanka made us turn our attention to the feasibility of establishing similar centres of excellence in South Asia. This was prompted by a sage piece of advice I had received from James Bever, an experienced and old AID/Washington hand who had worked for decades on energy and development in several South Asian countries. Jim's insight was priceless. 'Flow of ideas and information across the region should be the foundation on which a regional energy cooperation programme could be built,' he said at a staff meeting. This helped signal the pursuit of other energy efficiency centres in India and South Asia.

Around this time, a distinctive programme in the state of Kerala in south India was brought to my attention by Professor V. K. Damodaran, the vice chair of the Kerala Energy Management Centre (K-EMC). K-EMC had a longstanding programme for women in the energy sector. It comprised energy training programmes, energy clinics and demonstrations of alternative energy sources. A key component of K-EMC's programmes was its thrust on women energy service providers and entrepreneurs who would design, manufacture and market energy-efficient devices. Its activities had catalyzed over 100 women energy entrepreneurs in the state. K. M. Dharesan Unnithan, the director of K-EMC explained later in a meeting at his office '... the vital and central role women play in the management of energy – a full one-third of the total energy in the state is managed by women and yet there is no public institution available that can help women in making informed decisions on an issue such as energy that is central to their lives. As a consumer of energy, women are at a loss to truly understand the merits and demerits of various cooking fuels and cookstoves as well as electricity savings that have an impact on their family's budget and more importantly on their health.' Unnithan prompted his team to establish an energy conservation programme for women by women.

The state's energy conservation work included women

entrepreneurs who reached out to households to inform and motivate women with respect to energy savings. Like 'barefoot' doctors in Africa and elsewhere, these women service providers organized and conducted women-centric training programmes in homes on saving fuel while cooking and through an efficient use of electricity. The use of an insulating box made of coconut fibre that kept dishes warm and prevented reheating, and thus the box was a big hit among the women. Manufactured and marketed by women, the 'thapabharani', or hot box, became a calling card for energy conservation services in the homes of God's own country.

Thapabharani saves up to 75% fuel and was designed to suit the peculiar dietary habits of the people of Kerala where rice is consumed daily for both lunch and dinner, accounting for about 60% of the cooking energy needs in a typical home. Hot boiling rice from the stove is stored in the thapabharani and since there is negligible heat loss the rice continues boiling within the insulated vessel. Hot rice is served right through the day without the need to reheat, thus saving energy and time. Furthermore, the use of thapabharani resulted in several major co-benefits besides energy and fuel savings. Respiratory illnesses among women folk due to inhaling of fumes from firewood stoves declined, and, more time was available for other activities and leisure, Also since firewood used in cooking is transported from the interior forest areas of the state to cities and towns in coastal areas where the majority of the population resides, savings in firewood had reduced its vehicular transportation by an average distance of 75 km, thereby saving diesel used in trucks as well as arresting deforestation because of less felling of trees for firewood.[2]

We asked ourselves: Can this experience be replicated elsewhere in South Asia? To promote the idea, a South Asia Women in Energy network was first set up as a platform for dialogue and executive exchange among women stakeholders in the energy industry. The network included women from NGOs, the state and central governments, research institutions, consumer groups, academia and so on. During a women's energy executive exchange programme in Washington, DC, in May 2009, it was urged that such activities needed to be institutionalized formally. This laid the conceptual foundation of the Women's Institute for Sustainable Energy Research (WISER) which was established under a collaborative partnership between the state government and USAID at the K-EMC in Thiruvananthapuram.

WISER went on to serve as an information resource for the general public, research, business and policy groups interested in energy issues that affect women. It encouraged the application of clean energy technologies by starting a laboratory aimed at testing and demonstrating efficient household devices and systems. Training programmes were conducted on home energy audits to enable women entrepreneurs to offer energy efficiency services. WISER achieved global publicity in 2010, when it successfully conducted a training programme in Kathmandu for women from Afghanistan, with the assistance of faculty from USDoE labs and prominent Indian groups like Selco and Tata BP Solar.

Mother of Centres

The formula for setting up centres of excellence in energy efficiency had become familiar to us now. A regional centre for a small hydro development was established in Kathmandu in Nepal by the country's Alternative Energy Centre. Under USAID's bilateral programme in India, several more centres were established in quick succession – two of the most famous ones being the CII-GBC in Hyderabad (see Chapter Nine) and CenPEEP in Noida (see Chapter Five). Ahmedabad's

CEPT University established in 2009, a joint US-India Centre for Building Energy Research & Development (CBERD) to test and certify sustainable construction materials, advanced building designs and net-zero buildings. In a conversation with the director of the centre, Dr Rajan Rawal, elaborated on the mission of CBERD thus: 'The approach was to facilitate high performance building design through integration of building information technologies and building physical systems. To this end, CBERD has developed software tools, control platforms and energy monitoring solutions. In addition, we have focused on technologies for HVAC, lighting, low-energy cooling and mixed mode ventilation.' CBERD today is among the most sought-after source of information by architects, builders and vendors alike.

This was followed by the establishment of an energy efficiency information centre for civil society in Kolkata. Located amidst the sylvan surroundings of the city's premier park, the centre aimed at educating citizens and school children on energy conservation in homes, workplace, farms and industry. Recognizing the need to train engineers and operators in small and medium scale industry, a centre for capacity building and skill development was established by a private energy auditing firm in Nagpur, Maharashtra.

The lesson was not lost on the country's leading energy efficiency body, BEE. In a meeting called by its chief, Dr Ajay Mathur to review the role of the existing centres, he defined the broader strategic role that these entities should play. 'An energy conservation centre at a state or regional level will have the prime function of supporting the proper implementation and monitoring of energy efficiency programmes adopted by the government,' he opined. 'International experience,' Ajay further explained, 'had shown that such a centre operates more effectively as an independent, unbiased body under an autonomously managed structure.' Participants at the meeting recommended that a centre should preferably function with direct industry participation. They suggested besides its prime function of showcasing a specific end-use technology, the centre's activities could include conducting awareness campaigns, facilitating technology information sourcing, showcasing energy efficiency technologies, promoting technology cooperation and transfer and organizing audits. At the end of the meeting, Ajay walked up to me and with a wink and a genial smile, whispered, 'We plan to set up the "mother of all centres" soon.'

Sure enough, a few months later, an official BEE announcement followed. Recognizing the importance of regional energy efficiency centres, the official gazette notice informed the readers that they would be part of a major strategic thrust to promote electrical demand-side management in India promoting the adoption and commercialization of energy efficiency technologies and services which would have a direct impact on the reduction of greenhouse gas emissions. The notice went on to add that NPC, which was assisting BEE to conduct its Energy Auditors and Energy Managers Certification programme, would demonstrate industrial energy efficiency systems and practices at its training institute, the Dr Ambedkar Institute of Productivity (AIP) situated in the Ambattur industrial area at Chennai. NPC received support from outside of India as well. The Japanese government, along with the Indian government, awarded a ₹12 crore grant towards the centre established within AIP.

Arvind Asthana, a senior advisor at BEE responsible for designing and planning the centre, was working with NPC's energy efficiency professionals. I met with him several times over the course of the centre's early planning phase to share our experience and advice. I recall telling him, 'It should be interactive and not a museum piece. The energy efficiency centre should aim at imparting shop floor skills while accelerating business and market transformation.'

When NPC's Centre of Excellence for Training in Energy Efficiency (CETEE) was completed in 2011, it took its place as one of the country's premier educational exhibits on energy efficiency. Its laboratory provides hands-on efficiency training covering a wide range of industrial equipment and processes such as boilers, combustion burners, electric motors, prime movers, pumps, boiler, furnace, steam system and air conditioning and refrigeration system. Today, CETEE provides its services to large corporate as well as small-scale industry, public utilities, equipment manufacturers and university students in India and the Asia-Pacific. It has trained over a thousand professionals from India's leading public-sector companies like BHEL, Power Grid and Oil & Natural Gas Corporation as well as large private companies. Feedback on the quality of the training received has been excellent. Its fame has extended beyond the country's borders. CETEE has catered to several countries in Asia-Pacific. Interestingly, the centre has been replicated by several corporate organizations, like Reddy Labs, for their in-house training needs.

An Efficiency Association

The absence of an energy efficiency industry association dedicated to the development and growth of this nascent sector and business in India was a long felt need. Rightly, we asked ourselves that if the renewable energy industry were represented by a plethora of associations – each showcasing a renewable resource or technology, such as solar, wind or biomass – there was equal and compelling justification for an energy efficiency association in India. The experience of the US, UK and several other nations which had a number of such advocacy and catalytic agencies spurred us on.

Koshy Cherail, an energy analyst and journalist by

profession, reacted enthusiastically when I first suggested the idea in the summer of 2003. He drew upon his network of associates and mentors and plunged into the details of setting up such an association. The vision, ideas and interests of several energy professionals, consultants and trade associations were pooled together to develop the initial vision. There had been several efforts made in the past to set up similar associations. However, they floundered due to the lack of a core team of mentors and supporters, and most importantly, because of a lack of a funding model. After a few false starts that appeared initially promising only to disappoint later, Koshy was able to mobilize a small but significant coalition of private-sector supporters. In 2006, three years after the idea of a association was proposed, the Alliance for an Energy-Efficient Economy (AEEE) India was established.

Hema Hattangady, the CEO of Conzerv Systems, was an enthusiastic supporter who provided leadership and resources that helped launch and sustain the organization during its initial years. This was further augmented by the bilateral ECO programme and grants from Shakti Sustainable Energy Foundation which enabled AEEE to expand its activities and hire staff.

Dr Satish Kumar, the former COP of ECO joined AEEE in 2016 and took over as the executive director in 2018, and under his stewardship the association has grown into a globally respected think tank and policy analysis body. It's work in advancing private-sector energy efficiency services, developing M&V professional capacities, analysis of building energy efficiency potential, technologies and practices have been some of its activities. It has partnered with BEE and other governmental bodies in pioneering strategic efforts in developing the India Cooling Action Plan and Electric Vehicles. The AEEE has firmly placed India on the global energy efficiency map.

The establishment of AEEE signalled the acceptance of a professional body dedicated to the advancement of energy efficiency in the country. Today it is one of the leading policy advocacy and energy efficiency market enablers with a not-for-profit motive that works towards creating awareness about energy efficiency as a resource. The success of CETEE brought us the satisfaction of knowing that the journey of planning and establishing the citadels of energy efficiency excellence, though long and winding, was well worth the effort.

CHAPTER TWELVE

Defining Bedrock Documents

Rome, as they say, was not built in a day. So is the case with movements and campaigns. Oftentimes, it takes studies, research, analysis and experimentation extending over long periods before they are launched and tested in the field. The energy efficiency movement in India too went through several phases of reflection, discussion, deliberation and inter-ministerial consultations by official committees before it received the official seal of approval. This typically meant that the bureaucratic office, cell or department established for this purpose was vested with the authority to execute programmes or campaigns in coordination with the concerned arms of the government and other stakeholders. The official publication and launch of a report or a notification in the government gazette often signalled the success of an undertaking.

Today, there is a virtual explosion of study reports, documents and media presentations (print and digital) on energy efficiency on virtually every facet of the subject. This was not the case earlier. Reports were hard to come by. Only a few studies were conducted and fewer still were conferences and seminars on the subject. Of these, there are a handful that stood out for their vision and contribution to the development and growth of the energy efficiency movement in India. This is a brief recount of a few of those historical documents, the context in which they were produced, their contribution to a better understanding of energy efficiency and the people behind them.

Fuel Policy Committee (FPC) Report, 1970

The first official document released by the Indian government on the efficient use of fuel was the *Fuel Policy Committee (FPC) Report* published in 1970. It was released in response to the need expressed in ministerial and planning circles for a better grip on the supply-demand balances in the next two decades to enable a more scientific and optimal planning process to address the energy requirements of the country. It had become clear that ad hoc planning must give way to a robust methodological process involving scenario analysis and projections that reflected the national strategic goals of energy security and fiscal efficiency.[1]

The FPC was set up to develop the country's national fuel policy for the next fifteen years. It was headed by T. L. Sankar, an IAS officer of repute in energy circles. He later went on to head the Andhra Pradesh State Electricity Board and numerous governmental energy committees. Its report marked the official beginnings of energy efficiency or fuel efficiency as it was referred to at that time. The concept of efficient use of fuel, its categorization based on end-use necessity, inter-fuel substitution as well as promotion of specialized training in fuel efficiency was discussed for the first time.

The report caught the attention of economists and policy mandarins, not the least because of the theoretical underpinnings that characterized its analysis. It was, perhaps, for the first time that an energy report in independent India had espoused the use of computational techniques like econometric forecasting and end-use analysis in arriving at sectoral energy demand estimates. The report took a leaf out of the Integrated Resource Plans being widely implemented in North America in those days, which gave equal consideration to both energy supply and energy efficiency. Though the FPC fell short of that laudable objective, it must be said, in all fairness, that it brought more gravitas to the country's energy policy and opened the door for its integration with the national development plan.

As often happens, it gathered dust in governmental shelves for the next couple of years until the Oil Crisis of 1973.

The crisis called for a re-examination of the FPC report in light of the changing global oil situation and its implications for the Indian economy. The old report was taken off the shelf and a revised report with a sharper focus on fuel efficiency and included substitution of oil with coal was prepared. Justifying this retreat from its earlier policy of replacing coal with oil, Sankar in a discussion recalling this volte-face, said, 'One needs to approach energy efficiency from a broad perspective. The substitution of a costly fuel by a cheaper fuel is consistent with such an approach.'[2] The revised FPC report provided a fresh impetus to demand-side energy management and conservation. The rising intensity of fuel oil consumption by the Indian industry saddled with antiquated technologies and sub-critical production capacities was singled out as the area that required special attention. The immediate outcome was the constitution of an inter-ministerial body called the Standing Committee on Furnace Oil. This was followed by the growth of the fuel efficiency service of NPC and the establishment of PCRA which have been described earlier in the book.

A top-down, macro-economic report like the FPC report has its value in policy, economic and institutional planning. It however falls short of helping define the technological and other options needed to advance energy efficiency at an industrial sub-sector level. Identifying gaps, developing human capacity, establishing performance targets, prescribing codes and standards and so were some of the missing elements that needed to be strung together in any blueprint for a national conservation strategy. There was a need for a bottom-up study.

Report of the Inter-Ministerial Working Group on Industrial Energy Conservation, 1983

Nowhere was the need for such a study felt greater than in the Ministry of Industry's Department of Heavy Industry. Energy-intensive industries including steel, cement, aluminium, fertilizer and others were concerned about the rise in oil prices and the potential impact on their competitiveness and profitability. With this in mind, the secretary of the department, D. V. Kapoor, issued an office memorandum[3] on 27 August 1981 announcing the constitution of the Inter-ministerial Working Group on Energy Conservation.

> Energy saved is energy produced. If this axiom has any validity, it is obvious that in the absence of energy conservation both at the national level and at the enterprise level, the fall-out to the economy can be substantial. And yet a concerted drive in regard to energy conservation has so far been wanting. Diagnostic studies in the organized industrial sector have shown that through conservation measures, substantial savings can be made without affecting output ...

The memo went on to announce the composition of the working group and named NPC as its project secretariat with P. R. Srinivasan as the member secretary.

Five sub-committees were set up by the government's energy conservation working group to examine, deliberate and suggest policy, regulatory and institutional measures. Annexure 1 provides the summary report of each of the sub-committees. The working group also had access to the field studies conducted by NPC. Over the next twelve months, more than 200 industrial units in the country comprising engineering, textile, cement, chemicals, pulp and paper, jute, glass, edible oil and tea were visited by NPC engineers. Their observations were recorded in the final report which also prescribed 'dos and don'ts' for achieving 15%–20% energy savings in each sector through better housekeeping measures.

This went on to lay the foundations of a national energy conservation programme with a clear strategy and an action plan for ministerial responsibilities; budgeting and financing; training and capacity building; and technology and modernization.

The report was frank in its analysis.

> It will be appreciated that the subject of energy conservation has been discussed and debated in various forums for well over a decade in the wake of the global oil crisis. But what has been missing so far is the drive in its implementation and the lack of a coordination agency.

The working group proposed the creation of an apex national energy conservation steering team and suggested that it be linked to the erstwhile Energy Advisory Board of the Planning Commission.

The first move had been made.

The wheels of bureaucracy turned slowly. Too slowly, opined some. While the Ministry of Petroleum continued its support towards petroleum conservation with the Oil Industry Development Board funding to PCRA through the oil companies, notably IOC, the Department of Power took a more far-reaching step and instituted the Energy Management Centre (EMC) in New Delhi. It was set up as an autonomous entity to promote energy efficiency and develop human capacity. EMC was a forerunner to BEE, which was established in March 2002 under the provision of the Energy Conservation Act, 2001 – a full twenty years after it was envisaged as a policy and regulatory nucleus and pivot for the national energy efficiency programme strategy.

Report on Energy Conservation: The Indian Experience, 1989

It was a typically hot, dry summer day of June in 1989. K. L. Puri, the former chairman of the Central Electricity Authority was appointed as the advisor (Energy Conservation) in the Cabinet Secretariat of Rajiv Gandhi's government. It was a post created in recognition of his energy sector credentials. A tall, striking figure with silvery locks, he went about his work with gusto.

Once, at a meeting in his Delhi office with ministerial officials and invitees from public-sector companies like BHEL and NPC, he declared in a booming voice, 'National energy management efforts in conserving energy is beginning to yield dividends. Conservation consciousness is taking roots: it needs to be nurtured and strengthened. The downward trend in oil prices has provided us with much-needed respite. The gains in savings need to be consolidated. The need of the hour is to take stock of the situation.' He ended his rousing speech with a suggestion: 'Can NPC prepare a comprehensive document on energy conservation during the last fifteen years since 1973? We shall release it later this year on a day that would be designated as the National Energy Conservation Day.' The last bit took us by surprise since we were hearing about it for the first time. We fixed the date at the meeting itself: 14 December. And every year since then, for the past three decades, India has been celebrating that day as the National Energy Conservation Day with meetings, conferences, seminars on the subject. The grandest of the ceremonies is organized in Delhi at the hallowed conference hall of Vigyan Bhawan, where industry awards are presented in recognition of contributions to energy conservation. Teachers and school children and the general public are invited to participate in the celebrations.

The inaugural National Energy Conservation Day in 1989 was a memorable one. The first document to present the developments in energy conservation that had taken place in the country was released as suggested by Puri. The document titled 'Energy Conservation – The Indian Experience' with its eye-catching flaming red and yellow cover comprised two parts. The first part traced the evolution of the energy conservation movement and highlighted the landmarks of the same. The second part consisted of a hundred case studies on energy conservation achievements in various sectors of the economy – industry, transport, agriculture and domestic.

Between the time BEE was established in 2002 and the ascent of EMC through the late eighties and nineties, various efforts to bring about energy efficiency began to gradually emerge and gain some momentum and acceptance. It was an opportune time for the efficiency movement to look outside the country for ideas and inspiration.

Energy Efficiency Technology Cooperation, 2006 and 2009

Two important documents that served as the background papers prepared for the US-India Energy Efficiency Technology Conference held in 2006 and 2009 provided keen insights on the potential of technologies for energy efficiency, lessons from regulatory and policy-driven DSM programmes in the US and the role of market-driven strategies to foster and deliver energy efficiency services and projects in India.[4] The lead author of the documents was Dr Jayant Sathaye, an alumnus of IIT Mumbai and the founder of the International Energy Studies Group. He was also the senior scientist and strategic advisor at Lawrence Berkeley National Laboratory (LBNL). The conference informed the strategic foundation of the Indian government's subsequent efforts in advancing the Energy Conservation Building Code

(ECBC) and the development and commercialization of energy efficiency technologies.

A crucial contribution by Dr Sathaye was his study, analysis and evaluation of the macro-economic benefits of reducing electricity deficits through energy efficiency in India. The central premise was that efficiency improvement also had the potential to boost economic growth that could increase the tax revenue for the government. The study, carried out in the state of Maharashtra, illustrated that redirecting electricity saved through efficiency improvements to electricity-short businesses could increase economic output and tax revenue, which could reduce the state government's fiscal deficit by 15%–30% depending on the size of backup power generation.[5] Broadly, Dr Sathaye's analysis showed that improvements in efficiency combined with new and increased supply could eliminate electricity shortages at the same investment level as for a business-as-usual electricity supply scenario. This finding underscored the need to adopt integrated resource planning as an important tenet where investments in supply projects would be ranked alongside investments in transmission and distribution as well as DSM projects to enable a symmetrical approach to power sector development.

Opportunities for Electrical End-use Efficiency in India, 1992

In the fall of 1992, a utility DSM conference in New York led me to Steve Nadel, a young researcher from the American Council for Energy-Efficient Economy (ACEEE). Steve was talking about how electric and gas utilities in North America partner with consumers and introduce energy efficiency programmes and measures in their homes, offices and industry. What struck me at that time was the simulation model he had described which could assess the economic potential of energy efficiency projects and rank them in order of priority. This simple mathematical model combined utility data with data on energy use by consumers and generated important economic indicators such as cost of conserved energy and cost of avoided capacity.

It was a bit of a revelation to me. Here was a tried and tested method that compared investments in capacity addition to equivalent investments in energy conservation. The two sides of the energy equation – supply and demand – could be compared and contrasted. I returned to Washington and met Steve once again. This time at ACEEE's modest office on K Street, in the company of his colleague Howard Geller. I learnt more about Steve. He had testified many times before the US Congress on energy efficiency subjects and before multiple state legislatures. He was a major contributor to the national energy legislation passed by the US Congress way back in 1987 and, later on, in the 1990s and the 2000s as well. Steve had worked his way up at ACEEE, first as a promising researcher, rising to deputy director and then as the head of the organization in 2001. He continues to work to this day and his research interests include utility-sector energy efficiency programmes and policies; state and federal energy and climate change policy; and appliance and equipment efficiency standards.

Before long, David Jhirad and I spoke to Steve about the prospect of a project in India. He was enthused about it. The research report that he worked on was a quantitative analysis of energy efficiency opportunities in the Indian industry. We decided to look at electricity alone without looking at the thermal equation and to focus on developing empirical evidence and data that could contrast the cost-effectiveness of demand-side strategies against supply-side strategies.

For technical and logistical support, I turned to V. Raghuraman at NPC. He was helpful and willing to generate the data that would be required. S. Gopinath, a senior NPC consultant was appointed to assist him. I also got in touch with Virendra Kothari who was a consultant based in Delhi and an alumnus of Princeton University. He did his master's under the tutelage of Robert Watson and Eric Larson at the university's well-known Centre for Energy and Environmental Studies. A diligent researcher himself, he turned out to be a good choice for Steve to debate and deliberate with. The team comprising Steve, Gopinath, Kothari and myself as the team leader met in DC to prepare for the study. Steve laid out the methodology and we were quick to respond to his approach to design.

The bedrock report that eventually emerged from this collective effort – *Opportunities for End-Use Electricity Efficiency in Indian Industry* – became a reference guide and a mother lodestone for further work.[6] It served as a springboard for USAID's ECO project – the first of the three was designed on the basis of this report in 1998. It also provided some of the rationale that led to the creation of BEE in 2002.

The vision of this 1992 report is remarkably relevant in light of what India faces today as it moves into the third decade of the century with an exponentially rising demand deficit and the stark threat of a sharp decline in natural resources. Steve's interest in India, sparked by this study and the associations it engendered, did not die out. Much later, in 2015, Steve extended ACEEE's support to mentor the fledging, Delhi-based NGO Alliance for Energy-Efficient Economy (AEEE), India. Supported by a grant from the McArthur Foundation, the collaboration between ACEEE and AEEE has enabled the development of an Indian state-level energy efficiency scorecard and rating system modelled after ACEEE's work in the US. In Steve, India found a friend who helped inform its energy efficiency strategy and programmes.

From the humble information dissemination beginnings

of the Steam & Fuel Users Association of India in 1948 and its reliance on NIFES' vintage publications on efficient use of fuel and steam for information, India has come a very long way. The policy documents and reports which followed not only reflected upon the issues of the day but also provided a road map for institutional growth and capacity development. It was the result of works like these that energy efficiency has since gained acceptance as a resource in its own right and come to be referred to as the first fuel for India.

CHAPTER THIRTEEN

Moving beyond Energy Audits

An issue facing several energy efficiency programmes in India is their inability to rise and move beyond energy audits. The energy auditing exercise, important as it is, is viewed by corporate managements as an end in itself when in truth it is not the ultimate goal. The end result of an energy efficiency project is the stream of energy savings derived from its implementation. Beyond the energy audit exercise, an energy information management and accounting system that meters, measures, records and verifies the savings stream through discrete industrial processes is not always put in place. This leads to a gap in perception and a lack of understanding and appreciation of the benefits of energy efficiency. This gives rise to nagging questions such as these: Will the savings on account of the implementation of an energy audit study actually happen? Are the investments in money and time worth the effort? Answers to these and other related questions are critical for energy efficiency programmes to take root as an integral part of corporate business strategy.

At the heart of the debate is the philosophy of Measurement and Verification (M&V) and why it is critical for energy efficiency. It is equally important to understand *that energy audit is a mere process that identifies, analyzes, evaluates and ranks energy-saving opportunities and no more.* Since it is not possible to meter energy savings, the only way to establish the veracity of an energy efficiency project is to measure the energy consumed before (the baseline) and after the project is implemented and subtract the difference between the two measurements and thus arrive at the actual energy saved. M&V, as simply described here, needs to edge out energy audit as the pivot of any energy savings programme. While energy audits denote potential, it is M&V that actually connotes energy savings. The need today is to centre-stage M&V as the critical missing piece in energy efficiency projects and activities. An integrated M&V strategy would have a major impact on the success of national programmes such as Perform, Achieve and Trade (PAT) and the market-driven energy savings performance projects designed and financed by governmental agencies such as EESL.

The Growth of the Energy Audit Function

On 18 August 2001, the Energy Conservation Bill was enacted by the Indian Parliament. The act, called the Energy Conservation Act, 2001, provides for '… efficient use of energy and its conservation and for matters connected therewith or incidental thereto.'[1] BEE was established immediately thereafter to formulate a policy and regulatory framework for the planning and implementation of a national energy efficiency programme. The two decades preceding the formation of BEE, and the one succeeding it witnessed the emergence and growth of the energy audit discipline in industrial and commercial enterprises. Surveys and studies by governmental agencies (like PCRA, NPC, EMC and others) as well as commercial energy audit firms employed a host of audit programmes ranging from walkthrough audits to preliminary audits to detailed energy audits supported by diagnostic tools for measurement of operational parameters. As one wag put it '… Indian industry took to energy audits as a duck takes to water.'

The early energy efficiency programmes and related energy

audit exercises were conducted by the in-house engineering staff of the concerned organized sector of industry (for example, iron and steel, petrochemicals, refineries and fertilizers among others) and external energy auditors from engineering consultancy firms. In some cases, the energy audits at the surveyed facilities were followed by deployment of efficiency measures, practices and technologies. In a majority of the cases, particularly in the smaller enterprises that did not have in-house energy management departments, the energy audit studies and their recommendations were rarely acted upon, beyond any low-cost measures. There were several causes for this lack of application but the principal reason was the lack of confidence and understanding among corporates about the benefits of these investments. Deemed savings were widely used for evaluating energy efficiency projects, where savings calculation does not rely on measurements at the site but only permits determination of savings related to a single physical unit as a reference, a generic and ex-ante approach. The reliance on deemed savings as a means to establish the revenue stream from an energy savings investment did not find acceptance from managements who generally favoured top-line investments in the production apparatus over bottom-line investments such as energy efficiency.

The M&V Function

The lack of uniformity and transparency in deemed energy savings calculations called for an alternative that would be acceptable to corporate managements in industry and finance. The hallmark of this alternate approach to deemed savings is the robust, accurate and reliable in-field measurement of identifiable processes and operational parameters that enables the calculation of energy consumption as an integral outcome of the M&V process. This process was made stronger by incorporating energy monitoring plans, based on direct measurement of energy use before and after the project is implemented. Also, the emergence of the energy service company (ESCO) business model in this era drove the need for M&V systems. The M&V processes needed pre-approved methodologies and extended documentation for ex post validation. By the 1990s, M&V standards like ASHRAE, IPMVP, FEMP and others, established by the US, were in place with certification procedures for energy/cost savings.

Examples in the US show that the early M&V activities were identified to justify the expenses of energy efficiency programmes. These programmes included financial support for energy audits or the purchase of energy-efficient equipment. The state of California took the initiative to prepare a formal M&V protocol to evaluate the impact of its energy efficiency programmes to justify its significant yearly expenditure. In more recent times, many industrialized nation governments have prioritized energy efficiency by introducing regulations or voluntary protocols to investigate and analyze the nature of energy consumption in industrial sectors. Today M&V is critical to private energy efficiency projects (customer- or ESCO-based), utility-based DSM programmes, the European energy efficiency white certificate programme, the Clean Development Mechanism, the European Union Emission Trading Scheme, and lately, the much sought after international energy management standard, ISO 50001.[2]

M&V in the Indian Context

The Energy Conservation Act of 2001 and India's National Mission for Enhanced Energy Efficiency prioritizes energy use monitoring, verification and reporting by large energy users in India and prescribes energy consumption norms for these consumers. To this end, programmes were rolled out in India from 2006 onwards, many of which now require validation of their success to establish whether the savings justify the investments. While M&V is identified as a necessary component of any programme, there is a concern among India's energy efficiency stakeholders that the authorities have been rather lax in emphasizing the rigorous application of M&V. Harmonization of the verification processes is critical to avoid uncertainties, duplication of efforts and potential loss of credibility. For instance, the credibility of E-Certs in the PAT programme weighs heavily upon the transparent and reliable energy savings realized by the programme. While various international M&V standards are perhaps available for India to consider and adopt, the nation's techno-socioeconomic situation calls for its own model system.

The following section describes out some of the key elements that uniquely influence India's M&V systems and processes.

a. Energy Audit and M&V: Symbiosis, Difference and Hierarchy

As discussed earlier, the cult and culture of energy conservation in India is singularly dominated by the emphasis given to energy audit. *Instead of being regarded solely as a diagnostic tool, the energy audit process is perceived as the end result.* This leads to a gap in perception, hence understanding and appreciation of the benefits of energy efficiency among corporate managements. A large number of recommendations from energy audits remain unimplemented because corporate managements are not confident enough about the reliability to risk investment. M&V in India can redefine the energy audit scenario, by shifting the focus from auditing to the actual implementation of energy management services and verification of energy savings achieved.

b. M&V: A Corporate Decision

Energy efficiency as a corporate strategy can happen only when there is enough awareness about M&V and its implementation. Only when M&V becomes a corporate decision, opportunities for energy efficiency can be tapped into. Energy conservation measures have generally been always confined to the boiler room and rarely discussed in boardrooms. A robust M&V programme could change this by incentivizing boardroom interest and support to this vital area of activity that promises to improve the company's profitability and visibility. Globally, energy management processes and standards like ISO 50001 are now being widely deployed by organizations to monitor energy performance. The key driver here is to design and promote such programmes in a way that makes the management voluntarily commit to a target for efficiency savings.

c. M&V for Energy Efficiency Financing

Finance plays a key role in facilitating the large-scale implementation of energy efficiency projects and technologies. There is growing adoption of energy-efficient measures in India; however, several barriers continue to stall sufficient financing of such projects and technologies. A key barrier is the absence of formal M&V procedures and protocols for energy savings performance contracts. These have neither been sufficiently developed nor widely accepted in India, which limits the capacity of ESCOs to effectively deliver energy efficiency projects.

The lack of communication between financiers and developers is another significant barrier. This is perhaps the key reason why energy efficiency projects in India struggle to acquire the participation and support of financial institutions. While the concept of savings from efficiency can be tricky for the financiers to easily comprehend, M&V processes and their underlying principles can be used in narrowing the awareness gap. This drives home the need for simpler M&V processes for India. Simplifying M&V processes, however, needs to be carefully balanced against the level of accuracy of the estimation of energy cost savings.

d. The Challenge of Baselines

Defining an accurate baseline is highly dependent on the system boundary, availability and reliability of data and the cost of the study. The lack of reliable baselines poses a challenge to India's energy efficiency programmes, specifically in sectors where metering is not commonly practiced such as agricultural pumping and street lighting. It is considerably easier to develop baselines in the manufacturing sector since these companies have internal reporting systems including metering and billing data.

Energy audits can be very useful for defining the baseline which together with M&V could be the basis for computing the savings arising out of the implementation of the energy efficiency measure. M&V should be the basis of optimization methods; M&V and PAT should be discussed in the same language. The end result of PAT lies in the achievement of energy savings target or conversely its failure to do so. In either case, the resultant is monetary loss or gain which is determined through M&V.

e. Indigenous Concept of M&V

There are several challenges that are unique to the Indian context that call for tailor-made M&V protocol systems. For instance, the fixtures of street lighting in India are often non-standardized with varying luminosity levels and many street lighting units are non-functional. Over and above these drawbacks, the lighting systems are occasionally non-metered and, most often, the numbers of street lights installed are not known to the respective municipalities. Retrofitting programmes have been launched to tackle this problem but the challenge is in calculating energy savings programmes which become complex and expensive because of the lack of standardization. Thus, M&V systems are replaced by deemed measures in which savings calculation does not rely on measurements at the site but only permits determination of savings related to a single physical unit as a reference, such as the installed capacity of a street light and an estimate of its working hours.

Similarly, agricultural DSM has its own unique measurement problems which make the determination of baselines tricky. Apart from the fact that pump sets in most Indian states are not metered, the problem is accentuated by the poor quality and restricted supply of power, the non-standardized sizes and nameplate capacities of the motor pump sets. Measurement issues also crop up due to falling in groundwater levels, vagaries of rainfall, differing cropping patterns and other water-related problems. These factors thus require prior and careful consideration when designing the M&V systems.

The Next Steps

Recognizing the importance of M&V to accelerate the pace and direction of energy efficiency in India, AEEE has recommended a three-step integrative approach of stakeholder consultation, preparation of M&V protocols for critical end uses (such as street lighting, agricultural and municipal DSM and industrial energy management) and accreditation of M&V professionals through a national training, evaluation, testing and certification programme.[3]

It would not, therefore, be an exaggeration to state that the national energy efficiency goals are closely linked to the successful development and adoption of M&V systems in energy efficiency projects in the country.

CHAPTER FOURTEEN

Reimagining Efficiency: An Energy Productivity Storyline

Where do we go from here? If efficiency is all about how energy is used, should we not first question what it is used for? That being so, is it time for energy planners and analysts to embrace a new concept that is based on the principle of maximizing economic value in terms of GDP or corporate revenue society obtains from energy.

At the institutions of economic planning in many countries around the world, energy productivity is being increasingly seen as a key driver of sustainable development as a bulwark against climate change. The term 'energy productivity' has come of age as a way of framing energy planning and policymaking, most notably in Australia, the US and, surprisingly, the Middle East. The Gulf Cooperation Council (GCC) countries are increasingly conscious of the way oil could support their economies through a programme of diversification and value addition that includes advanced petrochemicals, oil-derived materials and non-oil exports. For instance, Saudi Arabia's vision for 2030 imagines a future where the kingdom is less reliant on oil exports and whose pathway to future economic growth would be centred around greater energy productivity. This is an indicator of a policy narrative aimed at rapid economic transformation.

Energy Consumption and GDP

There are fundamental differences in the decoupling of GDP and energy consumption in the major economies of the world based on the fascinating interplay between economic growth as defined by a country's GDP and its energy consumption. The indices of sectoral energy consumption and GDP for a selection of developed and developing nations showed some unmistakable patterns. While the US and Germany – among the industrialized countries – witnessed an absolute decoupling effect (that is, GDP grows as energy consumption falls), in China and India the decoupling effect has been relative (that is, GDP rises faster than the increase in energy consumption).

India's case requires some elaboration. The country's energy consumption from value-added activities had risen in index terms from a base of 1.00 in 1990 to almost 4.50 in 2014. During this period the size of the economy had also grown from a base of 1.00 to 4.50.[1] This suggests a close linkage between economic growth and energy consumption which was expected and is referred to by economists as the 'activity effect'. This relationship is relative and not absolute as is the case in G7 countries (like Germany, the US) since in India, GDP was rising faster than energy consumption. This relative decoupling is happening due to two reasons. The first is the efficiency effect. After a period of deterioration between 2003 and 2005, the efficiency effect brought about constant and consistent improvement in energy intensity which had declined from a base of 1.00 in 1990 to almost 0.7 in 2014.[2] Energy intensity is the amount of energy required to operate equipment or a process per unit of the physical output produced. The second is a structural effect. From a base of 1.00 in 1990, the degree of structural change has increased to almost 1.20 in 2014, indicating that the economy is slowly beginning to pivot towards the services sector but not as aggressively as one would assume.

The case of Gulf countries as exemplified by Saudi Arabia is quite different from both India and the G7 countries since decoupling had yet to take place here. In the case of Saudi Arabia, energy productivity was declining between 1990–2015 and stable thereafter. Ultimately, if this trend would have continued, it could have resulted in the decline of national per capita incomes and fiscal deficits as more and more energy resources were diverted to relatively low-value domestic consumption rather than be exported. To move beyond the business-as-usual path of declining or plateaued energy productivity, the Gulf countries needed to make targeted investments in infrastructure, technology and innovation that support a structural shift in the economy and energy efficiency.

This leads to an inescapable conclusion, that is, while energy productivity was improving in developed and developing countries the level of energy productivity was much higher in the former compared to the latter. On the other hand, many developing countries were catching up with faster rates of energy productivity improvement, especially China through their five-year planning targets. Between 1990 and 2015, energy productivity rose in almost all major economies around the world, including India where it grew by 72%.[3] This increase was in part due to India's economic and industrial reforms of 1991 and rising per capita energy consumption from a relatively low base. However, it was also due to the expansion and modernization of energy-intensive heavy industry reflecting higher levels of energy efficiency. China had greater success in improving energy productivity (203%) coming as it was from per capita energy consumption which was similar to India in the 1980s. This reflected a period of massive infrastructure expansion in China, which boosted the GDP and helped modernize the economy. Such modernization, which accelerated in India in the mid-2000s, a decade and a half after China, also improved energy efficiency in the country's overall capital stock.

The Kuznets Curve Hypothesis

I was oblivious to these global trends of energy productivity until I ran into Dr Nicholas Howarth (Nick) at the Global Energy Efficiency Conference in the summer of 2014 in Washington, DC. My professional and personal association with him has greatly influenced my thinking on strategic energy efficiency programme design and development over the past few years. Nick had the convivial manner of an Australian and the finely trained mind of an economist from Oxford. He had graduated from the University of Adelaide in 1998 before heading to Oxford University in England for a doctorate in Economic Geography in 2006, specializing in energy, technological change and climate change. In 2013, he joined the King Abdullah Petroleum Studies and Research Centre (KAPSARC) in Riyadh to lead their work on energy productivity.

My chance meeting with Nick and our preliminary exchange on energy efficiency and its potential global role led to an invitation to attend a KAPSARC workshop on energy in Paris later that year. It was there, over dinner on the opening day, that Nick shared his vision of the energy productivity research that was being launched. Economic development in nations by nature, he said, is an evolving process and can be tracked by calculating the relationship between per capita income and energy productivity. Applying the well-known – and a little controversial – Kuznets curve hypothesis, he suggested that in the early stages of economic development, energy productivity is typically high as the national economies may be small and energy consumption low due to the lack of industrialization and access to modern energy services such as heating, cooling and transport. As the economy grows, so does its energy intensity and per capita income due to infrastructural growth and industrialization. Kuznets theory submits that we should expect a decline in energy productivity during this phase. This changes as the economy matures and diversifies with industry moving up the value chain of production, including advanced manufacturing and services such as IT, health and education. This phase would be accompanied by a decrease in energy intensity and consequently a rise in energy productivity along with a rise in per capita income.

Clarifying this line of economic reasoning further, Nick explained concisely the research agenda that lay ahead for KAPSARC. It would be interesting, he concluded, to study the policy implications of Kuznets hypothesis on GDP growth, per capita income and energy consumption in the GCC countries as well as in developing and developed nations. To this end, he was assembling a small team of international experts as visiting researchers to KAPSARC to help them model the dynamics of energy productivity and develop a comprehensive strategy for economic transformation. Would I be interested in attending a follow-up workshop in Riyadh in February 2015? Fascinated and honoured in equal measure, I agreed.

The Productivity Argument

The energy productivity workshop at Riyadh was attended by a select group of experts from the world over including Nick's small, handpicked team of energy economists, econometricians, modellers and policy experts. It was a different world of academicians and practitioners than I was accustomed to.

Over the next two days, it became increasingly clear to me that the familiar subject of energy efficiency as an energy-related concept, had evolved, reflecting different periods and contexts. The energy conservation era of belt-tightening, sacrifice and curtailment of the early seventies as a result of the Oil Crisis (captured most famously by Jimmy Carter's fireside chat appearing in a sweater urging Americans to use less heating) had made way eventually for energy efficiency policies and programmes. This phase was directed at improving the end-use efficiency of industrial machinery, equipment and processes; home appliances, lighting fixtures, HVAC systems; and internal combustion engines used in vehicular transport. The emphasis was on energy intensity. Its value when broadened and applied economy-wide was used as a popular indicator to measure and manage the relationship between economic growth and energy consumption.

Energy intensity or specific energy consumption targets have been increasingly used by major economies such as China and India to help reduce energy consumption per unit of output in energy-intensive sub-sectors such as steel, cement and chemicals. The workshop pointed to the limitations of specific energy consumption as a meaningful indicator and extolled the benefits of energy productivity, which placed GDP at the macro level and company revenue at the corporate level as an alternative indicator, under which a broader range of energy and economic policies could be framed.

The argument for energy productivity as a superior, better-quality indicator to measure and manage energy consumption and economic growth was compelling. Developing further upon where he had left off at our dinner in Paris, Nick provided the strategic underpinnings of the proposed research on energy productivity. It was a masterly summation of the views and deliberations of the workshop participants. Energy productivity, he emphasized, echoing the views around the room, is affected by two main factors: the underlying energy efficiency of the economy and the structure of the economy. Improving the energy efficiency of the economy without any change in its structure can and will improve energy productivity. This can also be improved by an order of magnitude through structural changes. Modernizing from energy-intensive processes such as wet-process cement manufacturing to less energy-intensive methods such as dry-process cement manufacturing would also improve energy productivity. Diversification from the manufacture of mild steel to alloy steel used in precision machine tools would add value and improve energy productivity. Any energy productivity enhancement programme should consider a pragmatic blend of energy efficiency measures, technological modernization and industrial product diversification.

The workshop helped define KAPSARC's energy productivity research agenda for the next two years. The research work sought to empirically define and identify the economic benefits of improved productivity, develop strategic policy pathways and prepare policy toolkits covering the following sectors of the GCC and select Asian economies (China and India): industry, buildings, power/water and transport. I was invited to join Nick's research team and over the next two years made several visits to KAPSARC to research and prepare an industrial energy productivity policy toolkit.

KAPSARC

The KAPSARC campus, located on the outskirts of Riyadh and close to the King Khalid International Airport, never failed to impress. While driving into the city from the airport, the campus is hard to miss with its main building close to the highway. This mesmerizing architectural marvel has a unique visage of angular and interlocking hexagons set in white rising above the desert sand. Designed by the globally famous Zaha Hadid Architects and built by Aramco, the building's honeycomb-like exterior holds corridors that snake in no particular pattern and separate, unique offices with slanting walls, sharp corners and asymmetrical windows. As one wag put it, 'This is possibly the only building in the world where one can trip over walls rather than on carpets and furniture!' Spread over 70,000 sq m, the building houses prayer rooms, gyms, a library and numerous conference halls and meeting rooms, besides cabin space for researchers and support staff. While the size and shape of the building boggled one's imagination, it also, in a curious way, stimulated one's thinking. A veritable and fertile place to think outside the box. The 350-acre sprawling campus with villas, gyms, jogging tracks, football field, restaurants, supermarket and hostels was a self-contained entity. Electric buses constantly ferry the residents from their homes to the place of work. The air-conditioned buildings offer a cool respite from the unforgiving heat outdoors.

I found the environment at KAPSARC to be friendly and collegial. Recognizing that he needed a multi-disciplinary team, Nick and his research assistant, Kankana Dubey, had scoured the international energy research landscape for knowledge and talent. Alessandro Lanza was a highly acclaimed analyst from the International Energy Agency (IEA) and academic in energy planning from LUISS University, Rome. Lanza along with Marzio Galeotti, an eminent energy economist from the University of Milan, provided empirical evidence related to Kuznets hypothesis on energy productivity. While this provided the academic foundations of the research, the application of a new general equilibrium model for Saudi Arabia by Frederick Gonand – a professor at the University Paris-Dauphine and advisor to the French minister of the economy – showed how by reducing domestic oil consumption through efficiency and diversification policies, economic productivity could be enhanced. The saved oil could be exported for additional revenue for the government. Another set of team members comprising Moncef Krati, a buildings energy efficiency expert from the University of Colorado, Denver; Steven Fawkes, an internationally reputed expert on energy efficiency financing; and myself as the team's industrial energy efficiency expert worked on different aspects and sectors of the energy productivity policy toolkit. We called upon Ibrahim Gelil, a professor from Arabian Gulf University, Bahrain, and the former chairman of the Energy Planning Agency of Egypt, to benefit from his vast experience in energy pricing and environmental policies of the GCC.

I couldn't help but marvel at Nick's ability to effectively lead and mould the team, marshal and analyze the data and reports to present a synthesis of the results with clarity and consistency. Upon entering his chambers, one is mesmerized by the number of graphs and figures that he continuously worked on, drawing on the assorted data that came to his desk from the research team and his own investigations. He never said it in as many words over the period that I worked with him, but the message was silent and clear: Always seek substantiation of facts, diligently check every deduction and assumption, dissect basic beliefs and concepts and pursue leads to their logical conclusion. Slowly but surely, many of these attributes began to rub off on to several of the team members as well. It was much later, well into our research, Nick modestly let it be known that he was an Olympian who represented Australia in the 2000 Summer Olympics at Sydney in the 1500 m event.

It was in one or the other of the oddly shaped rooms of the KAPSARC campus that I spent a good part of my time working on the energy productivity policy toolkit. The toolkit enabled the assessment of the institutional readiness of the GCC and developing country institutions to plan, implement and deliver market-driven energy efficiency policies, programmes and services. It provided a strategic policy pathway for decision-makers to set energy reduction targets. An important contribution to this toolkit was the significance accorded to data analytics as a means to understand and benchmark performance to enable effective designing and implementation of industrial energy productivity programmes.

These broad interim results of the research team raised a question in my mind: What new sustainable development policy narratives can help policymakers in India advance the pace of decoupling and improve energy productivity? Nick was supportive of my research interest and suggested that the focus of the work could be on the development of a conceptual industrial energy productivity framework for India. Given the work I had just put into the industrial policy toolkit, I could devote some time to this new quest. Nick's encouragement and his offer of guidance strengthened my resolve.

Energy Productivity Policy Framework

While India had set clear goals regarding the objective of addressing energy efficiency through the Energy Conservation Act, 2001, the framework and pathway for delivering an energy productivity enhancement programme needed to be more clearly mapped out to assist in identifying problems, assessing impacts and developing an enhanced understanding of the underlying causes and effects.

The driving-force-state-response framework of the United Nations Commission on Sustainable Development (UN-CSD) is a useful structure to analyze the relationships mentioned above. It provides a template and conceptual basis that defines the scope, approach and methodology adapted for an industrial energy productivity policy mechanism. The modified framework comprised data and informatics on, i) nature of the eco-system that promotes energy efficiency and conservation: the *driving forces* of energy productivity; ii) factors that define the status and performance of energy productivity measures and policies: the *state* of preparedness or institutional readiness; iii) policy options and potential impact: the *response* that the policies should enable. The industrial energy policy framework suggests an integrated approach that can regularly review and update policies based on their measured performance.

This basic framework was used to develop the policy dimensions of the industrial energy productivity strategy in India.

Industrial Energy Productivity Policy Model for India

The Indian industrial sector is critical to the country's economic strength as well as the standard of living and well-being of its people. In India, 40% of the total energy consumption is attributed to the industrial sector and this is expected to exceed 50% by 2050 at a compounded average annual growth rate of 4.4%, with energy-intensive industries (iron and steel, pulp and paper, cement, chemicals and petrochemicals, non-ferrous, mining, fertilizers) accounting for over 50% of the total energy consumption in the country. The light industries – food processing, textiles, wood products, printing and publishing, metal processing and brick making account for the other 50%.

To understand how the Indian industrial sector contributes to energy productivity in the economy, it was important to analyze its energy intensity trends. Both industrial growth rates and energy consumption had been averaging over 7% and 5% annually. However, industrial energy intensity had been wavering over the period with an average decline of 0.6% per year. This contrasted with China where energy intensity had been falling by around 5% every year, one of the highest rates in the world.

There is significant, potentially exploitable, energy and emission-saving opportunities in Indian industry. The efficient use of energy is a function of good operating and maintenance practices as well as the choice of technology. Additionally, non-fuel feedstock and its efficient use is driven by a combination of factors such as structural change (moving towards less energy-intensive products) and new and improved process technologies (product and market innovation). Analysis of the pattern of specific energy consumption in key energy-intensive sectors in industrialized countries, developing countries and comparisons with India lead to several interesting conclusions:

1. The average specific energy consumption or energy intensity in India was higher compared to industrialized countries in petroleum refining, chemicals and petrochemicals (like ammonia and methanol), aluminium smelting, iron and steel (including alloy steel) and foundries.
2. India has the lowest energy intensity in clinker and cement manufacturing among all industrialized and developing countries including economies in transition.
3. India is also better than the global average in petroleum refining and ammonia production and compares satisfactorily with the global average energy intensity in iron and steel as well as glass and textiles.
4. India lags in the application of the best available technologies in almost all industrial sub-sectors. The gap is most pronounced in chemicals and petrochemicals (for high-value chemicals like ammonia and methanol), aluminium smelting, iron and steel, glass and foundries.

An economic restructuring and product/goods diversification strategy to move up the value chain towards a less energy-intensive (higher energy productivity) industrial economy including services will also improve energy productivity. For example, the share of India's steel production based on alternative technologies such as direct reduction iron-making and scrap-using electric arc furnaces has grown, accounting for over 65% of the country's installed steel manufacturing capacity and have replaced the inefficient integrated steel mills using blast furnaces and basic oxygen furnaces.

Energy productivity improvement plans must examine both approaches – short-term, less capital-intensive industrial energy efficiency measures that could yield a higher payoff in terms of improved productivity and long-term industrial diversification and modernization. In many situations, there are economic energy efficiency opportunities that could produce immediate impacts to slow down, or even reverse, the growth rates in industrial energy demand without negatively impacting industrial and economic growth. Enhancing industrial energy productivity based on available tools/measures/policies should be the priority. To this end, addressing the 'efficiency' gaps and identifying remedial actions are essential for improving industrial energy productivity. The study concluded that a national energy productivity enhancement programme should be a pragmatic mix of energy efficiency measures, technological modernization and industrial product diversification.

Moreover, it was clear that energy productivity policies and programmes in India could benefit from the creation of effective institutional capacity and enablers in a variety of areas, including infrastructure development, policy formulation, research, manufacturing and service capacity development, financing, engineering design and systems and market development. This called for the provision of a strategic pathway for policymakers in India to deliver market-driven energy productivity policies programmes and services in the industrial sector. Perhaps the most novel aspect of this approach making governments look beyond simply minimizing energy costs through energy efficiency investments is to pay attention to what was being produced and how more revenue could be generated by either expanding markets or developing new higher-value products. This shift in thinking around energy efficiency from cost minimization towards revenue maximisation and economic growth was the crux of the energy productivity agenda.

The energy journey in pursuit of understanding the demand side of the energy equation has been a long one, spread over forty years in India and across countries and continents. The stress on fuel efficiency in the early seventies, as mentioned earlier in the book, led to the broadening of its scope to include lifestyle changes and socioeconomic approaches. And fuel efficiency became energy conservation. Later, as the focus shifted to precise accounting of energy balances of inputs and outputs in appliances, equipment and processes, we moved on to energy efficiency. Today, we are at the threshold of a new concept – 'energy productivity'. As detailed in this chapter, energy productivity is based on the principle of maximizing economic value in terms of the GDP or corporate revenue from energy through modernization and structural diversification. It is still in the early phases of adoption and only time will tell whether this novel notion will take hold to lead energy efficiency from the boiler room to the boardroom.

CHAPTER FIFTEEN

Reflections on Water Balance in Farms

This account of my energy journey would be incomplete without a mention of an unexpected development along the way. When I left Delhi for Bangalore in 2013, I turned my attention to energy and water issues in urban and rural settings. It was my good fortune to run into an extraordinary individual, Chandrashekar Hariharan. A chartered accountant in the 1970s, Hari turned journalist by 1980 and during a stint in covering Indian villages, pioneered an enterprise for sustainable housing which grew into a ₹500 crore green company in the early 1990s. Deeply influenced by J. C. Kumarappa and Alvin Toffler's early models of decentralized solutions for water and energy, Hari spent the late 1980s and early 1990s working in fourteen districts in Gujarat, Maharashtra and Rajasthan on watershed and local command areas of irrigation. His involvement in the watersheds of these districts gave him powerful insights into what panchayats and local agencies could do for efficient agricultural practices. One of the most well-recognized green entrepreneurs of India, he has over fifty awards from four continents for his powerful pioneering of sustainability solutions.

In this chapter, I share his insightful and powerful reflections that I had the good fortune to listen to and record. They have been organized as separate themes and in Hari's own words, to present the larger narrative as well as possible.

Indian Agriculture: The Present and the Future

We don't often realise that out of the 3.3 million sq km of India's landmass, nearly 1.9 million sq km is under agriculture – that's over 60% of all of India's landmass. Of this, about 1.45 million sq km is the net sown area. We need to go back to what we were bequeathed as a legacy when the British left to get a perspective on agriculture. In 1947, India had to feed 380 million mouths with under 50 million tonnes of largely subsistence farming. Our food grains production in 1967 before the Green Revolution was about 70 million tonnes. By 1980, it rose 170 million tonnes and we achieved self-sufficiency. Yield per unit of farmland improved by more than 30% during those years. The figures for 2018 hovered around 285 million tonnes. But at what cost, and what suffering in the bargain?

Why did India not consolidate those dramatic gains with the second layer of better governance and the creation of healthy market-led ecosystems that favoured the farmer and not the middlemen? Why weren't hedges for pricing created with infrastructure for storing and for greater value addition in terms of food processing and desiccated produce options? To this day, cold storage options are few. The private sector has moved in, in the few places where such initiatives have sprung up, but at prices that again are exploitative. Dilapidated and poorly maintained silos for grain storage ensure that a third of our produce is feasted upon by rodents every year while a fifth of a year's produce rots away due to bad management. We have had a persistent deficit in the production of pulses (24 million tonnes produced in 2019 and 5 million tonnes imported) in a nation that depends on various *dals* or pulses for protein. We have for nearly all of the last fifty years imported pulses from Myanmar, Canada, Vietnam and China.

Pulses are dryland crops and there is a need for new and effective strategies for not merely making India self-sufficient but also ensure surplus for export. The potential for dryland crops is immense in a land that has over 100 million hectares – or over 60% of all of our cultivable lands – in areas that are not river irrigation-fed. Sunflower and soya are examples of other such crops that can boost farm yields and incomes in a country where close to 126 million small-holder and marginal farmers are dependent on an opaque system of auctions by cartels at wholesale markets that leaves them with little bargaining power. These farmers form the largest segment of the employed population.

On Farm Prices

Many of us as Indians are somewhat aware of the delightful variety of food available in our country, but very few of us know anything about how food is grown, stored, distributed, eaten, and wasted. We are ignorant of the yawning gap between the price a farmer receives and the retail price that we pay for their produce. Middlemen or intermediaries make twice or thrice the farmer's take. This has been at the centre of the 2020 legislative reform for rationalizing the market structure for farmers and offering them a fair deal.

Every year, we have hapless farmers gutting truckloads of tomato, for the price the market offers is often less than the cost of transporting it from their farms. We saw how onions have brought consumers to tears over the latter half of 2019, thanks to the complete lack of management of water need (both the lack and excess of it) for a crop that is the least fussy and is known, like pulses, to be a dry land crop. From ₹1 a kilogram in December 2018, prices shot up to ₹180 a kilogram. The government imported 12,000 tonnes of onions from Turkey in less than a month, though India's average annual production totals 24,000 tonnes! What went wrong with onions was the lack of governance – a malaise that afflicts every crop and region in the country. More so in the dryland districts that form over 70% of India's farmlands with no river-fed irrigation.

No one pays India's 126 million farmers a monthly salary, and their proceeds from sales barely cover the cost of seeds and other farm inputs. Farmers don't even impute notional costs of their own labour and the rent for the little handkerchiefs of land they hold onto fiercely. Fragmentation has been the bane of the farm economy since the 1960s. Three generations of farmers later, lands have been further fragmented as inheritances. Small and marginal farmers with less than two hectares of land account for 86.2% of all farmers in India but own just 47.3% of the cultivated area, as per the tenth agriculture census. Farmers owning between 2–10 hectares of land account for 13.2% but own 43.6% of the cultivated area.

How can we blame farmers for not paying for power and 'pilfering' it from long-distance power lines that pass through their regions to cater to the electricity needs of the rich? Development and planning are often looked at from the prejudiced and untrained lenses of an administrator who has no experience or knowledge of the pains and challenges of eking a livelihood by coaxing life out of lands that miss monsoon. Spending a day in any village of Vidarbha or Marathwada will open one's eyes to the sheer helplessness of farmers.

On Water and Energy Co-Management in Farms

This is a story that we explored earlier in Chapter Ten. Hari's thoughts lend it further import.

Does irrigation water and energy efficiency take precedence over the battle for farmers' self-sufficiency and business survival? Or are they two sides of the same coin? India's production of food grains is a decent enough indicator of the quantum of water that farming demands, and therefore, the amount of energy used to pump groundwater from deeper and deeper aquifers. Ironically, our farmers who grow staples like rice and wheat which claim over 4000 litres of water to a kilogram of such produce themselves subsist on millets as a staple food which claims less than half as much cultivation water! A news report in 2019 observed that more than 60% of the water available for farming in India is consumed by rice and sugar, two crops that occupy 24% of the cultivable area.[1]

What has this do with farm energy and the critical need to plan its future? Water, one must remember, is directly related to energy use. Every tonne or thousand litres of water is the equivalent of at least five units of primary source energy. When we talk agriculture, we are essentially talking energy. And what can India do to drop the levels of energy consumed per kilogram of every crop we produce? A few demand-side measures could help cut down farm energy consumption by half. For instance, the quality of seeds used and the chemicals pumped into the soil only make the land thirsty. A simple switch to non-pesticide management can halve the use of water for cultivation. With some streamlining, the energy profile for the agriculture sector can fall sharply.

India and China: A Comparative Study

China, which has three times the landmass of India, with nearly the same amount of arable or cultivable lands produces more to an acre. In other words, China feeds one-fifth of the world's population from just one-fifteenth of the world's arable land. In a way, India does that too, but not as effectively. Since the 1980s, when Deng Xiaoping stirred the sleeping dragon awake, farm productivity has risen even further. For the 3.5 tonnes of tomato that an Indian farmer harvests per acre, his Chinese counterpart produces 6 tonnes. Similarly, while India secures an average of 2 tonnes from an acre of paddy or wheat, the numbers are more than double in China.

Both countries have about a sixth of their cultivable lands under dam-based or river-fed irrigation. China faces the same vagaries of weather as India does. Cultivable lands that are rain-fed are much the same in both these ancient lands. In a sense, they are level playing fields. But the energy profiles of agriculture in the two countries are vastly different. Unlike China, which over the last three decades has managed to export a big chunk of its agricultural produce, India continues to reel under the wages of its sins – of not responding to the obvious need for smarter agricultural management in the 1980s and 1990s.

Need for a Technological Farm Revolution

India needs to be mindful of its biophysical capacity while attempting to meet the food challenge. For this, the young crop of engineers and trained extension officers in agriculture have to move to newer and more efficient technology and management in farming. The massive investment and annual spending on agri-research must turn their gaze away from poor precedents of the last half-century. The farm sector which consumes about a fifth of India's daily energy generation has to focus on water-efficient crop patterns and rain-fed irrigation. The one big flaw of the Green Revolution was that it did not pay much attention to India's ability to manage the process of agriculture or mechanizing. Instead, the transformation was primarily one of rapidly increased reliance on nitrogenous fertilisers and the use of high-yielding seed strains. Little was done to address the resilience needs of farmers by strengthening systems that shielded them from the vagaries of monsoon and unreliable weather and climatic conditions. This singular flaw that has not secured the attention of policy planners has left a staggering legacy as it has made the task of the two generations ahead of us that much harder, compounded as it is by the impact of climate change and global warming.

Given our resource constraint, what can one do now? Can we bring about feasible and effective changes in farming: efficient energy management on the distribution utility side of the meter; improvement in water conveying and pumping systems; independence from synthetic fertilizers and pesticides to heal the topsoil after many long years of abuse with potent chemicals; freedom from an external energy grid that has, in any case, failed far more often than helped; freedom from seeds that don't belong to the micro-region; independence from long-distance water resources, especially in the rain-fed regions of India that account for four times of the canal-irrigated areas, and last, but not the least, change in the urban consumer's eating habits to millets and grains that consume less water and are of higher nutritional value than rice and wheat?

We must return in effect to energy systems which are localized where energy is produced and consumed right at the village or gram panchayat or tehsil within the district. The smaller the unit, the more manageable and economical it will be, as has been proven by hundreds of isolated yet inspiring models of villages that are energy self-sufficient. The focus has to shift dramatically from the supply-side to address local challenges – environmental and economic – and not be snared by the centralized policymaking processes that administrators have learnt to love, for the control it offers them on public spending.

Reasons for Hope: Case Studies

Jakhni: An oasis amidst the crisis

In southern Uttar Pradesh, five districts of Bundelkhand fall under the state, with the rest spilling over into Madhya Pradesh. While most parts of Bundelkhand are reeling under severe water crisis, a village in the drought-hit Banda district, one of UP's five, has gone back to traditional conservation techniques to revive existing water bodies and is serving as a role model to others. While villages in this region grapple with water scarcity, Jakhni has come to be known as 'jalgram' (water village). It has its ponds, wells and other water bodies brimming with water. Not so long ago, Banda was one of the worst-hit districts in the Bundelkhand region. The village now has thirty-two wells, twenty-five handpumps and four ponds.

This was not the case always. Eight years ago, in 2012 Jakhni's farmers, fed up with their water problems, decided to adopt traditional water conservation techniques. The villagers say they did this without any assistance from the government. By the end of the decade, with the return of health to Jakhni's watershed and the relative abundance of water, farmers and youth who had migrated to big cities are slowly returning. Residents of the village have also formed an organisation – Sarvodaya Aadarsh Jal Gram Abhiyan Samiti – to take collective measures to harvest rainwater and thereby increase the groundwater level. Shanti, a Jakhni farmer, says: 'Eight to ten years ago, we decided to divert wastewater and rainwater to ponds and this measure has rejuvenated the water level and has made farming easier.'

Sonapura: A case of disbelief

Sonapura is a timeless little hamlet no more than an hour's drive away from the bustle of Bangalore. The landscape is green, with the massif of the Nandi Hills looming serenely on the horizon. If you stay still for a moment, you can hear the rumble of trucks on the distant Hyderabad highway. To a development worker, Sonapura poses a challenge that's typical of every water-strapped settlement in India. Until 1980, this land had groundwater at less than 200 feet under the ground. The rich Nandi Hills ecosystem served as home to six major east flowing rivers of the Deccan plateau in the broader doab between the rivers Krishna and Kaveri. Akravathi, Chakravathi, Papagni, Uttara Pinakini or Pennar, Dakshina Pinakini or Ponnaiyar and Palar are the east-flowing rivers which eventually join the Bay of Bengal. Sonapura hosts 52 homes and about 150 acres of cultivable lands.

The Minister for Rural Development in Ramakrishna Hegde's Karnataka government in the 1980s was a Nazir Saab. Upon the advice of engineers who saw an easy solution with borewells, he helped dig thousands of them across many districts and secured water for the farmers in the short term. But this led to severe groundwater depletion and the water levels plunged to 1800 feet.

In the race to chase the depleting aquifer, farmers started digging borewells across the landscape. Over the last thirty years, each farmer vied with the other to go deeper and drain the centuries-old aquifers that lay over 300 m underground. It didn't take long to exhaust the water tables that would take 5000 years to replenish.

Today, Sonapura is one among 37 hamlets where over 40,000 borewells are spread like a rash over an area of 70 sq km covering seven gram panchayats. That's an average of one borewell for every 1.5 acres. This is not a land that is on the lee side of the monsoon winds like the wide swathes of land to Karnataka's north or Marathwada or Vidarbha, all of which are part of central India's penumbra regions which get less than 500 mm rainfall, half the national average. This village in Karnataka gets a healthy 800 mm but farmers are steeped in debt over monies spent unwisely on borewells that never yielded what was promised and turned bone dry in a couple of seasons. Many farmers went against good technical advice and common sense and pushed their luck. Over 80% of the borewells in the region are dead with rusting metal pipes buried half a kilometre below the earth's surface standing in mute testimony to the folly of these farmers and governance directions.

Why did farmers not pay heed to the traditional ways of husbanding water? Why did they fill up the network of open wells and the intricate network of water canals that connected the cascade of lakes? Why was there no understanding of the simple relationships that exist between 'jan' (life), 'jangal' (forest), 'jaanwar' (animals), 'jameen' (earth) and 'jal' (water)?

There are no simple answers but the generation of farmers of the 1970s were led astray and had no one to mentor them about the balance they needed to maintain and they didn't pay heed to the sage advice of their forefathers who had over the centuries nurtured intricate water networks. The multiple schemes and sops for farmers that political parties promised while electioneering in the 1980s fed greed and weakened the farmer's ability to remain resilient. Nazir Saab was called Neer Saab for his borewells – the word 'neer' means water in Kannada. But that short-term measure – a disaster perpetrated in other states as well – has led us, forty years later, to a grievous water table that has altered the very geology of regions, especially in the low rainfall areas of the country and those that are not river-fed.

With a careful restoration of the micro watersheds of each farmer's lands and of the village, together with the creation of affordable bunds, revetments, tanks in every cultivable acre, combined with the healing of the water table, lands such as those in Sonapura can be transformed with yields over two crops a year if not three. It requires management, training and a bit of initial investment (less than the money invested in those unyielding borewells) to prove that intensive farming with massive water efficiency is possible.

Jalahalli taluka: A success story

Back in 2007, in the dry and dusty black soil terrain of Jalahalli taluka in the Raichur district of Karnataka began a journey in partnership with local NGOs to persuade farmers to move away from synthetic boosters and pesticides. They were assured that the use of non-pesticide managed systems would not hurt productivity but that it needed first the healing and sensitive stewardship of land with simple watershed systems of bunds and tanks and natural vegetation in common lands that fixed soils with nitrogen. Tree species that enriched soils with biological nitrogen-fixing microorganisms was part of the mission. A democratic process of debate and discussion was undertaken with equal participation from women and young farmers. It took three years before a set of pilot farms began to yield a second crop where for decades, they had not managed to secure more than one dryland harvest of millets every year. The demand for cultivation water fell, much to the disbelief of farmers, by half. With better water management, led by both women and men, it was possible for the villagers to cultivate a second crop in a year. Happily, the quantum of water used annually by the lands and the crops sown and reaped remained the same. With the first taste of success fever, a swathe of seven villages and two thousand land-owning farmers who saw results they did not think were possible, began a new phase of two crops every year no matter how bad or good the monsoon turned out to be.

Non-pesticide managed (NPM) farming has cut the amount of water used for cultivation by half. At the same time, yields have been protected if not increased for every farmer in the micro-region. Samuha, the organization that led the initiative, has taken these practices to the Ballari district and around Hampi, the ancient capital of the kings of the Vijayanagar Empire. Again, although these farmlands are canal-irrigated, the halving of water use has ensured water security for the farmers. This is no isolated example. NPM production has been taken up in many of the drought-prone districts of Adilabad in Telengana, Solapur in Maharashtra and other parts of the country.

In Conclusion

So why are such examples of village-wide good water conservation and management practices important in the energy context? At the September 2019 AEE (Association of Energy Engineers, US) World Energy Conference in Washington, DC, Jonah Schein, a researcher from the WaterSense programme of the United States Environmental Protection Agency (USEPA) made a telling remark that held important lessons for similar initiatives on the Indian farm front. As per Schein, an interesting data point that has been proven in California is that the energy savings due to water management and conservation in that state is greater than the combined impact of the state's energy efficiency programmes.

Our interest in food is an offshoot of a broader interest in the country's energy supply. This search for solutions should not stop at merely the production of food but cover the entire food production chain – including the environmental setting, post-harvest losses, food processing, access to food and actual nutritional requirement – because the energy supply chain cuts vertically through every segment of farm activity. Ask any villager or a committed development worker in the drylands that miss the monsoons, they will tell you the battle is to secure *sinchaai ka pani* (water for cultivation) and then *piye jal* (drinking water for humans and livestock).

What impact does energy have on the country's agriculture? How do we ensure efficient co-management of water and energy? How do we bring appropriate environmental management practices to these lands? It must be recognized that farming in the future has to move towards intensive agriculture. Any programme for the promotion of intensive farming has to begin with a thorough digitized mapping of the biophysical environment of every taluk or tehsil. A biophysical environment is the biotic and abiotic surrounding an organism or a population which also includes factors that influence their survival and development. A biophysical environment can vary in scale from a village to a tehsil or district. It can also be subdivided according to its attributes. India has nearly 700 districts and has over 5500 taluks or tehsils. Karnataka, for instance, has 31 districts and 175 taluks while Maharashtra has 36 districts and 358 taluks. A shift to intensive farming would result in water-efficient, climate-controlled and resilient farms without the 'steroids' of synthetics boosters. With the Internet of Things to aid and the infrastructure of telemetry stations already firmly in place in most states, we need to realize the convergence between such monitoring systems and agriculture.

A Sonapura or Jakhni model can serve as a good example of increasing crop productivity, water self-sufficiency with rainwater as the staple. Clearly, the benefits are manifold and include reduced dependence on groundwater; better nurturing of the natural ecosystems and the shallow aquifers in the area; multiple cropping possibilities; protection from the vagaries of weather and temperature offered by precision irrigation at affordable rates; bunds, revetments and storage tanks that buffer the seasonal need for water; crop patterns that are water-efficient and more suited to seasonal needs of the marketplace; and storage infrastructure that helps the farmers flex muscle to leverage better prices ... the list is long. All of these are centrally about energy efficiency. They are also about good and smart 'convening' of processes through deductive methodology and good on-the-ground thinking. And they all go back to India's need for 'managers' at the most basic units of agriculture in which are the 'gaon' (villages) and 'chhaani' (hamlets) under every panchayat.

The author adds: *Hari's insightful reflections elucidate that WENEXA (see Chapter Ten) addressed only a small sliver of the humongous challenge of bringing energy efficiency to farming that goes beyond merely the rationalizing of electricity distribution and groundwater pumping. There is a need for a more complex exploration of optimizing power and water co-management that Indian agriculture sorely needs. By extending the scope of programmatic interventions beyond the supply and demand sides of the energy equation to water-use efficiency and devolution of watershed management practices, sustainable use of natural resources can be greatly enhanced. Moreover, this new Green Revolution can help farmers enhance their income while drastically reducing the requirement of water for cultivation.*

CHAPTER SIXTEEN

Powering the India of the Future: 2020 and beyond

The Road Ahead

Where would India's energy journey lead us in the next thirty years? The climate change challenge is this century's most dangerous and intractable threat. It is dangerous because it places the health, safety, security and economic well-being of the world at risk. It's an intractable threat because it is largely due to emissions of greenhouse gases, particularly carbon dioxide due to the combustion of fossil fuels like coal, oil and natural gas. These fuels supply 70% of India's primary energy and over 60% of its electricity. The shares of electricity, as well as nonelectric energy, from fossil fuel can neither be rapidly reduced nor can their emissions be easily and inexpensively sequestered away from the atmosphere.

Earth's climate is characterized by a single factor, the global average temperature of its surface. It has been estimated that since the early twentieth century the earth has warmed up by 1.1°C. This seemingly modest increase has led to a spate of disastrous consequences today, such as deadly heatwaves, torrential downpours, wildfires, powerful tropical storms, increasing pathogens and pests. The global resolution of the 2015 Paris Agreement held by the United Nations Framework Convention on Climate Change which attempts to limit the earth's average surface temperature increase to 2°C above the 'pre-industrial' average is not likely to prevent the climatic disruptions and impacts of global warming. Given that the target of 2°C would have intolerable climatic consequences, an aspirational target of 1.5°C was also agreed upon by the global community at the 2015 Paris Agreement of the Conference of Parties to the UNFCC. Both developed and developing countries have made commitments to fulfilling their differentiated responsibilities to tackle this pressing issue. For instance, industrialized countries would have to reduce their emissions of heat-trapping gases by 80%–100% by 2050.[1]

Powering India through the tribulations of climate change to a future decarbonized world dominated by renewable energy and energy efficiency is a challenge of gargantuan proportions. The journey thus far, as evidenced by some of the experiences recounted in this book, provides a foundation and a foothold as we vault into the future.

In the past, nations ignored energy efficiency at their own peril. Countries that were energy inefficient with a high intensity of energy use were at a disadvantage in the global marketplace, apart from the cost of the environmental damage they incurred. It is now universally accepted that one can grow the economy by reducing energy use and attendant carbon emissions. Energy efficiency is an indispensable part of this proposed energy transition which has now become an important element of competitive economies. World over energy efficiency is seen as an integral part of sustainability as nations and people become conscious and mindful of the environmental consequences of unbridled energy growth.

The sharp contrast between the situations of the affluent (First World) countries and middle (Second World) and destitute (Third World) nations dominated international parleys on energy security and global sustainability last three decade. In 1990, the affluent OECD nations used 70% of the world's energy of 349 quads which was more than twice the energy used by the middle and destitute nations. Today, three decades later they account for only 30% of the world's energy use. It is no coincidence that the world's most energy-efficient economies – Japan, the European Union, the US and, more recently, China – have been the world's most successful economies as well. Conventional thinking dictated that First World countries to gradually reduce the growth rate of energy use and then proceed to reduce overall energy use. Second and Third World countries, however, were observed to be on a much different path. It was predicted that their mounting populations and climbing economic growth rates would lead to a dramatic increase in their energy use.

Unexpectedly, the First World countries reduced their energy use quicker than expected, and the energy use by the other two categories grew more gradually than anticipated in the 1990s. Expectations that the middle and destitute nations could catapult to advanced, energy efficient systems, processes and technologies were realized in only a few cases, notably China. One can draw a parallel between affluent nations' evolving shift to zero energy growth, and even net reduction, to the demographic transition towards zero natural population growth that they have passed through. While the Second and Third World nations, comprising 85% of the world's population, have been moving towards a demographic transition as well, they are at least a generation behind the affluent nations. The same will be the case for energy transition.

What is called for is a long-term, sustainable development strategy to be deployed at scale. To meet this exacting test would mean addressing squarely the task of engineering green and clean energy technology shifts. These are no ordinary transitions. They would have to be tectonic in both scale and application. The approach to planning and design would have to be innovative and consultative with synergistic partnerships among all the stakeholders: government, public and private enterprises. The management mantra has to be data-driven.

The green tectonic shifts in India should include the following prioritized listing of strategic policy and technological choices:

1. Shift to the demand side of the energy equation
2. Harness renewable energy at scale
3. Develop integrated energy network
4. Pursue the water-energy nexus
5. Optimize energy efficiency design approaches
6. Address the energy access challenge

Success in powering the India of the future hinges on the progress the country makes in ushering in these green tectonic shifts as elaborated below.

Demand-side Shift

Resounding through the pages of this book has been the clarion call to move energy policy planning from the supply side of the energy equation to the demand side. 'Integrated resource planning' (IRP) is a public process that involves examining energy generation, transmission and distribution and end use, symmetrically rather than sequentially. IRP considers a full range of power sector investments to meet the new electricity demand, not only through new energy sources but also through efficient techniques for transmission, distribution as well as demand-side measures on an equal basis. It seeks answers to the bottom-line question: Is it cheaper to save a unit of electricity than to generate an equivalent amount and distribute it to consumers? Thus, it compares the cost of saved capacity with the cost of equivalent generation capacity. With this in mind, power planners will work together with other interested parties to identify and prepare energy options that serve the highest possible public good. Unlike generation or network planning, the process of decision-making is decentralized. The stakeholders as part of the consultative process establish scope, investigate options, prepare and evaluate integrated plans, select preferred plans and establish mechanisms to monitor, evaluate and iterate plans as conditions change.

The IRP method was developed in the US in the 1980s as a response to the repeated complaints of unnecessary power plants, which saw serious cost and time overruns. In contrast to the limited choices considered in conventional power development planning processes, IRP plans use long-term (20–30 years) planning horizons and include careful consideration of risk. Best practice IRPs integrate environmental and other external costs and benefits. When done properly, IRP provides a structure and an opportunity for utility systems and stakeholders to learn and to develop plans in a cooperative atmosphere. Ultimately, better decision-making processes result in power plans more closely aligned with societal goals.

Although a comprehensive IRP process requires a substantial commitment of time, it leads to better outcomes: lower capital investment leading to low-cost electricity; clean energy-based processes means less adverse social and environmental impact. They can do so by emphasizing services (cooling, heating, lighting and others.) rather than just kilowatt-hours of electricity, through an evaluation that considers both social and environmental costs. These better outcomes involve considerably higher investment in energy efficiency and demand-side management.

There are institutional considerations that would greatly influence the shift to the demand side as well. A key prerequisite of a national energy efficiency strategy is its ability to harmonize actions among a number of disparate stakeholders. From an institutional perspective, the energy efficiency administrative machinery needs to be co-located within a governmental structure to enable it to coordinate cross-cutting programmes that involve multiple ministries and departments at both the centre and the states. An energy efficiency agency that is mis-situated is ineffective in the implementation of its mandates and programmes. The wrongful positioning of an energy efficiency agency within governments has been the singular reason adversely affecting the efficacy of its policies and programmes.

BEE, since its inception in 2002–03, has been located within the administrative precincts of the Ministry of Power. While initially there were good reasons to do so, not the least being the role of the country's power sector as a key energy efficiency driver in its formative years, there is a need now to examine the issue afresh. This is all the more important since it is now being considered as a key energy resource to serve multiple strategic objectives of climate change, energy security and economic competitiveness. That apart, an energy efficiency administrative unit co-located in a ministry that is essentially devoted to the growth and expansion of energy supply and capacity addition will have to compete for attention, have little visibility and will likely be passed over by the bureaucracy.[2] The other fallout is the fact that the energy efficiency programmes will typically be circumscribed within the jurisdiction that the parent ministry operates in. For instance, energy efficiency policies that impact energy intensive industrial sub-sectors such as mandatory targets in refineries or petrochemicals or steel would be difficult to prescribe and obtain compliance for, because of the simple reason that the ministries they report to might be less than forthcoming to participate.

Given the above, it is perhaps an opportune moment, in the 2020s, to consider alternative structures and arrangements. One such measure could be positioning the energy efficiency agency under Niti Aayog. This would have the advantage of not being limited to a technical or economic ministry's jurisdiction. Furthermore, energy efficiency as a fundamental strategy to advance multiple challenges of climate change and energy security would be better served if it's linked to the country's economic planning wing rather than to a line ministry.

There are drawbacks here as well. The foremost is that Niti Aayog is not structured to implement projects or programmes. It's function is largely advisory and while policy formulation is its responsibility, enforcement of policies is not its mandate. Perhaps an oversight arrangement by a supra-authority such as the Prime Minister's Office (PMO) might provide both the visibility and the impetus to stakeholders to coordinate and collaborate under a strict time-bound action plan.

Harnessing Renewable Energy at Scale

The case for renewables has been made, convincingly and irrevocably. Renewable energy resources are inexhaustible, emit lower or no carbon emissions, increasingly cheaper with price reductions over time caused by respective economies in volume. As against this, conventional energy sources are fast depleting and exhaustible, emit high levels of carbon emissions and are accompanied by price increases and volatility in supply. However, there are challenges that could thwart India's efforts to harness renewable power at scale.

Nationally determined contributions (NDCs) are at the heart of the 2015 Paris Agreement and the achievement of these long-term goals. NDCs embody efforts by each country to reduce national emissions and adapt to the impacts of climate change. As its NDC, India has committed to installing clean energy capacity equivalent to 40% of the total installed electrical capacity by the year 2030. To this end, India announced a very ambitious target of achieving 175 GW of renewable energy capacity by 2022. About 100 GW of it is expected to come from only solar energy.

The target of renewable energy capacity was further scaled up to 450 GW by 2030 in September 2019, at a meeting of the International Renewable Energy Agency held in Abu Dhabi. As of March 2020, India has installed a power generation capacity of 370 GW, of which about 81.3 GW or 22% is generated through clean energy projects such as solar and wind. With the addition of large hydroelectric plants to the clean energy generation basket, the total renewable power capacity constitutes 132 GW or 36% of the country's total installed capacity. The plan is to reach 220 GW by 2022, a higher target than the one set in 2019.

The country passed an important landmark of its energy journey in 2018, when the renewable energy capacity added was 11.8 GW – more than double the capacity additions from coal, gas and large hydro, totalling 5.4 GW. Also, encouragingly, India has emerged as the lowest-cost producer of solar electricity ahead of China, Germany, Italy and France. The costs for utility-scale solar projects in India dropped by 80% in the country between 2010–2018. While the journey of renewable power in terms of capacity addition and fast falling price discovery of solar energy bids have been quite exemplary, some problems could threaten the future growth in capacity additions. Addressing these would be critical for the country to meet the target set for 2030.

The aggressive downward spiral of low tariffs in solar power bidding auctions (ranging from ₹2.47/kWh [$0.035/kWh] to ₹2.91/kWh [$0.041/kWh]), termed by many in the industry as 'a race to extinction', has resulted in regulatory and contractual disputes.[3] Existing feed-in tariffs for wind power were non-competitive with the falling solar tariffs, and thus, had the effect of stalling private wind farm projects. The objective of 'discovering best tariff' through audacious, exhausting electronic reverse auctions (e-RAs) set in motion a trend of declining tariffs in each subsequent solar auction. This unintended consequence of the e-RAs triggered insecurities among utilities that had committed higher prices for their earlier solar power procurements and caused them to retrospectively renege from their purchase commitments. Several states proceeded to renegotiate legally binding power purchase agreements with renewable energy developers only to be hauled to court for cases pending judicial decisions. If this backtracking was not enough to slow the tempo of renewable energy power project developments, delayed payments by distribution utilities proved to be yet another stumbling block. According to the Central Electricity Authority's (CEA) report, *Payment Dues to RE Generators*, as on August 2019, the total dues from discoms amounted to ₹11,500 crore ($1.60 billion). Furthermore, the report mentioned that the average waiting period for outstanding bills was in excess of two years!

The problem was compounded by falling grid availability due to the intermittent nature of renewable power and the attendant need for costly balancing power. Despite the efforts of the government to restrain all state utilities from curtailing renewable energy production and accord 'must-run' status to renewable power-generating stations, the fast-increasing penetration of renewable power is bound to increase the balancing costs.

Another issue is the threat posed by the thin margins owing to the precipitous fall in solar tariffs to industry partners, like original equipment manufacturers (OEM), engineering, procurement and commissioning contractors (EPCs) and operation & maintenance companies (O&M). With extremely competitive tariffs, the quality of plant constructions and services offered have been put under intense 'bottom-line' constraints causing the industry partners to turn to 'value engineering', a euphemism for cutting corners. Due to inconsistent power offtake in both the wind and solar segments of the business, only few O&M companies have been able to sustain their operations. India's largest wind turbine manufacturer and developer Suzlon almost going bankrupt is a testimony to this pertinent problem.

Given all of the above constraints and barriers, there is an overwhelming possibility that unless long-term, tested and validated sustainable solutions are developed, the pace of renewable power development in India might slow down and the 450 GW target by 2030 would remain an elusive dream.

Integrated Energy Networks

To meet India's demand for increased energy use, while reducing emissions significantly, it will be necessary to produce energy (electricity) in a much more integrated way and use it more efficiently. This cannot be achieved by focusing separately on electricity, coal, oil, gas and renewable forms of energy. It will require an integration of all energy sources with electricity produced from renewable energy, nuclear power and fossil fuels using carbon capture and storage, a process that removes carbon dioxide emissions from sources like coal-fired power plants and either reuses or stores it so that it does not enter the atmosphere. The 'integrated energy network' (IEN), or 'sector coupling' as it is also referred to, is the convergence of four system elements: customer engagement with energy resources and providers; dramatic emissions reductions in generation through clean energy (renewable and efficiency) including carbon capture; application of information and telecommunications technologies; and an integrated grid enabling economy-wide emissions reductions through end-use electrification.

Why do we need an IEN? What are its benefits? IEN advances deep decarbonization through electrification through an optimal mix of conventional energy, renewable sources and energy efficiency. Deep decarbonization is the process of mitigating and totally eliminating the use of carbon in all its forms in the generation and utilization of energy. To reach a fully decarbonized economy by 2050, we need to eliminate emission from power utilities as well as difficult-to-abate, carbon-intensive end-use sectors such as industry (steel, cement and petrochemicals) and freight transport by road, shipping and aviation. These sectors currently account for 30% of the total global emissions. For India, the carbon emitted on the demand side of the energy equation, namely, in industry, transport, buildings and farms is greater than on the supply side through coal-fired power generation.

A clean energy network that comprises a grid-connected renewable energy system can be used to produce green hydrogen from the electrolysis of water. This hydrogen can be used to produce biofuels to substitute petroleum fuels in transport and industry. It would involve major scaling up of grid-connected renewable energy generation and the creation of a smart grid infrastructure to deliver it for the production of clean carriers like green hydrogen as feedstock for the manufacture of biofuels. Although IEN sounds like a futuristic concept, its seeds have already been planted. Technologies, such as hydrogen manufacture, storage and conversion to biofuels including electrolysers, fuel cells, battery storage and electric vehicles are either at an embryonic or near commercial stages. A global IEN programme to collectively transition to cleaner technologies on both sides of the energy equation is central to meeting the global target of net zero emissions by 2050.

Tackling the Water-Energy Nexus

The unpredictable global temperature and weather patterns suggest that we are living through a time of momentous and tumultuous environmental change. Compounding these climate change-induced disasters is the exponential demand for water and energy in cities, agriculture and industry.

Energy for water and water for energy – the two are tightly interlinked and highly interdependent. The interconnection between the two – known as the water-energy nexus – has been relatively underexplored. In particular, the nexus that prevails in the end-use segment (wherein energy is used for various water-related purposes within industrial facilities, for agriculture and in buildings) is frequently overlooked. This end-use segment has been identified to have among the highest energy and carbon emissions intensity in many regions of the developing world. Reduction in carbon emissions through energy and water end-use efficiency improvements is a feasible option to pursue.

Global water withdrawal and its utilization varies between sectors and essentially determines the water-use profile of a country or region. Key developing countries account for 43.5% of the total global withdrawal of freshwater as compared to 22.1% in the leading developed nations. Agriculture uses 80% of the water withdrawn in the developing countries, while only 9.5% and 10.5% are attributed to the domestic and industrial sectors respectively. In India, industry is the second-highest consumer of water. Estimates of sectoral water demand in India indicate that the largest user of freshwater (surface and groundwater) is agriculture followed by industry (including thermoelectric) and then residential. In 2010, agriculture accounted for a total freshwater withdrawal of 388 MGD, industry and electric utilities was 30 MGD and residential was 84 MGD.

Unlike in the developed countries, there are very few comprehensive water-energy nexus studies in India that include the results of pilots and case studies as well as workshops and conferences for utilities, planners and policy advocates. Few detailed studies exist that audit embedded energy in water and wastewater systems, but no such assessment has been done at the city, regional or national level. What does exist are only high-level, generalized assessments. Most of the WEN research currently underway is focused on the economic and energy efficiencies associated with water supply and wastewater treatment with little information on secondary energy uses such as end-use pumping, distribution and industrial processing. Research in the area of energy-efficient technologies for water is focused more on the treatment water and wastewater and less on the consumptive use of water in industry (that is, process efficiency). Even so, while it appears that energy efficiencies for treatment technologies is well researched, most of the funded research work narrowed their conclusions and recommendations to implementation and management strategies, rather than on new technologies and barriers to their use. In addition, these studies tended to look at individual actions or measures, with few paying attention to the planning and implementation of a portfolio of options across an entire system.

Despite the interdependency of the energy and water sectors, policy frameworks, research agendas and related technological developments are pursued largely in isolation from one another – a degree of policy fragmentation that is seeing erroneous outcomes in several developing countries including India. The current status of water and energy use in end-use sectors in India are briefly described below.

Water-energy nexus in industry: In aggregate terms, the manufacturing sector is not a significant water user as compared to thermo-electric generation or agriculture. Globally, the manufacturing sector accounted for 19% of freshwater withdrawal in 2000. However, opportunities for water conservation including reduction in energy-related carbon emissions are substantial. For example, in India, annual industrial wastewater discharge accounts for roughly 77% of all the total industrial freshwater withdrawal. The majority of this discharge (>85%) can be attributed to four sub-sectors – namely, engineering, pulp and paper, textile and steel – and accounts for roughly 3,093 MGD of freshwater (equal to the total freshwater supply to India's four largest metros). A 25% reduction in industrial wastewater discharge in the aforementioned sub-sectors through efficient distribution, utilization, recycling and reuse could completely offset the 2% of the total national energy consumption used by public water utilities to convey, treat and distribute water to its residential customers. This strong interdependency offers a great opportunity in the energy-water nexus to impact both energy and water consumption.

Manufacturing plants use water for a number of purposes, including process mixing (dilution), chemical reactions, process cooling and heating, steam generation, product drying and washing, extraction, room humidification, and equipment sanitization. While energy is required to power electric motors; operate pumps, blowers, compressors and other motor-driven equipment; provide illumination; heat and cool processes; and generate steam. The water-energy nexus in manufacturing provides many opportunities for the co-management of water and energy use through integrated design approaches and technological innovations. However, within the manufacturing sector, the water-energy nexus is not well understood.

Water-energy nexus in urban areas: The variants of sustainable urban growth (like smart cities, green cities, resilient cities, low carbon cities, sustainable cities) have brought renewed opportunities to create pathways for sustainable urban development. Nearly all energy and water needs(except transportation) in the cities are confined to spaces within various buildings (residences, offices, institutions and so on). At the outset of any city-wide attempt at bringing sustainability, resilience, liveability, equity and economic efficiency, many questions come to mind: Why do we need to advance water-energy conservation? How can this be achieved citywide? Who needs counsel among the various stakeholder groups? How should advice and information be disseminated to various stakeholder groups of users? What are the costs and benefits involved in this process? What are the potential savings in capital expenditure on public infrastructure that shall be accrued? How do we move into a new era of demand-side thinking that cuts public expenditure and enhances governance values across the board from policy to end use?

A study of such a nature would be multidimensional and span ethnography studies, literature and web research, including interviews with experts in the domains of lighting, energy management, energy and water efficiency, renewable energy, sustainable buildings, HVAC, waste management and appliances manufacture. Such a process of 'solutioning sustainability' will need a host of resource persons – environment engineers, ethnographers, electrical engineers, mechanical engineers, energy analysts at applied research levels, vernacular architects, civil engineers, geophysicists and geologists, project and task managers, documentation specialists and, above all, a process to innovate. The intent should be to better understand the prevailing water-energy situation in a given country or region and to demystify inefficiencies and sustainability practices for urban settlement.

Integrative Energy Efficiency Design

If you were to walk into the basement of an office building or hotel or apartment and go to the water supply section, you would likely see big pumps and small pipes. The network of small pipes connects equipment that are typically far apart, skirt around objects that obstruct the pipes, are often at the wrong height and occasionally face the wrong way. Pipe friction falls as pipe diameters increase: small diameter pipes mean greater friction and more energy consumed for pumping. So, the piping in most installations has three to six times more friction than a straight shot. Pipe installers of this kind, since paid by the hour, mark up a profit on the extra pipes and fittings and do not pay for the extra electricity towards pumping or the bigger pumping equipment. A smart owner prefers fat, short, straight pipes to thin, long, circuitous pipelines. For such an owner, the capital cost of pumping equipment – pump, motor, inverter and electricals – needed to overcome pipe friction falls. Their size and roughly their cost fall proportionately as the fifth power of diameter whereas the cost of the fatter pipe rises as the second power of the diameter. Optimizing the whole system yields fat pipes and small pumps with smaller capex and tiny opex. These 'integrative' design changes can cut pumping power by seven or more times, with lower capital cost and better performance. Following integrative design principles of laying out the pipes first, then the pumping equipment, a factory owner was able to redesign a 70.8 kW of pumping power and use 9.7 kW – 86% less than before. There are several such examples in other areas of energy use as well where integrative design can dramatically reduce energy consumption.

At an international energy efficiency conference in Jaipur in November 2017, Dr Amory Lovins, chairman of the Rocky Mountain Institute in the US and considered by many as the foremost proponent and champion of energy efficiency in America and globally, observed, 'Energy end-use efficiency's potential is large and little-tapped. Yet all official studies substantially understate its potential and overstate its cost, because they focus on individual technologies without also counting integrative design that optimally combines those technologies. He went on to state, 'Integrative design remains nearly invisible, unrecognized, untaught and practised only by a small subset of exceptional designers.' Dr Lovin's observation has been supported by several reports such as United States National Academy of Sciences (NAS) by *America's Energy Future* that conservatively estimated US buildings can profitably save more electricity (35%) than projected growth *in all sectors* through 2030, while McKinsey and Company found profitable potential savings by 2020 totalling 23% of the US energy, worth $1.2 trillion but costing less than half of that.

As discussed in Chapter One, optimizing whole systems, not just individual components, often results in much greater energy efficiency benefits. Developing efficient technologies for and around stand-alone equipment or sub-systems instead of designing inclusive methods for the entire system has several limitations. Some of them have been illustrated in the example discussed below.

Consider the overdesigned chiller systems in a typical Indian hotel. Cooling a space such as a room is basically the abstraction of indoor heat. Changes in illumination technology – the large-scale use of LEDs that run cold, unlike incandescent lamps and tube lights that run hot – as well as a reduction in other hot spots in a room due to natural ventilation or better insulation, the amount of heat required to be abstracted has come down and so has the cooling load. One can save on capital cost by using a smaller chiller – and possibly a smaller standby diesel captive plant that hotels usually install as a safeguard against power blackouts. Thus, one could reap capital savings and energy savings simultaneously if one were to follow an integrative approach.

Addressing the Energy Access Challenge

Access to energy is critical for a country's economic growth and development. It improves the quality of life and helps meet basic lighting, cooking, transport and telecommunication needs. India is the world's fifth-largest electricity producer, but a third of all households remain without access to electricity. Nearly 93% of these households are in rural areas with most depending on kerosene to satisfy their basic lighting needs.

While it has been widely recognized that a lack of access to the modern and sustainable sources and modes of production of energy has major implications for development, it also needs to be understood that the energy access gap is also a potential market. As incomes rise, access to electricity increases at a faster rate, since governments prioritize electrification because of the great developmental benefits it provides. Distributed generation and renewable energy systems that can deliver electricity through mini-grid/off-grid networks can play a significant role in influencing such development outcomes.

Over the past fifteen years, India has churned out several initiatives to provide energy access to all, especially in rural areas. Notwithstanding numerous expired and ongoing initiatives by the central and state governments, expanding energy access remains a daunting challenge. Business opportunities that use low-cost local renewable sources to bridge the access gap are, as yet, limited and nowhere near their true potential. Energy service providers operating in the off-grid domain have been hampered by a plethora of obstacles, including unsupportive policies, inadequate financing, lack of a skilled workforce, inferior-quality products and limited opportunities for effective networking and collaboration.

The policy drawbacks are key and tend to erode investor confidence. There is a need for improved policy guidelines designed to safeguard against perceived risks such as grid extension to currently underserved areas. What would happen if the state grid were to expand and reach areas that are being serviced by off-grid systems? It might force the off-grid system owner to close shop. Another important policy challenge relates to subsidies. Multiple layers of bureaucratic hurdles and delays in the disbursement of subsidies give rise to reluctance towards using renewable energy among potential customers.

Lack of access to finance is another major constraint. Any off-grid solution will require entrepreneurs to tap into as wide a variety of sources of capital as possible. Essentially, there could be three 'colours' of money: grant financing, public funds and private capital investments. Each would have different criteria, conditions and financing eligibility. Intermediary entities that can facilitate the flow of funds from these three sources is the need of the hour. The role of the intermediate entity would be to interact with the full spectrum of financing sources ranging from non-returnable capital (like grants) and concessional loans from banks, all the way to private equity from investors and capital markets. Deployment at scale requires standardization and bundling of projects. There are currently a few regional and national business entities capable of preparing not just individual projects, but whole portfolios of sustainable and resilient off-grid distributed renewable energy projects on a large scale.

It is quite apparent that for the rapid advancement of off-grid distributed generation project, there is a need to adopt a 'distributed strategy' of stakeholder mobilization across the organizations and individuals, comprising technology vendors, entrepreneurs, local banks or lenders, donors, local government (such as Panchayati Raj institutions), self-help groups and NGOs. The missing link is a multi-stakeholder alliance. Such an alliance could address the access-to-finance gap by linking investors with entrepreneurs. It could serve as a one-stop shop for access to information on policy, business models, environmental and statutory clearances and avenues for support. It could also help provide technical and management skills and workforce training.

Ensuring universal energy access is the key challenge as India marches forward on its energy journey. It is critical for its economic growth and development. Multi-stakeholder networking and collaboration can serve as a promising solution for bridging India's energy access gap by accelerating deployment at scale and business-driven off-grid renewable energy systems by leveraging equity and debt finance from private and public sources. This, coupled with sound policies and an effective regulatory environment, will help India achieve development outcomes in a faster, cost-effective and sustainable fashion. This has the potential to be a game-changing solution to India's quest to deliver sustainable energy solutions to its unserved and underserved population.

Annexure

Summary Report of the Inter-Ministerial Working Group on Utilization and Conservation of Energy[1]
20 September 1983

Industrial Energy Conservation Policies and Programs (Sub-Committee I)

As brought out by several Governmental and other studies on Energy matters, and in particular the Report of the Working Group on Energy Policy, Planning Commission, Govt. of India, the Industrial Sector is the second largest consumer of total energy (commercial and non-commercial), accounting for about 30% of this total. Energy for industry comes predominantly from coal (32%), electricity (31%), oil (5.5%) and non-commercial energy (31.5%). If non-commercial sources are excluded, the contribution of the commercial energy sources, namely coal, electricity and oil, are about 47 percent, 45 percent and 8 percent respectively.

The trends in the industrial consumption of commercial energy indicate the following:

- The intensity of commercial energy use in the industrial sector has been steadily increasing.
- Commercial energy consumption in the industrial sector increased at the rate of 6.7 percent between 1953 and 1978; the rates for coal, electricity and oil being 5.3 percent, 10.0 percent and 3.7 percent respectively.
- Throughout the twenty-five-year period, coal has contributed to meet about half the energy needs of the industrial sector.
- Over 50% of the commercial energy is used in six industry sub-sectors: Steel (24.4%), Textiles (9.3%), Cement (8.6%), Fertilizer (6.5%), Brick making (4.9%), and Aluminium (3.3%).

Despite the low values of total and per capita energy consumption in India, the rapid post 1973 escalations in oil prices has led to a situation wherein the country imports 60% of its oil requirements at an astronomical cost of over Rs. 5,000 crores – representing 70% of its total export earnings. This already impossible situation can only worsen if historical growth rates in energy demand persist. Hence, many policy interventions are imperative. This report attempts to explore issues and suggest policy for promoting energy conservation in the industrial sector.

The broad components of this policy as explained in the report could include industrial energy audits, educational strategies, energy substitution, development of energy conservation technologies, etc., as indicated below:

1. National Industrial Energy auditing and reporting.
2. Establishment of a comprehensive Energy Conservation Data base.
3. Education and training of managers, professionals and technicians in the field of energy conservation; development of consultancy and design expertise in selected areas.
4. Programme for substitution of energy in industrial processes.
5. Programme on Industrial Waste Heat Management.
6. Industrial cogeneration systems including accompanying technical, administrative, financial and legislative policies.
7. Development of suitable technologies for energy conservation, improvement of processes and efficient utilization of energy.
8. Appropriate financial, taxation, and pricing policies to encourage energy conservation.
9. Authorization/licensing of new projects based on an examination of energy related issues.
10. Development of house-keeping standards, energy labelling of products.
11. Institutional mechanisms to provide continuous feedback system from users to policy makers and energy suppliers; mechanisms to administer relevant programmes in energy conservation.

The report points out that steps to bring into motion such a broad range of actions in the industry sector is imperative, and more so when the benefits are considered. Management of energy demand in the industrial sector through improvement in fuel efficiency, shift to less energy intensive technologies, inter-fuel substitution, reducing energy intensity of the industrial sector by adopting different strategies of industrial growth, etc., represents an energy savings of Rs. 1,100 crores/year by 1987–88 – within four years from today provided urgent steps are taken to implement policies. By 1992–93 the likely savings figure would increase to Rs.2,750 crores/year and would be over Rs. 5,000 crores/year by 2000 when the long-term energy conservation measures yield desired results. These costs of energy savings are based on today's prices of energy and in reality would be higher as energy costs in real terms increase in the future.

The realizable potential deserves close attention and priority through the formation of an Energy Conservation Policy that provides implementation programmes at the national, regional and unit levels. Special emphasis is laid on technological imperatives and on an institutionalized system for energy conservation in the report.

Summary of Report on Energy Conservation in Energy Intensive Industry (Sub-Committee II)

Energy intensiveness can be measured in terms of indices such as energy consumed per unit value of goods produced, ratio of energy cost to the total manufacturing cost and ratio of energy cost to the total of raw materials and energy cost. Keeping in view the above indices as well as the sectoral energy consumption on the national basis and relatively large quantum of energy in a single unit, the following industry sub-sector were taken up by the Sub-Committee for analysis and finding out the scope for energy conservation:

1. Aluminium industry
2. Integrated steel plants
3. Mini steel plants
4. Fertilizer industry

The report gives details of the steps to be taken in these industries which could lead to Energy Conservation, some of which are given below in brief:

Aluminium Industry

In view of the increasing energy costs, the aluminium industry all over the world has made efforts in reducing their energy consumption. Since the major quantity of energy consumed is in the form of electrical energy in the electrolytic cells, greater emphasis has been on the smelting operations. In India, the aluminium industry has on its own implemented several measures and savings of over 15% during the period 1975–80 have been recorded, although the basic process remained essentially the same.

The report gives the various measures that have already been taken up by the industry as well as it recommends certain medium and long- term measures that could lead to further energy conservation. It is estimated that these measures would result in additional savings in energy consumption to the tune of 10 to 15%. It also recommends that the industry should go in for new technologies/processes which have been developed keeping in view energy conservation and mentions details of these like Fluidized Bed Calcination, Sumitomo Process, Alcoa Chloride Process, etc.

Integrated Steel Plant

From the figures of specific energy consumption in steel plants of various countries it is found that the figures in India are roughly 1.5 to 2 times of that in other countries like USA, UK, West Germany, Japan, etc. From this it is evident that there is enormous scope for reduction in energy consumption in Indian steel plants. The major area of energy economy in the steel plant is in iron making zone and blast furnaces as about 60 to 65% of the total energy is consumed in this stage. The report analyses the factors responsible for the higher energy consumption in the Indian Steel plants and mentions one of the main reasons being due to the processes being adopted for steel production which are out dated. The report also mentions the various constraints which are responsible for the higher energy consumption and suggests several short, medium and long-term measures which could lead to energy conservation and also recommends that adequate care may be taken in the future plants at the planning stage itself to achieve energy consumption levels comparable to other countries.

Mini Steel Plants

In this industry the major energy source is electricity and as the energy cost as a percentage of sales comes to about 10–14%, the industry itself is very keen on reducing its energy consumption levels. The report discusses the various factors that are responsible for higher energy consumption like lower capacity utilization, unstable and unreliable power supply with voltage fluctuations and sudden interruptions, etc. It is estimated that it is possible to bring down the energy consumption by 10–20% if energy conservation measures are implemented and these measures could be considered by the industry for achieving savings and these are listed in the report.

Fertilizer Industry

The report mentions the details of the existing fertilizer plants along with their capacity utilization and energy consumption patterns. In the case of ammonia production, the cost of energy constitutes 60 to 80% of the total cost of production. The major factors contributing to energy savings are discussed and the different measures that could be taken by the industry for effecting savings in energy are also discussed. One of the major areas for energy savings is replacement of low efficiency steam turbines by higher efficiency steam drives or by electric motors, wherever feasible. The report also mentions that apart from the energy savings recommendations, various process modifications and mechanical modifications could also be incorporated which would lead to further savings and these modifications have been explained. It is estimated that it will be possible to bring down the energy consumption by 15 to 20%, if the various measures are implemented.

It is recommended that for implementation of various Energy Conservation measures, Energy Conservation technology plans in these energy-intensive industries should be prepared by working cells consisting of representatives of industry associations, experts in the field and the concerned Ministries in the Government.

Summary of Report on Energy Conservation in Transport Sector (Sub-Committee III)

In India, the transport sector is one of the largest consumers of commercial energy, consuming nearly 33% of the total. 84% of the energy consumption by transport sector is in the form of gasoline and diesel. During the last two decades, the energy consumption in the transport sector has increased faster than the national income and population. Many analysts have forecast that for the remainder of the century, the energy problems will be most acute among middle distillate users which form the backbone of India's transport sector.

The above sub-committee was constituted to draw up energy conservation strategies in transportation sector through modification of transport hardware, improved design of equipment, and better operation and maintenance practices. The findings of the committee are based upon feedback from various agencies on the energy conservation studies taken up during the last decade, discussions with experts and extensive literature survey. The findings of the sub-committee are not supported by detailed investigative, field or analytical studies. Besides the above sub-committee, Transport Development Council under Ministry of Shipping and Transport is currently engaged to work out conservation strategies for the transportation sector as a whole including road transport, railways, air and waterways, coastal shipping as well as other unconventional modes.

The major of the report has been on road transport and to some extent, on the railways. Road transport and railways account for over 80% of the commercial energy used in the entire transport sector. Various recommendations highlighted in the report would produce significant energy savings; however due to various financial, social, political and infrastructural limitations, implementation of some of these could be difficult. The recommendations have been highlighted giving implementing mechanisms, cost-benefit analysis, wherever feasible and implications on long term goals. Some important recommendations include policy measures on increase in railway's share in the mechanised transport sector for transport of goods, intensification of programme of electrification of trunk routes and phasing out of steam locomotives; development and implementation of an action plan to upgrade road quality; adoption of newer technological innovations in the field of heavy vehicles, automobiles, 2 and 3 wheelers and promotion of energy efficient technologies by Government through fiscal incentives, stepping up the pace of education campaign, introducing a practice of pre-licence training at license renewal stage for drivers, setting up of model depots in organised state transport sector, enforcing speed limits and abolishing octroi check posts.

The considerable scope and breadth of the suggested policy measures as well as the need to co-ordinate, enforce and implement conservation strategies justify the setting up of a central body for the above task. The agency may be created based upon PCRA's experiences and may be linked to the Department of Petroleum.

Summary of Report on Energy Conservation in Lift Irrigation Pumps (Sub-Committee IV)

Studies by various organizations have indicated that through remedial measures in the existing pump-sets, 25 to 30% energy savings is possible. This would amount to an annual savings of Rs 200 to 240 crores. In order to achieve this level of savings, there is a need for formulation of a policy that would take into account the following:

1. National educational and awareness campaign.
2. Planned rectification programmes to rectify the defects in the existing pump-sets.
3. Standardization of lift irrigation machinery through efficient designs of pumps, oil engines, etc.
4. Improvement of production technology in the manufacture of lift irrigation machinery.

For achieving the above objectives, it would be necessary to take action on the following:

1. Rectification facilities of low interest loans for purchase of approved standardized equipments.
2. Initiate launching of a mass media campaign with immediate effect.
3. Producers of life irrigation machinery in the small-scale sector to obtain ISI rectification within a time frame not greater than 5 years.
4. Setting up standardization, R&D and testing facilities at major centres of manufacture.
5. Promote transfer of technology amongst the reputed manufacturers and small-scale producers.

The considerable scope of the suggested policy measures as well as the need for coordination among Central and State Government agencies, financial institutions, etc., indicates the need for a central body to initiate and coordinate programmes on conservation in lift irrigation pump-sets. It is recommended that a separate cell may be created in the Rural Electrification Corporation for this task, with the corporate objectives of achieving a minimum of 10% savings in energy consumption in this sector within the next five years.

Report on Organizational Matters and Listing of Do's and Don'ts (Sub-Committee V)

The promotion and implementation of energy conservation programmes at macro level should be tailored to national conditions. The Government should ensure that the energy implications of all its policies and operations are harmonised towards efficient energy use. At the macro level several actions could be taken up to implement energy conservation programmes. It is estimated that around 15–20% energy savings could be achieved by simple short-term or better house-keeping measures. Accordingly, do's and don'ts for all sectors have been developed in this report.

The areas which need immediate attention are listed below:

1. Planning, execution, co-ordination and monitoring of nation-wide education campaign on simple conservation measures.
2. Identifying and concentrating on key areas of potential energy savings in all sectors.
3. Demonstrative programmes specifically designed to suit the requirements of small farmers, drivers and mechanics.
4. Development of a cadre of trained personnel and extension agencies.

Education and training are the two important means of both informing and involving people in a nation-wide energy conservation programme.
It has been recognized as a major strategy towards energy conservation. The training and education campaign should aim at specific and special needs of target groups and it should cover both organized and unorganized sectors.

Acknowledgements

Regardless of whose name is on the cover, this book is the work of many. I owe a huge debt of gratitude to Chandrashekar Hariharan who started me off on this endeavour by assisting me in setting the tone and tenor of the contents.

My strongest supporters from the very beginning were, of course, my close family members – my wife Uma, my daughters Aarthi and Anjana and Anjana's husband Niel. Uma provided the perfect ambience for me to carry out my research and exploration that made this book possible, for which I am truly and exceptionally grateful to her. It was her understanding and patience that gave me the strength to draw upon past experiences and memories of a four-decade-long journey across two continents and several regions. And my girls have been both my sternest critics and strongest supporters.

I am grateful to the remarkable people whose work and writing directly (and as often indirectly) inspired and defined the ideas and outcomes presented in this book – particularly P. R. Srinivasan, Radha P. Krishnan, David Jhirad, P. Raghavendran, Naren Nadarajah and Nick Howarth. I remain indebted to Chinmaya Acharya, Arvind Asthana, Anupama Anand, Gaurav Bhatiani, Shrikant Bhonsle, Romir Chatterjee, Amit Dalal, Vinay Deodhar, Richard Edwards, Anna Jhirad, Balakrishnan Kalyanaraman, Ravi Kapoor, Niranjan Khatri, Steve Nadel, P. G. Narasimhan, Prabir Neogi, Tallapragada Prasad, V. Raghuraman, Sridhar Ramamurthy, Datta Ray, Arun Sanghvi, Ashok Sarkar, Scott Smouse, S. Srinivas, Kalyani Subash, R. Suryanarayanan, Tanmay Tathagat, P. H. Vaidya, K. S. Venkatagiri, Archana Walia and Kath Williams, for their thoughts and encouragement. A special thanks to the organizations that I had the opportunity to work with, including the National Productivity Council of India, the World Bank and the United States Agency for International Development in New Delhi and Washington, DC. Each of them left an indelible imprint on my thinking.

The field of energy efficiency is filled with some of the most remarkable and inspiring individuals, and it is an honour to have learned from them and introduce them to you, dear readers. I could not have written the book without the active input of some of these individuals whose 'energy efficiency' spirit continues to inspire me and many others.

I am thankful to Teesta Guha Sarkar, my publisher at Pan Macmillan India, and copy editor Elizabeth James, who elegantly and skilfully steered it through several tenuous moments on the path to completion, and my agent Anish Chandy, who advocated for this project. Last but not the least, I owe a huge debt of gratitude to Koshy Cherail, who patiently read through the manuscript while jogging my memory of events past and providing unfailing insights on the unfolding energy efficiency saga of this country.

Additional Readings

1. Blumenfeld, Yorick, ed. *Scanning the Future: 20 Eminent Thinkers on the World of Tomorrow.* London: Thames & Hudson, 1999.
2. Coates, Joseph F., John B. Mahaffie and Andy Hines. *2025: Scenarios of US and Global Society: Reshaped by Science and Technology.* Greensboro: Oakhill Press, February 1997.
3. Gottfried, David. *Greed to Green: The Transformation of an Industry and a Life.* Berkeley: WorldBuild Publishing, 2004.
4. Khan, Mansoor. *The Third Curve: The End of Growth As We Know It.* Mumbai: TRIKKON Press, 2013.
5. Lovins, Amory. *Integrative Design: A Disruptive Source of Expanding Returns to Investments in Energy Efficiency.* Colarado: Rocky Mountain Institute, March 2010.
6. McDonough, William and Braungart Michael. *Cradle to Cradle: Remaking the Way We Make Things* New York: North Point Press, 2002.
7. McKenzie-Mohr, Doug. *Fostering Sustainable Behavior: An Introduction to Community-based Social Marketing*, Academy for Educational Development, Washington, DC (Canada: New Society Publishers, 1999).
8. Nadel, S. *Regulatory Incentives for Demand-Side Management.* Washington, DC: ACEEE, 1992.
9. Nadel, S., S. Gopinath and V. Kothari. *Opportunities for End-Use Electricity Efficiency in India.* Washington, DC: ACEEE and NPC, 1993.
10. Raghuraman, V., et al, *Energy Conservation: The Indian Experience.* New Delhi: NPC, 1989.
11. Sarkar, A., Neha Mukhi, Padu S. Padmanaban, Amit Kumar, Kulbhushan Kumar, Manoj Bansal, Shyamasis Das, Shuboday Ganta and Anurag Verma. *India's State-level Energy Efficiency Implementation Readiness.* Washington, DC: World Bank, 2016.
12. Sarkar, A., Neha Mukhi, Padu S. Padmanaban, Amit Kumar, Kulbhushan Kumar, Manoj Bansal and Shuboday Ganta. *Utility*

Scale DSM Opportunities and Business Models in India. Washington, DC: World Bank, 2016.

13. Shukla, P.R. et al. *Electricity Reforms in India: Firm Choices and Emerging Generation Markets.* New Delhi: Tata McGraw-Hill Publishing Company Ltd, September 2004.
14. Worley, Heather, Ashok Sarkar, Neha Mukhi, Padu S. Padmanaban, Amit Kumar, Jayakrishnan Nair and Manish Soni. *Communication Research on Energy Efficiency in India: Communications Needs Assessment and Stakeholder Mapping.* Washington, DC: World Bank, 2016.
15. Zolli, Andrew and Ann Marie Healy. *Resilience.* London: Headline Publishing Group, 2012.
16. *An Integrated Water/Energy Strategy for India.* New Delhi: USAID, January 2000.
17. *Best Practices in Rural and Agricultural Power Delivery: A Manual.* New Delhi: USAID, January 2004.
18. *Electricity End-Use Efficiency.* Paris: International Energy Agency, 1989.
19. Inter-Ministerial Working Group, Government of India. *Utilization and Conservation of Energy: Summary and Sub-Committee Reports.* New Delhi: NPC 1983.
20. Office of Energy, Environment and Technology Center for Environment and Bureau for Global Programs, Field Support and Research. *Strategies for Financing Energy Efficiency.* Washington, DC: USAID, July 1996.
21. Office of Energy and Infrastructure and Bureau for Research and Development. *Advancing Cogeneration in the Indian Sugar Industry: Three Mills in Tamil Nadu and Maharashtra.* Washington, DC: USAID, May 1993.
22. *Partnership to Advance Clean Energy – Deployment (PACE-D): Concept Note.* New Delhi: USAID, May 2013.

Notes

Preface

1. Sherif Aziz, 'The First Fuel,' Lead Digest, 23 February 2021, https://leaddigest.com/the-first-fuel/.
2. 'Let's Make Energy Efficiency Our First Fuel,' YouTube video by Efficiency Nova Scotia. The video serves as an introduction to the concept of energy efficiency as 'first fuel' for our daily use of energy in homes, transport, offices, industry and on farms. Watch here: https://www.youtube.com/watch?v=FGnh0uzZmmU.
3. Jipson John and Jitheesh P. M., 'The Pandemic Has Only Exposed the Suicidal Tendencies of Capitalism: Noam Chomsky,' *Wire*, 18 May 2020), https://thewire.in/world/noam-chomsky-interview-covid-19-pandemic-capitalism-neoliberalism-us-hegemony.

1. The Tryst with Energy, 1974–85

1. Jillian Ambrose, 'Oil Prices Dip below Zero as Producers Forced to Pay to Dispose of Excess,' *Guardian*, 20 April 2020, https://www.theguardian.com/world/2020/apr/20/oil-prices-sink-to-20-year-low-as-un-sounds-alarm-on-to-covid-19-relief-fund,
2. 'Coal Mining in India: The Past,' Ministry of Coal, Government of India, http://www.coal.nic.in/about-us/history-background. This statement was made in defence of the Indira Gandhi administration decision to nationalize coal mining in 1973. With the enactment of the Coal Mines (Naturalization) Act, 1973, all coal mines were nationalized on 1 May 1973.
3. Bernard Weinraub, 'India, Slow to Grasp Oil Crisis, Now Fears Severe Economic Loss,' *New York Times*, 20 January 1974. Available at: https://www.nytimes.com/1974/01/20/archives/india-slow-to-grasp-oil-crisis-now-fears-service-ecomomic-loss-a.html.
4. 'India's Fuel Demand Posts First Annual Growth since February,' *Economic Times*, 13 November 2020, https://economictimes.

indiatimes.com/industry/energy/oil-gas/indias-fuel-demand-posts-first-annual-growth-since-february/articleshow/79207723.cms?from=mdr.

5. Twesh Mishra, 'Domestic LPG Price Hiked by Rs 25 per Cylinder, to Cost Rs 819 in New Delhi,' *Business Standard*, 1 March 2021, https://www.business-standard.com/article/current-affairs/domestic-lpg-price-hiked-by-rs-25-per-cylinder-to-cost-rs-819-in-new-delhi-121030100161_1.html.
6. Shantanu Bhagwat, 'The Nonsense about the "Hindu Rate of Growth",' Reclaiming India (blog), *Times of India*, 8 February 2013, https://timesofindia.indiatimes.com/blogs/reclaiming-india/the-nonsense-about-the-hindu-rate-of-growth/.
7. James H. Muhl Jr, *The Iranian Revolution: Revalidating Crane Brinton's Model of Revolutions for the Operational and Strategic Planner* (School of Advanced Military Studies United States Army Command and General Staff College Fort Leavenworth, 1990).
8. EESL website, https://www.recindia.nic.in/eesl.

3. Hard Thinking, Soft Solutions, 1985–90

1. J. B. S. Haldane, quoted in K. R. Dronamraju (1987). 'On Some Aspects of the Life and Work of John Burdon Sanderson Haldane, F. R. S., in India,' *Notes and Records of the Royal Society* 42, no. 2 (1987): pp. 211–237.
2. Amarendra Dhaneshwar, 'Why despite Several Controversial Moves, George Fernandes Continues to Inspire Us,' *DailyO*, 4 June 2018, https://www.dailyo.in/politics/george-fernandes-socialist-leader-atal-bihar-vajpayee-indira-gandhi-janata-party-emergency/story/1/24642.html.

4. Tiruchy, Tennessee and Technology, 1986–2010

1. John B. Taylor, 'Discretion versus Policy Rules in Practice,' *Carnegie-Rochester Conference Series on Public Policy* 39 (1993): pp. 195–214.
2. USAID, USDOE and NETL, *USAID-USDOE/NETL*

Cooperation on Clean Energy and Environment: A Legacy of Partnership and Accomplishment, June 2013.

3. Scott Mouse, in conversation with the author.

5. Energy Options and Hobson's Choice, 1986–97

1. 'About Us,' USAID, https://usaid.gov/india/our-work.
2. K. C. Kapoor, in conversation with the author.
3. 'The Tarapur Fuel Controversy,' *Business India* 85 (1981): pp. 74–78, https://inis.iaea.org/search/search.aspx?orig_q=RN:13700197. Reference No. 13700197, INIS volume 13, INIS issue 19.
4. *The Inter-Ministerial Working Group Report* (IMWG) *on Energy Conservation in Indian Industry – Policies and Programmes*, 1983. Also known as the D. V. Kapoor Report, it was among the earliest studies conducted by NPC on policy, institutional, capacity building and technologies to advance energy efficiency in India. Subsequent steps adopted by the Government of India such as the establishment of the National Energy Management Centre, the Bureau of Energy Efficiency under the Energy Conservation Act, 2001, and others can be traced to the suggestions and recommendations of this landmark report. Annexure 1 provides the summary document of the IMWG report for its historical role and significance in India's energy journey.
5. Program for the Acceleration of Commercial Energy Research (PACER), *Project Activity Completion Report* (New Delhi: USAID/India, September 1998).

6. The Deep South Shows the Way on Cogeneration, 1992–95

1. P. R. Srinivasan and Durgesh Chandra, 'Application of Total Energy Concept to Indian Industry', *Proceedings of Total Energy and Energy Substitution Seminar,* National Productivity Council, New Delhi, March 1973.
2. *Cogeneration Potential in Indian Industry*. An NPC report submitted to Department of Science & Technology, New Delhi, in 1978.

3. Office of Energy & Infrastructure, USAID, *Advancing Cogeneration in the Indian Sugar Industry – Three Mills in Tamil Nadu and Maharashtra* (Washington: USAID, May 1993).

7. Power, Pelf and Pandemonium, 1991–2000

1. Munde Sub-committee, Government of Maharashtra, *Report of the Sub-committee to Review Dabhol Power Project*, May 1995. Excerpts available at: https://www.it.iitb.ac.in/~damani/enron/ Home_files/doc/munde/intro.htm.
2. Heinz Vergin, 'Cover Letter', *India: Dabhol Power Project* (World Bank, 30 April 1993), www.it.iitb.ac.in/~damani/enron/Home_files/WBreport.htm.
3. *Report of the Energy Review Committee (Part 1)* (10 April 2001), www.it.iitb.ac.in/~damani/enron/Home_files/doc/godbole/godbole-report.html.

8. Greening Buildings and Urban Habitats, 2000–2010

1. 'Green Building Movement in India,' Indian Green Building Council, https://igbc.in/igbc/redirectHtml.htm?redVal=showAboutusnosign.
2. Kath Williams, in conversation with the author.

10. The Water–Energy Nexus: A Silent Passage, 2003–2010

1. T. L. Sankar, All India Conference on Power Sector Reforms, November 2008, Administrative Staff College of India, New Delhi.
2. Padu S. Padmanabhan, 'India's Water Crisis,' SAISPHERE, 2011-12, p. 41, *Journal of the Paul H. Nitze School of Advanced International Studies*, Johns Hopkins University, Washington, DC.
3. Power Finance Corporation, *Performance of Distribution Utilities in India from 2006–07 to 2008–09,* (May 2010).
4. 2nd Indo-US Energy Efficiency Technology Cooperation Conference, 16–17 November 2009, New Delhi.
5. USAID/India, Water and Energy Nexus Project 6 Task Team,

Water Reuse Guidelines and Policy Recommendations for Nagpur Region, 8 February 2006.

6. Balakrishnan Kalayanaraman, *Nagpur City MSGPCL Water Reuse Project: Case Study*, 2019.

11. Energy Efficiency Centres of Excellence, 2006–2012

1. Announcement of Architectural Competition for Proposed Lighting Information Museum & Energy Centre, BESCOM, Bangalore, June 2007.
2. 'Conservation Tips,' Energy Management Centre Kerala, https://www.keralaenergy.gov.in/index.php/conservation-tips-menu.

12. Defining Bedrock Documents

1. For more information on the history of energy efficiency in India, see Koshy Cherail, et al, *Energy Efficiency in India: History and Overview*, Alliance for an Energy Efficient Economy, December 2011, https://aeee.in/wp-content/uploads/2016/03/AEEE-EE-Book-Online-Version-.pdf.
2. T. L. Sankar, in conversation with the author.
3. Inter-ministerial Working Group, Government of India, *Main Report on Utilization and Conservation of Energy*, (New Delhi: September 1993)
4. J. Sathaye, Padu S. Padmanabhan, et al, 'Implementing End-use Efficiency Improvements in India: Drawing from Experience in the US and Other Countries' (Paper presented at the US-India Energy Efficiency Technology Cooperation Conference, New Delhi, May 2006). Sathaye, J., Padu S. Padmanabhan, et al, 'Theme Paper: Energy Efficiency and Sustainable Development – Potential for US-India Collaboration in Buildings, Industry and the Smart Grid,' (Paper presented at the 2nd US-India Energy Efficiency Technology Cooperation Conference, New Delhi, India. November 2009).
5. J. Sathaye, A. Phadke and S. Padmanabhan, *Economic Benefits of Reducing Maharashtra's Electricity Shortage through End-Use Efficiency Improvement (LNBL Report 57053)* (Lawrence Berkeley National Laboratory, 2005).

6. Steve Nadel, S. Gopinath and V. Kothari, *Opportunities for End-Use Electricity Efficiency in India* (India, Washington, DC: NPC, ACEEE,1993).

13. Moving beyond Energy Audits

1. Energy Conservation Act of 2001. Available at: https://legislative.gov.in/sites/default/files/A2001-52.pdf.
2. *Energy Efficiency Measurement and Verification Issues and Options: An Overview of International Measurement and Verification Experience* (World Bank, 31 July 2013).
3. Padu S. Padmanabhan and Reshmi Vasudevan, 'The Philosophy of M&V: Why Is It Critical to Energy Efficiency,' (AEEE, March 2016).

14. Reimagining Efficiency: An Energy Productivity Storyline

1. Nicholas Howarth and Padu S.Padmanabhan, *Towards an Industrial Energy Productivity Model for India*, KAPSARC discussion paper, 30 November 2017.
2. Ibid.
3. Ibid.

15. Reflections on Water Balance in Farms

1. Soutik Biswas, 'India Election 2019: How Sugar Influences the World's Biggest Vote,' *BBC News*, 7 May 2019, https://www.bbc.com/news/world-asia-india-48173677.

16. Powering the India of the Future: 2020 and beyond

1. Eric Larson, Chris Greig, Jesse Jenkins, et al, *Net-Zero America: Potential Pathways, Infrastructure, and Impacts* (New Jersey: Princeton University, 15 December 2020).
2. Padu S. Padmanabhan, Member, CII Advisory Committee, Policy Dialogue for Energy Efficient India 2030. Note submitted on *Institutional Positioning of Energy Efficiency in India*, October 2018.

3. Vishal Pandya, 'Is Orange the New Black?' *Business India Magazine*, 6 October 2019.

Annexure

1. *Utilization and Conservation of Energy: Summary and Sub-Committee Reports*, (New Delhi: NPC, 1983).

This historical document on industrial energy conservation policies and programmes was prepared by the government in 1982–83. The document provided a summary of several sub-committee meetings across ministerial and departmental lines, each chaired by a senior government official with members drawn from industry, research and civil society. The deliberations of the sub-committees and their recommendations offered one of the earliest records of the consultative process that helped lay the foundation for energy efficiency policies and programmes and related institutional and regulatory framework in the country. Of interest is the *Report on Organizational Matters and Listing of Do's and Don'ts* (Sub-committee V) which laid out the rules for industrial energy consumers to ensure efficiency in the use of fuel and power.

Index

O

P

R